Patricia Neville

Janet Frame's World of Books

STUDIES IN WORLD LITERATURE

Editors:	Advisory Board:
Prof Janet Wilson, University of Northampton, UK	Dr Gerd Bayer, University of Erlangen, Germany
Dr Chris Ringrose, Monash University, Australia	Dr Fiona Tolan, Liverpool John Moores University, UK

The book series STUDIES IN WORLD LITERATURE is devoted to the analysis of global literature, and the multiple, sometimes contradictory, tendencies it accommodates. Its field of enquiry is the 'new' world literature, a category currently emerging through multiple changes from the old Romantic concept of *Weltliteratur*, attuned to the challenges posed by postcolonialism and multiculturalism, the increasing globalisation of literature (but also its reverse trend, regionalisation), and the diversification of the market place. STUDIES IN WORLD LITERATURE encourages research which celebrates and critically assesses a phenomenon that can be understood, as Pheng Cheah points out, as the 'literature of the world—imaginings and stories [...] that track and account for contemporary globalization as well as older historical narratives of worldhood'.

World literature can be brought into dialogue with postcolonial writing through scrutiny of how it is written, read, circulated, and received transnationally within the contemporary circuit of global cultural capital. The series also responds to the need to examine the inherent contradictions in the concept of a world literature and dependence on a hegemonic (often English-centred) literary and critical discourse.

The series seeks to address these tensions, and consequently welcomes:
1) volumes which debate such matters theoretically (including definitions of what counts as 'world literature' and the place of postcolonial literary production within this larger category);
2) comparative studies of texts and genres from different countries and cultures under common headings or concepts such as memory, ethics, and human rights.

Volumes on national literatures, when these are set in a world/comparative or generic context, will also be considered, and the series will include discussions of other complementary aspects of discourse, narratology, and media. While writing by 'canonical' authors will be covered, the series will additionally propose wider cultural and intellectual genealogies for 'minor' or occluded writers. A key aim of this series is to redeploy the familiar rhetoric of postcolonial theory and discourse in relation to concepts relevant to world literature by introducing arguments that will be integrated with the evidence of individual literary practice. This emphasis on contesting definitions of 'diasporic' or 'postcolonial' writing, 'transnational' or 'transcultural' literatures and 'world' literature as used by writers, critics and thinkers may lead to a reconsideration of the boundaries that divide and intersections that link these related fields.

Recent volumes:

3 Bruce King
From New National to World Literature
Essays and Reviews
ISBN 978-3-8382-0876-3

4 Gareth Griffiths, Philip Mead (eds.)
The Social Work of Narrative
Human Rights and the Cultural Imaginary
ISBN 978-3-8382-0958-6

5 Johanna Emeney
The Rise of Autobiographical Medical Poetry and the Medical Humanities
ISBN 978-3-8382-1128-2

6 Gerri Kimber, Janet Wilson (eds.)
Re-forming World Literature. Katherine Mansfield and the Modernist Short Story
ISBN 978-3-8382-1113-8

Patricia Neville

JANET FRAME'S WORLD OF BOOKS

ibidem-Verlag
Stuttgart

Bibliografische Information der Deutschen Nationalbibliothek
Die Deutsche Nationalbibliothek verzeichnet diese Publikation in der Deutschen Nationalbibliografie; detaillierte bibliografische Daten sind im Internet über http://dnb.d-nb.de abrufbar.

Bibliographic information published by the Deutsche Nationalbibliothek
Die Deutsche Nationalbibliothek lists this publication in the Deutsche Nationalbibliografie; detailed bibliographic data are available in the Internet at http://dnb.d-nb.de.

Cover pictures: Janet Frame visiting Pegasus Press in 1964 (Photographer Albion Wright) and working at home in 1983 (Photographer Michael Willison). © *New Zealand Listener*. Reprinted with kind permission.

ISBN-13: 978-3-8382-1242-5

© *ibidem*-Verlag
Stuttgart 2019

Alle Rechte vorbehalten

Das Werk einschließlich aller seiner Teile ist urheberrechtlich geschützt. Jede Verwertung außerhalb der engen Grenzen des Urheberrechtsgesetzes ist ohne Zustimmung des Verlages unzulässig und strafbar. Dies gilt insbesondere für Vervielfältigungen, Übersetzungen, Mikroverfilmungen und elektronische Speicherformen sowie die Einspeicherung und Verarbeitung in elektronischen Systemen.

All rights reserved. No part of this publication may be reproduced, stored in or introduced into a retrieval system, or transmitted, in any form, or by any means (electronic, mechanical, photocopying, recording or otherwise) without the prior written permission of the publisher. Any person who does any unauthorized act in relation to this publication may be liable to criminal prosecution and civil claims for damages.

Printed in the EU

For Sarah and Bryan

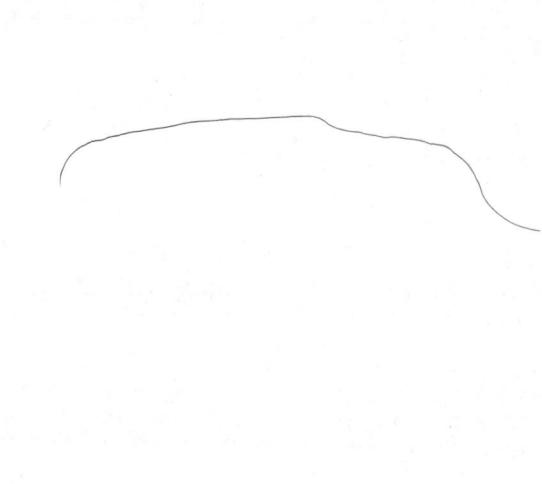

Table of Contents

Abbreviations 9
Introduction 11
   Intertextuality 20
   Mikhail Bakhtin and Polyphony 21
   Janet Frame and Intertextuality 23

Chapter One: Janet Frame's Books
   Leaving New Zealand 27
   Early Years and Dot's Little Folk 45
   School Days 60
   At College and In Hospital 65
   Later Reading 68

Chapter Two: Poets and Poetry
   The Importance of Poetry 81
   Poetry at School and College 85
   Poetic Visionaries: Blake, Yeats, Rilke and Dylan
   Thomas and their Celebration of the Natural World 90
   The English 19th Century Romantics and *A State of Siege* 106
   New Zealand Poets 111
   Walt Whitman, Frame's America and *Daughter Buffalo* 115

Chapter Three: Frame's Use of Poetry in the Novels
   Prose, Poetry and Poetic Prose 121
   Sylvia Plath and *Intensive Care* 127

Chapter Four: The Bible—Eden and Apocalypse
   Biblical Poetics 137
   Ethics and Spirituality 148
   Biblical Narratives 158

Chapter Five: Engaging with Shakespeare
- Upon the Heath 167
- Wild Waters 175
- Shakespearean Dreams 178

Chapter Six: Tending the Myths
- Folklore 185
- Fairy Tales 190
- Anglo Saxon Poetry and *The Adaptable Man* 193
- The Ballad Tradition and *Intensive Care* 195
- Myth and Survival 198
- Memory, Language and *The Carpathians* 205

Afterword 217
Index 219
Selected Bibliography 225

Abbreviations

Unless otherwise indicated, all references to Janet Frame's works are to the following editions and abbreviated as shown:

AM	*The Adaptable Man* 1965. New York: Braziller
CA	*The Complete Autobiography* 1999. London: The Women's Press
CP	*The Carpathians* 2005. Auckland: Random House NZ
DB	*Daughter Buffalo* 2008. Auckland: Random House NZ
EA	*The Edge of the Alphabet* 1995. New York: George Braziller
FW	*Faces in the Water* 2009. London: Virago Press
IC	*Intensive Care* 2008. Auckland: Random House NZ
LM	*Living in the Maniototo* 1981. London: The Women's Press
MM	*Mona Minim and the Smell of the Sun* 2007. Auckland: Random House NZ
MR	*In the Memorial Room* 2013. Melbourne: Text Publishing
OC	*Owls Do Cry* 2002. London: The Women's Press
PM	*The Pocket Mirror.* London: The Women's Press
RB	*The Rainbirds* 2006. Auckland: Random House NZ
SG	*Scented Gardens for the Blind* 2000. London: The Women's Press
SS	*A State of Siege* 2006. Auckland: Random House NZ
ST	*Storms Will Tell* 2008. Tarset: Bloodaxe Books
TS	*Towards Another Summer* 2007. Auckland: Random House NZ

References to unpublished papers held in archive collections are abbreviated as shown.

In the Hocken Collections, University of Otago, Dunedin, New Zealand:

CBH	The papers of Charles Brasch.
FSH	The papers of Frank Sargeson.
HMH	The papers of Heather Murray.
JBH	The papers of James K. Baxter.

At Princeton University Library, Manuscripts Division, Department of Rare Books and Special Collections, USA:

GBP	The papers of George Braziller.

ODT   *Otago Daily Times.*

Grateful acknowledgement is made to the Immediate Media Company for permission to use the illustrations of BBC radio programmes from the *Radio Times*; to the Janet Frame Literary Trust for the extract from *The Adaptable Man*; to the Hocken Collections, University of Otago, Dunedin, for extracts from the papers of James K. Baxter, Frank Sargeson and Charles Brasch; to the Estate of James K. Baxter for permission to quote from James K. Baxter's correspondence; to the Estate of Charles Brasch for quotations from the poems and prose of Charles Brasch; to the Sargeson Trust for quotations from Frank Sargeson's unpublished letters; to Princeton University Library for access to the archives of George Braziller, Inc. Every effort has been made to contact all copyright holders, and the publishers would be pleased to hear from anyone who believes their rights have been overlooked.

A Note on the Text: All inset poetry quotations, including Janet Frame's juvenilia, are as faithful as possible to the published lineation. All translations, unless otherwise stated, are the author's own.

Introduction

> She weaves her prose from the thread and idiom of everyday speech. [. . .] Janet Frame's stories echo with voices. (Dorothy Ballantyne, 4YA Radio Review, June 9, 1952)

> What I admire no end are her brilliant verbal associations—and they're not merely verbal or literary. (Frank Sargeson, Letter to William Plomer, September 15, 1957)

These comments on Janet Frame's early fiction by two of her fellow New Zealanders, written before she left New Zealand for Europe and America, indicate a perception that even at the very beginning of her adult writing career Frame was doing something that was both innovative and unrestricted by her New Zealand nationality. Frame's interweaving of different voices is identified by Dorothy Ballantyne, the eminent New Zealand librarian and critic, and Frank Sargeson, who was at that time one of New Zealand's foremost writers. Frame references literature from across the world and this interconnectedness or "intertextuality" was central to her identity as a writer, and a key characteristic of her mature style. Ballantyne is reviewing *The Lagoon and Other Stories* (1952), Frame's first, award-winning book of short stories, and Sargeson is commenting on Frame's first novel, *Owls Do Cry* (1957). Both critics are stunned by her brilliant originality, their observations pointing towards Frame's imaginative, creative mindset and her intensely allusive, intertextual style. Sargeson is puzzled, unable to pinpoint precisely the range or complexity of this novel, which departs so fundamentally from the social-realist style of New Zealand fiction which prevailed in the 1930s to 1960s.

Early critical writing about Frame in New Zealand, largely biographical in orientation, tended either to focus on her account of repressive, puritanical and punitive New Zealand society in the postwar years, or to interpret her novels predominantly in relation to her extraordinary life history. However, in his 1957 review of *Owls Do Cry* in *Landfall*, Winston Rhodes, while sympathizing with those watching for "the great New Zealand novel", perceives that Frame is giving us something much wider when he asserts that she "brings us closer not to the average New Zealander, but to common humanity in its suffering and search" (328–29). For all its identifiable locations and New Zealand English, *Owls Do Cry* deals with universal themes and events which are not dependent on their setting for their significance. Small-minded, puritanical and provincial attitudes are not confined to New Zealand. The conditions in mental hospitals which Frame delineates were common everywhere at that time. Ken Bragan (1993), who came to work at Seacliff Mental Hospital in 1955, near Dunedin, where Frame had been a patient, recalls conditions in the Scottish mental hospital where he worked in the 1950s as "so appalling as to be beyond description; these conditions would have been similar to those endured by Janet Frame for months on end" (133). Her years as a patient in these hospitals gave Frame access to universal experiences of mental suffering endured by the inmates of such institutions the world over.

At this early stage, Frame was largely regarded as a specifically New Zealand writer, an exciting new local talent writing in the tradition of the New Zealand short story, although Ballantyne was clear from the start that Frame "also extends that tradition" (Ballantyne 1952, 2). *Owls Do Cry* was published in the USA in 1959 and all her novels appeared in Britain and the USA as they were completed. By the early 1960s her work began to appear in translation in France, Germany, Spain, Italy and the Netherlands. Publication overseas began to change the way Frame was perceived, and within a decade she had gained international recognition. Her novels, short stories, poetry and autobiography have now been translated into 14 European languages and three from the Far East, Korean (2012), Japanese (1991, 1994) and Chinese (1993), forming a further extended transnational exchange of creativity, and confirming Frame's place in world literature. This book explores the verbal echoes and associations with which Frame locates herself in a world-wide community of writers.

Janet Frame was awarded the Commonwealth Writers' Prize in 1989 for her final novel, *The Carpathians*. The shifting terminology used for literature written in English, or translated into English, from outside the British Isles or by immigrants to Britain—Commonwealth, Postcolonial, World Literature in English—owes much to the changing political scene, especially since the end of World War II, and the dismantling of the former British Empire, as well as to the globalization of the publishing industry. Increasingly, multi-cultural Britain has honoured migrant and second-generation writers, both from its former empire and from other countries, often people whose mother tongue was a minority language, and who chose to write in English. These include writers like Joseph Conrad (1857–1924), the former Polish seaman, writing during the British Empire's heyday; Salman Rushdie, who was born in India in 1947, and came to Britain as a schoolboy; V.S. Naipaul, born in 1932, who grew up in Trinidad, came on a scholarship to study at Oxford, and later worked for the BBC; and Kazuo Ishiguro, born in 1954, whose Japanese parents came to England when he was a small child. English has remained, through an accident of history, the world's dominant language in literature as it is in science. The re-adoption of Goethe's broad term *Weltliteratur*, "World Literature" is especially useful given the range of backgrounds of non-British writers in English from within the former colonies and elsewhere.

David Damrosch (2003) defines "world literature" as "all literary works that circulate beyond their culture of origin" (4), stressing that world literature is less of a fixed canon and more "a mode of circulation and reading" (5). Damrosch's mode of thinking is the antithesis of an approach to World Literature as a canon, a semi-fixed body of masterpieces, added to occasionally, which can be arranged as an anthology. Other critics take a more heavily politicized view, for example the Warwick Research Collective (2015) which defines world literature as "the dialectics of core and periphery that underpin all cultural production in the modern era" (51). They argue that the key element is the imposition of capitalism on previously non-capitalist countries and that the Euro-American literary tradition is responsible in the peripheral world for "capitalism's bewildering creative destruction (or destructive creation)" (51).

By contrast, Pascale Casanova (2004) argues in *A World Republic of Letters* for "a lost transnational dimension of literature" (xi). Casanova takes up this theme again in an article of 2005, when she asserts that "the world literary space [...] is formed by the Republic of Letters, each of them differently situated within their own national literary space" (2017, 281). Casanova is criticized by the Warwick Research Collective for the way in which her views "abstract too strongly from the world of politics" (2015,9). For her part, Casanova argues that literary domination should not be confused with forms of political domination but acknowledges that in many ways literary and political worlds are interdependent (2004, xi). She acknowledges also the value of having her own work, originally published in French in 1999, translated into English.

Casanova's view of a World Republic of Letters makes an interesting parallel with Frame's concept of a world of the imagination, the "room two inches behind the eyes" (*SS*, 36) the space she comes to call "Mirror City". The final volume of Frame's autobiography is entitled *The Envoy from Mirror City,* at the end of which she writes: "I stare more closely at the city in my mind. And why, it is Mirror City, it's not Dunedin or London or Ibiza or Auckland or any other cities I have known. It is Mirror City before my own eyes. And the Envoy waits" (*CA*, 435). Frame's writing reconciles her sense of her place in New Zealand, the "land of the mythmakers" (*CA*, 415), her "own national literary space", with the skilful interweaving of her transnational literary borrowings.

Writers like Frame, working on the periphery of the world's major languages and literary centres, geographically isolated and far from centres of publishing, face a considerable challenge, as the publication industry is dominated by voices from Euro-American sources and the world's major publishing centres in Europe and the USA. Such Euro-American dominance can have deleterious consequences for minority languages and cultures, as it tends to promote widely spoken languages over those local and national languages which have fewer speakers and may possibly be under threat. The novelist Milan Kundera, for example, was born in Czechoslovakia but writes in French. In his 2005 article, *"Die Weltliteratur"*, he cites as an example of the self-importance of powerful nations Neville Chamberlain's dismissive 1938 comment on Czechoslovakia as "a faraway country of which we know little" (2017, 290), one of those small countries who never have a seat at the top table, and whose existence and language are always at risk. Kundera wonders what might have happened to Kafka's work if Kafka had written in Czech rather than German. The same question might be asked about Rilke; or Conrad, who wrote in English rather than Polish, and August Strindberg who wrote his plays in French rather than his native Swedish. Kundera complains of being sidelined as "slavic" or as "an East European exile", in spite of living in France and writing in French.

Frame took up this theme of linguistic power in a Pacific context in 1977, in a paper given to the East-West Centre in Honolulu, where she deplores the stereotyping attitudes of powerful cultures, for example, to the cliché of the "mysterious" East (2011, 57), and expresses her concern that "in every cross-cultural encounter there is a dominance, a submission, a merging, or a resistance" which the dominant culture tends to win, and "can almost vacuum-clean, overnight, another culture and language" (64). Frame's starting-point was New Zealand forms of English, and the inclusion of common Māori words. Kundera, writing in a specifically European context, perceives the interrelation of texts as a kind of literary baton being passed from one writer to another across Europe and beyond, from the Icelandic sagas on through the centuries to the present time, and views the classification of literatures solely in their national groups as a betrayal of Goethe's testament to *Weltliteratur*.

In his "Footnote to *Weltliteratur*", written in 1979, George Steiner discusses Goethe's enthusiasm for translation and his own facility with languages other than German, and asserts that Goethe's "insistence on the interrelations between literatures, the conviction that no man knows his own language thoroughly if he knows it alone—these stand" (2017, 121). Frame's suggestion in her talk for the East-West Centre is that future education programmes might consist of learning "first, one language, and then many". She is generous in her praise here for translators, "who so often have been accused, rightly or wrongly, of 'losing' the 'genius' of the works they translate". They are, she insists: "Beasts of burden. Water-carriers. Bearers of the spirit of life" (2011, 66).

Damrosch asserts that "works become world literature when they gain on balance in translation, stylistic losses offset by an expansion in depth" (2003, 289) a proposition which might arguably depend on the nature of the works in question and the quality of the translation. Damrosch argues for the importance of translation and appears to share the same generosity of spirit towards translators that Frame expresses in Honolulu, although she could be a stern critic of translation practices. The balance of losses and gains in translation in—particular of poetry and poetic prose—is a contentious issue, which Damrosch arguably overlooks. J.B. Leishman's 1936/46 translation of Rilke's *Sonnets to Orpheus*, for example, was initially the only translation available to Frame in English, and its bilingual format enabled her to access Rilke's verses. However, access to other translations from the early 1970s through her visits to the USA highlighted for Frame just how poor much of Leishman's translation was. She was disappointed to find that her eagerly awaited Penguin Modern European Poets edition of Rilke consisted of Leishman's translations. Of "Autumn Day" ("Herbsttag") she tells Bill Brown "I think it is a shocking translation [...] and all are pretty bad" and that she is going to "prepare some bombs for when the Great Translation Revolution is at hand" (2016, 104). One of Rilke's most recent translators, the Scottish poet Don Paterson (2006)—also highly critical of Leishman—describes his own poetic rendering as "A Version of Rilke", and is a set of poems in its own right. Paterson advocates collaboration in the translation of poetry, and this is a view endorsed also by the Australian poet Clive James (2013) in his translation of Dante's *The Divine Comedy*. James acknowledges the substantial contribution made by his wife, a Dante scholar, who assisted him in spending half a life-time in attempting to unpick and understand Dante's verse effects in relation to Dante's themes, and to find a style of English verse which served Dante's pace and tone. James began by trying to emulate the tercets of Dante's *terza rima*, but found "it was creaking with strain the longer it went on" (xv), and turned to the quatrain to do justice to Dante's "interplay of form and content", with masculine rhymes "to match Dante's gravitas" (xvi) and to create "a mutually reinforcing balance of tempo and texture" (xix).

Frame appears for the most part to have been well served by translators who have taken great pains to convey her underlying sense, often in collaboration. When, however, the translation is poor, inaccurate, misses cultural nuance, or loses the spirit of the original, the outcome has been a loss to the target culture as well as to Frame's work. The result may be unpublishable, or not sell, or go quickly out of print, as detailed further in Chapter 1. The "circulation and reading", in Frame's case, depend very much on there being not too many "stylistic losses". The testimony of effective translators, however, tends to support the view that losses are inevitable, even when translators are working within a European language family and even more so, as Spivak (2005) suggests, with literature from Africa, Oceania and Asia where western readers are "out of touch with the idiomaticity of nonhegemonic languages" (10). Professor Nakao, who successfully collaborated on a translation of Frame's autobiography into Japanese, found that Frame's "poems (especially the early ones) were not so easy to translate" (Nakao, personal communication). Even translation from one European language to another is fraught with cultural and linguistic pitfalls, and there are some examples from Frame's work in Chapter 1.

Western European academics working in the field of Commonwealth Studies have been at the forefront of Frame criticism from the late 1970s to the present day, especially in France and Belgium. I am especially indebted to the inspiring work of the Belgian scholar Jeanne Delbaere, who pioneered an approach to Frame's metaphorical prose, highlighting Frame's sense of connectedness with other world writers, among them Virginia Woolf, Emily Brontë,

T.S. Eliot, William Blake, Rainer Maria Rilke and Ovid. Delbaere began reading Frame's novels in 1974 at the suggestion of the French scholar Victor Dupont, who was full of praise for her work, and had visited Frame during her Katherine Mansfield fellowship in Menton earlier that year. The influential collection of essays edited by Delbaere, *Bird, Hawk, Bogie* was published in 1978 and revised in 1992 as *The Ring of Fire: Essays on Janet Frame* after the publication of Frame's autobiography. By including the work of scholars from America and Europe as well as Australasia, Delbaere (2001) was able to widen discussion and emphasise Frame's worldwide appeal rather than her nationality. She notes that Frame "is beginning to receive more and more attention all over the world" and that the essays bring together Frame's "most ardent admirers scattered through the world" (13). Outside New Zealand, Frame has long enjoyed academic and popular recognition in Western Europe and the USA, especially during her lifetime when she was well known among American artistic and publishing communities. Frame's international outlook was further developed during the 1970s when she spent several months at a time in the US artists' colonies of Yaddo and McDowell, as well as with friends in the USA and she had an active champion in her American publisher George Braziller.

Frame had been a voracious reader from childhood. Her autobiography and her correspondence reveal that she read widely—an eclectic mix of New Zealand, British, American, and European literatures, and had an interest in Buddhist thought—and all of these writers, from all parts of the world, form a rich and diverse transcultural literary hinterland which leaves its mark on her novels. As well as the British canonical writers she encountered at school and college, Frame read New Zealand and American poetry, Rilke's poetry in French and in a variety of translations from German all her life, as well as French poetry, short stories and fiction from Balzac and Maupassant, to Camus and the *nouveax romans*, in particular those of Nathalie Sarraute. She read Kafka and Chekhov, as well as fiction written by emergent Māori writers in the 1970s. She draws on this wide-ranging and extensive personal reading, over the course of 13 novels, to construct form, pattern and meaning. Frame creates a space for herself in a worldwide community of writers, and it is fitting that her œuvre, in its turn, is made available to a global readership in English and through translation of her work which began in the early 1960s.

Frame lived her life through her reading, composing her novels with purposeful allusions to the poetry and fiction she loved—a deliberate strategy of interconnection—and this study shows how her literary sources and multiple voices interconnect, in "coexistence and interaction" in Bakhtin's (2011, 28) phrase and create an intertextual relationship with the writers Frame felt were her community. She immersed herself in her reading, taking her cue from the poets especially, and developing for herself a world of the imagination. Frame's style is intensely poetic, and she held poetry to be the highest form of verbal art. As a student she was dazzled by Coleridge's view of imagination in *Biographia Literaria* and wrote, that "the most magical word to me was still *Imagination*, a glittering noble word, never failing to create its own inner light" (*CA*, 121; Frame's emphasis). She was keenly aware of her debt to the poetry of Shakespeare, Blake, Wordsworth, Yeats, Eliot and the King James Bible. Frame had a considerably familiarity with the language of the Bible from her mother's strong Christadelphian faith and the family Bible-readings. She also draws on poetry from oral traditions—mediaeval ballads, Anglo-Saxon poetry, nursery rhymes, myth and traditional stories, European and Māori—as well as lyrics from songs and contemporary New Zealand poetry. All these sources contribute to the sense of her felt connection with literary traditions as they stretch back to time immemorial. In a 1955 review of Faulkner's *A Fable*, Frame summed up her sense of the value of artists and poets, commenting that "perhaps one may doubt whether William Faulkner is a novelist, but never that he is an artist who can take and transform, and never that he is a poet" (2011, 29), an observation which applies equally well to Frame herself. A self-consciously intertextual author, she weaves the work of other literary creators into her own through reference, quotation, pastiche and echo, and saw herself as part of a world-wide family of writers, spanning all ages and cultures. She creates what the Russian scholar Mikhail Bakhtin has termed "polyphonic" texts, the orchestration of different voices, literary and non-literary, as Ballantyne and Sargeson both saw at the outset in their comments on her first published fiction.

Intertextuality

T.S. Eliot (1997) expresses the view that "No poet, no artist of any art, has his complete meaning alone. His significance, his appreciation is the appreciation of his relation to the dead poets and artists" (41). Intertextuality is the most common theory used to explore the ideas that Eliot expresses here. He views the work of later writers as a conscious, cerebral culmination of a long process of literary interaction. W.H. Auden (2006) makes the point rather more pithily when he writes in "In Memory of W.B. Yeats" that "The words of a dead man/Are modified in the guts of the living" (149). Auden's image is a more organic, natural take on the same idea, suggesting that intertextual reference is an inevitable part of the cycle of living matter. In a different image taken from the cycle of life, Frame, also a purposefully intertextual writer, takes up this theme in *In The Memorial Room*, commenting that, "In authorship, the author is not the tree scattering his books like leaves; the books are the trees; the author is shed, blown away, dies, to make compost for other leaves and other trees" (*MR*, 113). Frame's "composting" images occur regularly in her novels, and she uses these images to express this aspect of her art and the interconnectedness of literature which Auden and Eliot felt.

Analogies between the cyclical nature of horticultural and agricultural growth and the cyclical nature of literature have a long history. The 18th-century novelist Henry Fielding (2004) devotes a whole chapter of *Tom Jones* to "Showing What is to Be Deemed Plagiarism in a Modern Author, and What is to Be Considered as a Lawful Prize". With a metaphor taken from the age-old right of English peasants to graze their livestock on common land, Fielding sums up his view that "the antients [sic] may be considered as a rich common, where every person who hath the smallest tenement in Parnassus hath the free right to fatten his muse" (250-51).

The French-Bulgarian theorist Julia Kristeva coined the word "intertextuality" in the 1960s and introduced the work of Mikhail Bakhtin (1895–1975). She acknowledges Mikhail Bakhtin's insight, that "any text is constructed as a mosaic of quotations; any text is the absorption and transformation of another" (1986, 37). In her essay "Word, Dialogue and Novel", Kristeva discusses intertextual relationships—in a broader context than poetry—and views "the literary word" as "an intersection of textual surfaces rather than a point (a fixed meaning), as a dialogue among several writings: that of the writer, the addressee (or the character) and the contemporary or earlier cultural context" (36).

In a similar vein, in "From Work to Text", Roland Barthes (1977) uses the image of textiles rather than "mosaic" in referring to "the *stereographic plurality* of its weave of signifiers (etymologically, the text is a tissue, a woven fabric). The reader of the Text may be compared to someone at a loose end" (159; Barthes's capitalization and emphasis). Barthes and Kristeva argue that intertextuality is an essential part of the fabric of a novel, whether the author is conscious of it or not, while Frame—conscious of her extensive literary hinterland as the roots of her own writing—is deliberate and explicit in her own weaving of the threads of language, in her repeated use of metaphor from weaving and textiles, "the rich, wide tapestry of language" (*LM*, 27).

Mikhail Bakhtin and Polyphony

Mikhail Bakhtin frequently mentions his love of the 18th-century English comic novel. He refers several times to Henry Fielding and would have been aware of Fielding's comment on the process which 20th-century commentators call "intertextuality". Bakhtin's observations and insights stem from his love of the novel as an art form, and in particular his love of Dostoevsky, rather than from a starting-point of linguistic theory. He sees language not as a system, but as a social activity: not as a "sign", but as an interactive "act", a "dialogue". He argues for a view of the novelist as a listener with an acute sensitivity in a comment which relates very much to Frame's style:

for the prose artist the world is full of other people's words, among which he must orient himself and whose speech characteristics he must be able to perceive with a very keen ear. He must introduce them into the plane of his own discourse, but in such a way that this plane is not destroyed (Bakhtin 2011, 200).

Bakhtin stresses the social context of language, its essential "dialogic" or conversational nature, in an insight which has linguistic value far beyond academic literary discussion, but which Bakhtin relates to the creation of prose fiction, and more specifically to the novel of the 18th and 19th centuries.

In addition to his comments on Dostoevsky, Bakhtin references the novels of Smollett, Sterne, Fielding and Richardson, Walter Scott and Dickens, Stendhal, Balzac and Flaubert, Goethe and Shakespeare. In his later years he also refers to Proust and Thomas Mann. His understanding of the interconnected development of literature over time and across cultures is especially enlightening in relation to Frame's interest in folklore and what might lie beyond it. Bakhtin's insights illuminate her intertextual practices and it is worth summarising briefly the main elements of what Bakhtin termed dialogic, or polyphonic novelistic prose.

Bakhtin seems to have at one time thought Dostoevsky initiated the polyphonic style of novel, but later came to the conclusion that dialogic prose is an inherent aspect of the genre—which Dostoevsky developed in his own style. Bakhtin distinguished between three categories of literary discourse:

1. Direct speech – the voice of the novelist
2. Represented speech – the speech of the characters
3. Doubly-oriented speech – speech which refers to something in the world as well as another speech act.

Bakhtin refers to this third category also as "double-voiced discourse", and describes it as his "chief hero" (2011, 185), the subtle and sometimes almost imperceptible transition from one style to another. He sees how novelists lessened the hold of authorial discourse in rapid shifts of linguistic register—the kind of literary ventriloquism in which Frame excels—and gives an extended example from Dickens's *Little Dorrit*, in which Dickens merges language from the voices of different characters, their hypocrisy, greed and sycophancy, the language of ceremonious speech, the legal discourse of the law courts and of official documents, the voice of "general opinion", and the Bible. Bakhtin asserts that "there is no formal—compositional and syntactic—boundary between these utterances, styles, languages, belief systems; the division of voices and languages takes place within the limits of a single syntactic whole, often within the limits of a simple sentence" (2008, 305). Dickens's "entire text is [. . .] washed by heteroglot waves from all sides" (307). Bakhtin's view of the freedom and flexibility of the novel chimes also with the ambiguities and uncertainties of Frame's novels when he writes in relation to the novel genre of "an indeterminacy, a certain semantic openendedness, a living contact with unfinished, still evolving contemporary reality (the openended present)" (7).

Bakhtin uses the language of music—"polyphony", "counterpoint" and "orchestration"—to consider how novelists in their varying ways incorporate and orchestrate "other people's words" in their novels. These musical metaphors can be used to illuminate Frame's use of language in her fiction; and in particular how she exploits those polyphonic aspects of dialogic language with increasing sophistication in the course of her career, a process which Bakhtin sees as reaffirming the creativity and imaginative power of the writer.

Janet Frame and Intertextuality

Frame's first novel, *Owls Do Cry*, illustrates her early use of polyphonic language. In this novel Frame separates with italics the most densely poetic sections from the narrative, mostly Daphne's songs from the dead room, densely interwoven with the echoes of William Blake, G.M. Hopkins and Dylan Thomas. Elsewhere the reader hears an interplay of voices of different characters from the novel. Jennifer Lawn (1990, 87–105) gives a detailed account of Bakhtin's theories with reference to *Owls Do Cry*, the most striking examples of which serve to convey the nature and thinking of Toby, Daphne's epileptic and barely literate brother: "Commitments. It was a long word for him because he had left school early on account of his fits, and his spelling had always been shaky, but heavens, what he had picked up in the meantime" (*OC* 2002, 56). In this brief piece, we hear Toby use his father's favourite word, "commitments", i.e. money; the voice of the general community, "left school early [. . .] fits"; a school-teacher trying not to be too discouraging, "a bit shaky"; and Toby's over-brightly optimistic mother, "but heavens".

In later novels, Frame develops her use of this kind of interplay to include a broader interweaving of personal voice and literary allusion as well as language from other kinds of text, an eclectic discourse including Anglo-Saxon and other texts from a variety of literary and non-literary sources. Consider, for example, this extract from *The Adaptable Man*, in which the Rev. Aisley Maude muses on the nature of the post-war English county of Suffolk:

> The self remains: a complex doodle or pattern like those menacing structures you see in the lonely places of East Anglia – the incongruous temples built upon layers of destruction, where bombers fly in and lay their eggs in the concrete towers, and where the bell tolls for all. When men are like flies to be exterminated, there is no refinement or distinction of 'me' and 'thee.' It is 'us,' and 'all.' A yellow fire of light streaks down the sky, there is a taste of ashes in the mouth, the eyes expand, like frogs about to commit a spring vision on the surface of the weed-infested pond. (*AM*, 78)

Frame links Suffolk's vulnerability to invasion in World War II with the contemporary threat of nuclear war and she includes the language of the guide book, "the lonely places of East Anglia" and nature notes, "lay their eggs" and "like frogs", interspersed with references to poets and orators, Shakespeare and John Donne. Suffolk's massive ancient wool churches, its "temples", have been overtaken in size by the vast hangars and flight-towers of wartime American airbases, "menacing structures", which continue to operate during the Cold War, after the end of World War II. Wartime propaganda still insists on "us" and "all" rather than "me" and "thee", taking the words of Donne's (1967) sermon, "send not to know for whom the bell tolls; it tolls for thee" (101), distorting and manipulating them for support in "the bell tolls for all". Aisley cites *King Lear*—"men are like flies"—in his sense of man's abject powerlessness. He despairs at the possibility of a nuclear missile, "the yellow fire of light", causing a final human instinctive reaction, "the eyes expand", not in re-creation, "a spring vision", but in a final expression of horror before destruction. He echoes J.F. Kennedy's warning during the 1962 Cuban Missile Crisis that in a nuclear war "even the fruits of victory would be ashes in our mouth", a nuclear annihilation (Roberts 2012, 196). From his reveries about a 20th-century world threatened with nuclear extinction, Aisley then recalls lines from the Anglo-Saxon elegy, "The Wanderer"—a kind of Anglo-Saxon blues—mourning the loss of another older world in the words of an anonymous 7th-century poet, "How that time has passed away, has grown dark under the shadow of night as if it had never been" (Gordon 1967, 74). Frame's evocative piece of polyphonic writing, with its brilliant interplay of different voices, typifies the complexity and constant allusiveness of her mature style.

Frame's multiple voices coexist and interact, as she locates herself in the literary world. She had a sense of the timelessness of literature, its cyclical nature, and a sense, like Goethe, of the interrelationship of literary works. Drawing on her reading of the world's literature she incorporates and transforms all their voices into a wondrous fabric of her own. She creates a place for herself within a transnational community of poets and artists, taking and using the voices of a whole host of other writers from around the world, writers who inspired her, as if there were no temporal or spatial frontiers, and encouraging the onward progression of her work in a variety of world languages.

Chapter One: Janet Frame's Books

Leaving New Zealand

Janet Frame set off for Europe in July 1956 before her first novel, *Owls Do Cry*, was published in New Zealand in 1957. She returned to New Zealand in October 1963 as an established novelist, having published three more novels and two more collections of short stories with British and American publishers, and having had four titles translated into German, one in each of French, Italian and Dutch, with a Spanish translation in the pipeline. After her return to live in New Zealand, Frame continued to travel frequently and widely, spending long periods of time at writers' colonies in the USA, and visiting friends in London, New York, and California. She spent six months in Menton, France as a Katherine Mansfield fellow, having been awarded New Zealand's prestigious annual Katherine Mansfield fellowship in 1974. She occasionally attended overseas conferences, for example in Honolulu (1977) and in Toronto (1984), so that her life, cultural interests and reference points were quite international early in her career even before publishing became the global business it is today.

The time span of Frame's career as a published writer in the second half of the 20th century saw huge changes in the organisation and culture of book publishing, and in the technological means by which readers can access literature. As Sarah Brouillette (2011) illustrates, the implementation of new technologies has revolutionised the publishing industry. The tradition of family-run publishing which existed from the 18th century to the mid-20th century has been transformed, and small-scale independent publishing houses have largely become subsumed into transnational companies, or ceased to exist, and in Brouillette's words "the conglomerates control the rules of the game" (53). A business which was traditionally as much about culture as commerce is now perhaps at least as much about commercial considerations as about cultural values, although even in this climate, there have been a few ardent small publishers prepared to establish a publishing house on a more traditional basis.

When Frame was discharged from Seacliff mental hospital, near Dunedin, in March 1955, after eight years in and out of various mental hospitals, she was offered a home by Frank Sargeson. He was then New Zealand's foremost writer, and she came to live in the army hut in his garden at Takapuna, on Auckland's North Shore, at that time a quiet place. There Frame had the time and space to write. Sargeson encouraged her to feel she could become a full-time writer, and in the 18 months she was living there, she completed her first novel, *Owls Do Cry*. She entrusted her manuscript copy of *Owls Do Cry* to Sargeson in 1956 and left New Zealand for Europe, at a time when book publishing in New Zealand was still largely in the hands of small, independent publishers.

The Caxton Press was founded in Christchurch in 1935 by Denis Glover, a New Zealand poet, who also published the pre-eminent New Zealand literary quarterly, *Landfall*, established and edited by the poet and critic Charles Brasch, in 1947. In 1947 the publisher Albion Wright founded the Pegasus Press in Christchurch, with a philosophical outlook similar to that of the Caxton Press—both Glover and Wright aimed to publish New Zealand writing of literary merit. Frame's friend John Money sent Frame's first book of short stories, *The Lagoon and Other Stories*, to the Caxton Press in 1952, and Frame sent *Owls Do Cry* to Albion Wright herself in 1955 and became a Pegasus author. The Caxton and Pegasus print runs were limited and profits small, and Albion Wright looked for overseas publishers to produce co-editions to boost sales, profits and royalties.

The basic facts of Frame's New Zealand, British and American publication history are covered in meticulous detail in Michael King's biography, *Wrestling with the Angel* (2000), but in the published and unpublished correspondence between Brasch, Sargeson and Frame, we learn more about the overseas and New Zealand publication of Frame's work. In his letters, Sargeson (2012) expresses considerable frustration with Albion Wright and Pegasus for being very slow and for not giving "preference for a vocational writer" when Frame is short of money and she has to take her place in the queue with "academics who expect only pocket-money from their writings" (249). He is frustrated by Albion Wright's lack of urgency which prevents him from sending a copy of *Owls Do Cry* to William Plomer, a reader for the British publisher, Jonathan Cape, who "might have made her an offer" (251), and he asks Frame to let him know which US publisher would be interested, so that he can send them a copy (253). Sargeson tells Brasch that he is trying to interest both US and UK publishers in *Owls Do Cry*, that he is "tied up pushing it along" (FSH June 28, 1957), and that he has heard from Frame that *Owls Do Cry* is being published in the USA. Sargeson continues to send Frame advice about dealing with publishers during the late 1950s (FSH October 30, 1959). By 1960, Sargeson (2012) reports that "Albion Wright is feeding the Press with nice pieces of praise for you from your American publisher" and was also "negotiating publication in England & France. So you may soon benefit financially" (282). Sargeson in fact discovered that Pegasus had about £300 to Frame's credit, and became suspicious that Albion Wright was not giving Frame her fair share of the royalties. In July 1960 Sargeson asks her "have you received this yet?" (283), and in January 1962, Sargeson reports to Brasch that news from Frame was not generally very encouraging, "after all the publicity she has been getting", and that he thinks Frame's New Zealand publisher, Albion Wright, is getting too great a share of the rewards. In the same month he wrote to Frame to say that he had come to the conclusion that Albion Wright was "soaking you far too heavily for his over-share of income" (294).

Early in the 1960s, however, European translations of Frame's novels and short stories were beginning to appear. The foreign language licences may have been arranged by Frame's London agents at the time, A.M. Heath, either on behalf of Frame directly or on behalf of Pegasus Press. They would have lasted for a specific number of years, usually five, before they expired. In a letter dated May 25, 1960 Frame tells Brasch that a German translation of *Owls*

Do Cry and *Lagoon and Other Stories* is "in the pipeline". The Hamburg-based publishing house Nannen Verlag released three titles in German in the early 1960s, *Wenn Eulen schrein*,1961 (*Owls Do Cry*); *Die Lagune*, 1962 (*The Lagoon and Other Stories*); and *Am Rande des Alphabets*, 1963 (*The Edge of the Alphabet*). Editions of *Faces in the Water* appeared in 1963 in Italian (*Volti nell'acqua*) issued by Rizzoli, French (*Visages noyés*) by Éditions du Seuil, in Dutch (*Schimmen in het water*) by Van Ditmar, and in Spanish (*Rostros en el agua*) by Plaza & Janés in 1965.

There was also a Spanish edition of *The Edge of the Alphabet* (*Al margen del alfabeta*) published by Ediciones G.P. in 1966. There is then a considerable gap in time until the 1980s when further French, German, Spanish and Italian re-issues and new publications begin to appear in those languages and others, sometimes with a different title. Sargeson tells Brasch that the UK publishers Curtis Brown, "very tough agents", had "just begun to look into" Frame's work. However, there is firmer news from the USA and "her American publisher is going ahead with a new book" (FSH July 1963).

In the USA, George Braziller (1916–2017) was one of a handful of independent publishers, establishing his publishing house in 1955. Frame had an active champion in her American publisher, and their working relationship became a friendship which endured to the end of Frame's life. Braziller (2015) was in many ways an ideal publisher for Frame, an outward looking New Yorker, describing himself in his memoir, *Encounters*, as "looking for books representing what was new in publishing" (76). The son of Russian Jewish immigrants, Braziller grew up speaking Yiddish and listening to the voices around him talking in "every conceivable foreign language" (13). He declared his support for the Republicans in the Spanish Civil War, when he "learned to see the world through other people's eyes", and also spent two years as a US serviceman in Europe at the end of World War II. Before the war, he had established a book club, making good writers available in cheap editions (34), and after the war he set up his own publishing house. He made regular visits to Paris and

Frankfurt for the Book Fair, meeting and making friends with writers and publishers from all over the world.

Braziller admired writers from beyond Europe, such as Salman Rushdie and Orhan Pamuk, for example, from whom he learnt about "the conflicts and contradictions of Eastern and Western culture" (88). He was especially excited by the work of Natalie Sarraute and Claude Simon and other practitioners of the *nouveau roman*, who were "pushing the boundaries" (68) of the conventional novel. Braziller was very much an "old school" publisher, more interested in the quality of the writing than in making huge profits. By chance one evening in 1959, he picked up the New Zealand edition of *Owls Do Cry* from the office slush pile. Expecting Frame to be "just another local talent", he was surprised to find himself reading the novel in one sitting. He felt the form was "less consciously new" than that of the *nouveau roman*, but that it was "equally striking and powerful" (69). Braziller came to admire Frame's work immensely, and introduced her to other writers he published over a period of time he refers to as his "thirty year journey with Janet Frame" (Alley 1994, 15).

Owls Do Cry sold about 800 copies in its Braziller edition of 1960. The next book of Frame's they published, *Faces in the Water*, sold 5000 copies, vindicating Braziller's faith in Frame as "a poet of genius, a Rimbaud who chose to write in prose" (GBP 11/6). Braziller was on a mission, and in writing about *Scented Gardens for the Blind* he asserts that "Janet Frame is our girl, and we can be proud of her, because there is no publishing house here or in England that has an author who for sheer writing genius can come anywhere near her." (GBP 11/6)

Years later, in his tribute to Frame in *The Inward Sun*, the festschrift celebrating Frame's 70th birthday, Braziller (Alley 1994) wonders about his right to claim the rôle of Frame's publisher "when it is in fact Janet who struggled to make her experiences and voice available to readers of all ages, from all over the world" (19). Braziller managed to keep Frame's work in print in the USA, through his policy of publishing cheap editions. His publishing strategy seems to have worked in that sense, since in San Francisco in 2015, I noticed that the City Lights bookshop carried a full stock of Frame titles, across the whole range of her work, whereas London major bookstores rarely display more than one or two.

Frame's first British publisher was W.H. Allen, who published *Owls Do Cry* in 1961, some five years after it had been written, and remained Frame's British publisher for over a decade, publishing five more novels, the last of which was *Daughter Buffalo* in 1973, and some short stories shortly before W.H. Allen ceased trading as an independent publishing house. Thereafter, Frame's novels and autobiography were published by The Women's Press, established in 1978 with a stated mission to publish "incisive feminist fiction and non-fiction by outstanding women writers from around the world" until it ceased trading at the beginning of this century. They published four of Frame's novels: *Faces in the Water* (1980), *Living in the Maniototo* (1981), *Scented Gardens for the Blind* (1982) and *Owls Do Cry* (1985), as well as a collection of short stories, *You Are Now Entering the Human Heart* (1984), a book of poems, *The Pocket Mirror* (1993) and an edition of Frame's three-volume autobiography (1990). Her final novel, *The Carpathians*, was published by Bloomsbury after Frame took issue with the over-zealously feminist stance of The Women's Press, which according to Michael King (2000, 484) did not want to publish *Daughter Buffalo* because its protagonists were men. Currently, Virago—part of the Little, Brown Book Group—which aims "to champion women's voices and bring them to the widest possible readership around the world" has Frame's autobiography in print in Britain and three Frame novels, *Towards Another Summer*, and *Faces in the Water*, the latter reissued in May 2018 as one of a "baker's dozen" of significant fiction to celebrate the 40th anniversary of Virago, and *Owls Do Cry*, issued in 2016 with an introduction by Margaret Drabble.

In the rest of Europe, the 1970s and 1980s were very quiet years in publishing terms for Frame. There was a new French translation of *Owls Do Cry* in 1986 from Alinéa, given the title *La Chambre close* [The Closed Room] and a Dutch edition of *Owls Do Cry* (*Uilen roepen)* in 1982 from De Geus. The German publishers, Suhrkamp, issued further editions of *Owls Do Cry* (*Wenn die Eulen schrein*) in 1981, and *Auf dem Maniototo* in 1987. There is then a veritable explosion of publications in the 1990s, following the award of the Commonwealth Writers Prize to Frame for *The Carpathians* in 1989. The success of Jane Campion's film, *An Angel at My Table*, the prize-winning appearance of which at the Venice Film Festival in 1990 generated a very considerable degree of publicity, and both the film and the award doubtless sparked the interest of a wide range of publishers.

The preface to the 1986 edition of *La Chambre close* (*Owls Do Cry*) by Viviane Forrester, who won the Prix Goncourt in 2009 for her biography of Virginia Woolf, focuses entirely on the autobiographical aspects of the novel and the social setting of the characters in New Zealand, children of "rudes pionniers" (9) [rough pioneers] in the land of the Māori. Forrester appears to be interested solely in the novel's setting and its relationship to Frame's life, and in taking a biographical approach overlooks entirely the quality of its language and its poetry. She suggests that the success of Frame's novel comes "peut-être parce qu'elle a traversé elle-même ce récit presque autobiographique, mais qu'elle a pris, qu'elle a su prendre la distance de l'écrivain" (9). [Perhaps because she has herself traversed this semi-autobiographical narrative, but has taken, knew how to take a writer's distance.] Forrester's focus is on character and the part played by memory: "Chaque épisode, chaque instant, chaque sensation se répercutent tout au long de leurs vies, les rendant chaque fois plus sensibles, plus vulnérables" (10). [Each episode, each moment, each sensation reverberates through their lives, each time making them more sensitive, more vulnerable.] There is no mention of Frame's poetic use of language, her imagery, or the connection to *The Tempest* as pursued in Jeanne Delbeare's collection, *Bird, Hawk, Bogie* (1978), and none of the perceptive appreciation of Frame's style that is found in Ulrich Walberer's 1963 review, discussed later in this chapter, though Forrester's approach may perhaps have brought new French readers to Frame's work.

By contrast with Forrester's preface, Christine Jordis—an eminent writer and editor specialising in English literature—wrote a review of *La Chambre close* for the literary periodical *La Quinzaine Littéraire* in May 1986 : "Désir, rêve, imaginaire dans un monde aveugle" [Desire, dream and the imaginary in a blind world], which gives French readers a much more wide-ranging view of Frame's skill as a writer. She focuses on Frame's blending of dream and reality, her use of imagery, and her references to *The Tempest*. She translates the English title of Frame's first novel as "les hiboux crient", and comments on its significance with its reference to Ariel's song from *The Tempest*, "le chant d'Ariel, qui n'est pas cité ici, porteur des notions de mort et d'enfouissement, de magie et de métamorphose" [the song of Ariel, who is not named here, carrying the ideas of death and burial, magic and metamorphosis]. Jordis had read a number of Frame's novels in English, and comments on the connections of theme and language among them, making a link with the themes of *Owls Do Cry*. She quotes from *Intensive Care* in her own translation, "Tous les rêves, [. . .] ramènent au jardin du cauchemar" [all dreams lead back to the nightmare garden], and adds "Et tous les cauchemars, après maints détours, à une vérité" [and all the nightmares, after many detours, [lead] to a truth]. Jordis remarks on the poetic nature of Frame's prose, and its relation to poetry and music:

> Des mots reviennent, chansons d'enfant, poèmes ou phrases en italiques, motifs musicaux qui marquent l'alternance du souvenir et des faits, le glissement continuel des événements, dans les passage narratifs, aux images incohérentes, heurtées, étouffantes, que charrie malgré elle la mémoire [words return, children's songs, poems or phrases in italics, musical motifs that mark the alternation of memory and fact, the continual shift of events, in the narrative passages to the incoherent, colliding, suffocating images carrying her [Daphne's] memory, in spite of herself].

With warm words of praise for the translator, Catherine Vieilledent, Jordis concludes with a comment on the "traversé de voix" [the criss-cross of voices] recognising the polyphonic nature of Frame's prose and "un tissu serré d'images et symboles" [a tight fabric of images and symbols] in a review which both demonstrates her total immersion in Frame's œuvre and provides an attractive, informed and perceptive introduction for French readers. This edition was reissued in 1994 by the publishers Joëlle Losfeld, who changed the title from *La Chambre close* to *Les Hiboux pleurent vraiment* [The Owls Do Weep]. If the publishers thought this was a more appealing title, it is nevertheless sadly an inaccurate and nonsensical translation of the Shakespearean lines. There is a standard translation of the lines from *The Tempest* as an epigraph in this edition, "quand crient des hiboux"—which would have made a perfect title—and whose significance Jordis so clearly elucidates in her 1986 review.

The autobiography and film, however, also sparked further academic interest amongst French academics currently based in Paris and working in the field of Commonwealth literature. Twenty years after Jane Campion's film, during 2011–2012, *The Lagoon and Other Stories* was on the syllabus for the French *agrégation*, a prestigious, competitive post-graduate national teaching qualification, prompting a French monograph, *Janet Frame: The Lagoon and Other Stories: naissance d'une œuvre* in 2010, co-authored by Claire Bazin and Alice Braun, *Chasing Butterflies* in 2011, a collection of essays edited by Vanessa Guignery, and a special edition of Paris University's *Commonwealth Essays and Studies* devoted to Janet Frame in 2012. Bazin (2011) also authored an overview of Frame's work in the "Writers and Their Work" series for the British publisher, Northcote House.

By 1981, Frame was becoming increasingly concerned about royalties and sales and engaged Tim Curnow, a New Zealander she had known for some years, as her literary agent. He felt that however committed George Braziller was to Frame "his enthusiasm was not reflected in the sales of her work". Frame (Alley 1994) had complained to Curnow that "the returns are incredibly bleak" (29) and

Curnow has confirmed that Frame wasn't receiving royalties which were due to her from Albion Wright (Curnow, personal communication). Curnow set about improving on this situation, and Frame asked him to represent her throughout the world except in the USA. He set about winding up the old literary rights of Frame's early publishers in Britain and New Zealand, and by 1983 Curtis Brown had negotiated for Random House to acquire the New Zealand rights, enabling them to reprint and republish Frame's backlist, and in editions which restore Frame's idiosyncratic formatting and punctuation.

By the end of the 1990s, French, German, Spanish, Italian, Danish, Swedish, Norwegian and Polish publishers had all issued a translation of the autobiography and most of them published or reissued some of Frame's novels. Generally, publishers translated titles as near the original as possible, but the Italian Edizione Club decided on *Dentro il muro* [Inside the Wall] in 1990 for *Faces in the Water*, and *An Angel at My Table* became *Un été à Willowglen* [One Summer at Willowglen] in one French edition, though a Hungarian edition of *Owls Do Cry, Ejjel, ha bagoly huho,* published in 1999, keeps closely to the English title. The changes of title are a reminder of the marketing problems created for Braziller and Bloomsbury by Frame's insistence on *The Carpathians* as the title, when they first published the book, rather than "The Orchard" or something similar.

The correspondence in the Braziller archives at Princeton University library indicates that Braziller had proposed *The Orchards of Puamahara,* and felt that *The Carpathians* suggested "a travelogue". Frame (2011) was outraged and in an undated letter from New Zealand protests that the title "has been carefully chosen" (216). George Braziller (Alley 1994), ever alert to the letters from Frame which "came on different coloured paper", was "always on guard when the ones on green paper arrived, as Janet usually complained on green" (15). Braziller clearly relented, as Frame's preference for *The Carpathians,* as a title "(travelogue or not)" prevailed (Frame 2011, 217). The British publisher, Bloomsbury, also used *The Carpathians* as the title, and made it clear on the cover of their publication of this title in 1993, that the author was a Commonwealth Prize winner, and in an introduction to the novel's plot, that *The Carpathians* was indeed fiction.

Beyond Europe there were Chinese (1993) and Japanese (1994) translations of the autobiography during Frame's lifetime. The Japanese translation of Frame's autobiography was undertaken by two translators working as a team, Professor Masami Nakao, a poetry specialist at Tokyo University and Naoko Torwaiwa. Nakao reports that there were a "few good reviews" but not "big sales" (Nakao, personal communication). Frame's short story, "The Winter Garden" was included in a Japanese publication of *Contemporary New Zealand Short Stories* in 1981, and *The Lagoon and Other Stories* was published in Japanese in 2014. Nakao's fascination with Frame lies in "the complex mixture of domestic and European cultures and traditions incorporated in Frame's growing literary mind. And, more than anything, appreciating her rich and imaginative text was a real pleasure to me" (ibid.). There was also an edition of the autobiography in Korean (2012) and a Korean edition of *The Carpathians*. A proposed Russian edition of the autobiography does not appear to have reached publication. It is more difficult to pursue and verify details of translations into languages which use alphabets other than Roman, or use writing systems which are not European, but the Public Library in Oamaru—appropriately given that this was Frame's home town where she lived from 1931 and where she went to school—has a reference collection of Frame titles in translation, listed in its online catalogue, with details of translators.

During the 2000s, French, German, Dutch, Italian, Spanish, Norwegian and Swedish publishers have continued to issue or reissue Frame's novels in translation, perhaps encouraged by Frame's second nomination for the Nobel Prize in 2003. Further encouragement may well have come from the posthumous publication by the Janet Frame Trust of two novellas, *Towards Another Summer* (2007) and *In the Memorial Room* (2013), both written much earlier, but not published in Frame's lifetime for reasons of sensitivity to people easily identified in the novellas and still living. The Trust published a volume of non-fiction, *Janet Frame: In Her Own Words* (2011), and a volume of previously unpublished or uncollected short stories, *Gorse is Not People* (2012). Beyond Western Europe, there was a Mexican Spanish edition of poems, and a Brazilian Portuguese edition of *Towards Another Summer* (*Rumo a outro verão*) in 2009, a Turkish one (*Bir Başka Yaza Doğru*) in 2012, as well as a Turkish edition of *Owls Do Cry* (*Baykuşlar Öterken*) in 2010, a Romanian edition of *The Rainbirds* (*Familia Rainbird*) in 2013 and a Slovene edition of *The Carpathians* in 2009.

Frame's work also inspires creators of other media—Jane Campion's film, famously—but also radio drama and a chamber opera. Frame's autobiography was the subject of a prize-winning adaptation for BBC Radio by Anita Sullivan, first broadcast in January 2013, and re-broadcast periodically. The American composer Aaron Siegel of *Experiments in Opera*, who has read most of Frame's novels, composed an opera, *Rainbird*, based on *The Rainbirds*, attracted by what he saw as its use of the Orpheus myth, and this was premiered on November 30, 2017 in New York.

Most readers outside the English-speaking world, however, read Frame in translation. Although it is difficult to gauge to what extent the difficulties of translation have affected the publication of non-English editions of Frame's novels, and whilst a comprehensive consideration of literary translation is beyond the scope of this study, we can see that translation *is* an issue, understandably, given the densely poetic nature of Frame's novelistic style. Rosanna Masiola Rosini (Alley 1994), who taught Commonwealth Literature and literary translation at the University of Pisa, writes with feeling in a tribute to Frame about the translation difficulties her students encountered because "the text was just too beautiful" (140) and the need for the translator to be "at one with the text, the author, the land and the landscape" (139). Rosini writes about the value of collaboration in translation and respect for the author's intentions, and her words are echoed by Nadine Ribault and Jean Anderson (2011) in their fascinating, detailed account in *Commonwealth Essays and Studies* of their collaboration on a translation into French of *The*

Lagoon and Other Stories. They completed this translation in 2004, having "spent considerable time and energy exploring the 'undertext' of the stories" (21), and were concerned "to set down the writer's inner voice on the page" (24) and in considering word choices to pursue "the best option until it was finally 'cornered' to the satisfaction of both partners" (25).

In her paper for the 2017 New Zealand Studies Network conference, held in London, "Islands on Sale: New Zealand and Pacific Arts in the Global marketplace", Andreia Sarabando used the 2004 Portuguese translation of *The Carpathians*, the only translation of Frame's work in Portugal, to give an enlightening account of the effects of poor translation choices, bearing in mind that Frame's text poses some very difficult translation problems. Simplification and the use of generic words impact on cultural specificity, style and nuance. Awkward choices for words with specific New Zealand connotations, for example "creeks", "paddocks" and "dairy", and a lack of distinction between different variants of American, British and New Zealand English add to the confusion for Portuguese readers. Māori phrases are printed without comment, and Sarabando suggests that greater use might have been made of footnotes to explain cultural, linguistic and pronunciation issues. At least the Portuguese title, *Os Carpatos no nosso jardim,* [The Carpathians in our Garden] is simply an extension of Frame's title taken from the words of one of the characters, rather than something entirely different. This Portuguese edition is now out of print. It is difficult to see how it could even have been considered publishable, and can have done very lttle for Frame's reception in Portugal.

The earliest European edition of a Frame novel was the German edition of *Owls Do Cry,* published by Nannen Verlag in 1961, and reviewed in *Die Zeit,* on October 13, 1961 by Ulrich Walberer, who notes that the publishers had, "ein Stück großer Literatur engagiert, ganz großer" [issued a truly great work of literature]. The title of his review reflects his assertion that "Ein Riß geht durch die Welt" [The World is Ruptured]. Janet Frame, he said, was "eine Schriftstellerin die Beachtung verdient" [a writer who deserves attention]. He notes that the Withers children "dringen zufällig in die Welt von Grimms Märchen ein" [randomly penetrate the world of Grimms' Tales] and he perceives the interwoven texture of Frame's prose. Walberer says of the events in the story that "Sie sind nur Kettenfäden in einem Gazegewebe, bei dem die Schußfäden von der Poesie und Phantasie zur Realität hin- und hergezogen sind." [They are only the warp threads in a gauze fabric, in which the weft threads of poetry and fantasy weave in and out.] Finally, he has warm praise for the translator, Ruth Malchow. It is difficult to know how much involvement Frame had with translated editions, but Malchow came to visit Frame in London in 1963, and Frame told friends how much she enjoyed the visit from her German translator and how well the two women got on. Walberer clearly believes that Malchow has been true to Frame's intentions and "Werkgetreu zieht sie die Linien nach, die ihr die Autorin vorzeichnet". [She is true to the work and follows the threads that bring you to the author.] The passionate tone of Walberer's words reminds us of the powerful feelings behind Ballantyne's 1952 New Zealand radio review of *The Lagoon*, and H. Winston Rhodes's 1957 review of *Owls Do Cry* in *Landfall*, which he begins by declaring that:

> The emotional effect of *Owls Do Cry* is such that instead of confining myself to the language of criticism, I feel tempted to talk about life and human suffering, about the values of civilization and the search for meaning, about the empty heart and the disturbed mind. (327–28)

The considerable interest in Germany evidenced by Walberer's 1961 review of *Owls do Cry* is matched by the interest of French and Belgian academics in the 1970s, notably Delbaere at Liège and Victor Dupont at Toulouse, whereas in Spain, according to Paloma Fresno-Calleja (2015) New Zealand literature has been largely disregarded, and the newspaper *La Vanguardia*, for example, commenting on New Zealand's place as guest of honour at the Frankfurt Book Fair in 2012, described New Zealand literature as *"un peso pluma"* [featherweight].

The 2014 publication of *Un pais de cuento: veinte relatos de Nueva Zelanda* [A Country of Tales: Twenty Stories from New Zealand], translated by Paloma Fresno-Calleja and edited by Janet Wilson was awarded a translation prize, and includes Frame's short story, "The Lagoon". The excellent translation and careful editing in this Spanish-New Zealand collaboration may go some way to address Spain's dismissal of New Zealand literature and increase the global reception of New Zealand literature, and Frame, in Spanish-speaking countries.

New Zealand's status as guest of honour at the 2012 Frankfurt Book Fair highlighted the very considerable interest in New Zealand literature in Germany. Early 20th-century German immigrants to New Zealand made up one of its largest non English–speaking communities, and Charles Brasch, for example, was a member of one of New Zealand's German-speaking families. At the time of the Book Fair, the German publishers C.H. Beck reissued Frame's novels, partly in a revised translation, and German paperback editions of *Towards Another Summer* and *An Angel at My Table* were published in 2012 and 2016 respectively. Beck's publishing blurb for *Auf dem Maniototo* (2013) speaks of Frame as "eine meisterhafte Erzählerin, die brilliante Pirouetten dreht und funkelnde Reflexionen zum Besten gibt. Daraus ensteht ein irrgarten der Emotionen und die wunderlichen Bilder, der die Lesenden bezaubt". [A masterly story-teller who turns brilliant pirouettes and creates sparkling reflections. This creates a whirlpool of emotions and whimsical images which enchant readers.] However, even before the boost afforded by the Frankfurt Book Fair, there were encouraging reviews of *Den neuen Sommer entgegen* (*Towards Another Summer*) in the German press. Verene Lueken, writing in the *Frankfurter Allgemeine* of November 27, 2010, shows that in spite of anything that might be lost in translation, she grasps the essential character of Frame's prose when she writes that

> Janet Frame schreibt entlang der Grenze zwischen wirklicher und eingebildeter Welt, wobei der Blick der Autorin immer beide Welten erfasst und die Wörter mühelos zwischen ihnen hin und her springen, Verbindungen bilden

und die eine, die sichtbare Welt, mit der anderen sozusagen infizieren. [Janet Frame writes along the border between real and imaginary worlds, where the author's gaze always captures both worlds and the words leap effortlessly between them, forming connections and infecting the visible world with the other, so to speak.]

Leuken also expresses her thanks to the translator, who, she says, has unusually but helpfully supplied some notes on New Zealand items. For example, she chose to leave the word "godwit" in English with an explanation, as the German name for this bird would mean nothing to most German readers.

Dieter Riemenschneider, Emeritus Professor at Frankfurt University, assures me that there is interest in Frame's work in German universities, especially the autobiography and *Owls Do Cry*, but that it tends to be taught in introductory courses, and according to the interests of particular academics. In the 1990s he included *The Carpathians* in a course on "The Motif of the Journey" and recalls how difficult Frame's novel was compared to the other texts, but that his students "got into it", and that Frame's novels "once readers have taken note of them are highly appreciated" (Riemenschneider, personal communication).

The significance of the individual interests of influential academics and critics is borne out in the case of the Italian market, where the enthusiasm for Frame's work of the late Professor Claudio Gorlier of the University of Turin is published in the book pages of *La Stampa*, and contrasts markedly with the "featherweight" Spanish view in the *La Vanguardia* article. Writing about Frame on September 18, 1990, Gorlier argues that

> La letteratura neolandese ha sì e no cinquant'anni di vita, ma possiede una fisionomia autonoma e originale, [. . .] Inoltre, vi occupa un posto centrale la scrittura femminile, a cominciare da Katherine Mansfield. (16) [New Zealand literature has only fifty years of life, but it has an autonomous

and original physiognomy [. . .] In addition, it occupies a central place in women's writing, beginning with Katherine Mansfield.]

He refers to Frame's magical use of language, to her "consciente alchimia della parola" [her conscious alchemy with words] with which she is "rifiutando le coordinate tradizionali del tempo e dello spazio" [rejecting the traditional co-ordinates of time and space]. He takes great delight at the Venice Film Festival of 1990 in his written interview with Frame, asking in the September 29 edition if she felt "una certa parentela" [a certain kinship] with Prospero and about her affinity with Māori culture. In the same edition Gorlier provides his own translation of an edited extract from *Owls Do Cry*, taken from the end of Chapter 13, where Daphne is receiving shock treatment. In his commentary, Gorlier notes that Daphne may be reduced to silence, "ma interiormente le rimarrà fino all'ultimo la forza di immaginare, di articolare la magia della visione" [but inside the strength will remain to the last to imagine, to articulate the magic of vision], the "magic" which Gorlier sees as the essence of Frame's writing. ("Tuttolibri" 1)

A selection of Frame's poetry translated into Italian, *Parleranno le tempeste* [Storms will Tell] was published in 2017, selected from *A Pocket Mirror* and *The Goose Bath*, and it had a very enthusiastic reception in the Italian press, with a number of detailed and lengthy press reviews. The words "gem" and "virtuoso" are used a number of times, and the critics note that as well as conveying Frame's lyric voice, imagination and universal themes, the translators have also managed to communicate her wit and word-play. The collection has made a profound impression on the Swiss-Italian poet Daniele Bernardi. Writing in *Azione*, a Swiss weekly, on November 20, 2017, and quoting lines from "The Clown", he comments that in this poem "si recepisce una forza dolorosa, frutto di un sapere che si misura col profondo patire umano" [we perceive a painful force, the fruit of a knowledge that is measured by profound human suffering]. By way of contrast, Bernardi also quotes from "Napalm", in which

Frame combines wordplay with the most serious of themes, "il gioco linguistico [. . .] e la denuncia delle violenze del proprio tempo" [linguistic games ... and the denunciation of violence in one's own time]. He describes this collection as "una gemma preziosa" [a precious gem] and that Frame's poetry shows "potenza visionaria" [visionary power] and "poesia intesa come destino" [poetry understood as destiny] (4).

One of the translators, Francesca Benocci, completed her PhD in translation studies at Victoria University Wellington, and she and her collaborator, Eleonora Bello (2017), both attest in their translators' notes to the translation experience as being "complessa, divertente, emotivamento onerosa, illuminante" [complex, entertaining, emotionally onerous, enlightening] (20) and point out that both they and the translations benefitted from their collaboration, completing their task with a sense of achievement and satisfaction, "in questa rinnovata quiete dopo *le tempeste*" [in this renewed quiet after the storms] (20). The book's cover makes reference to Jane Campion's film and Frame's autobiography, and gives a list of further Frame titles available in Italian.

The success of Jane Campion's film, *An Angel at My Table*, at the 1990 Venice Film Festival, already noted, brought Frame to the notice of a much wider international audience, encouraging further translations and publication of her work. Frame's autobiography sold well, and brought her, finally, financial security. It has become her best known, and by far her best-selling work, acclaimed as "one of the greatest autobiographies written this century", by Michael Holroyd, the eminent British biographer, in his contribution to the *Sunday Times* "Books of The Year" on December 8, 1985. The US publisher, Counterpoint, which in 2016 published a collection of Frame's letters to her American artist friend Bill Brown, *Jay to Bee*, brought out a new edition of her autobiography in 2017, and it is the most frequently translated of her works. Braziller's (Alley 1994) anecdote about his meeting at the Frankfurt Book Fair with a young German girl who picked up one of his newly published Frame titles because she had seen Campion's film, and "would like to read everything about Janet Frame" (19) is repeated frequently in the reviews posted on the websites of online book-sellers across Europe. Comments from people who have bought one of Frame's novels in translation, almost invariably reference Campion's film and Frame's autobiography. As even a cursory glance through the websites makes clear, the internet is now making literature published beyond the reader's own national and cultural borders so much more readily accessible.

Nevertheless, however far Frame's reputation eventually extended, her writing career began, very locally indeed in her home town, Oamaru, in New Zealand's South Island. In the 1930s Frame was writing, as a child correspondent, letters and poems for the children's page of her local newspaper, the *Otago Daily Times*, showing something of the imagination, talent and interests which she later developed as a mature writer, and this correspondence is the subject of the next section.

Early Years and Dot's Little Folk

Janet Frame's childhood home had few books, but her parents, her mother Lottie especially, had a keen interest in stories, poems and songs, which helped to sow the seeds of Frame's lifelong devotion to the literary world. Her mother published poems in the *Wyndham Farmer*, an Otago newspaper, and came to be known as "Lottie C. Frame, the local poet" (*CA*, 25). One of Lottie's resolutely cheerful poems appeared in another local newspaper, the *New Zealand Mercury* on January 10, 1938, and begins: "I should not choose to criticise/A poet of the sunset skies". She concludes with a comment that makes clear her sense of the superiority of poets' perception: "I leave the satire for the fools/Who care not for the poet mind" (8).

For Lottie, poetry does not reside in satire and criticism, but in a grateful appreciation of the beauties of the natural world. The adult Janet Frame valued the mind of the poet as a privileged person, and we see here that this was a view that Lottie also took, though Lottie's style of poetry adheres to the Georgian conventions of the time. A poem Lottie had published in July 1933 in the monthly *New Zealand Railways Magazine* begins:

> Where straggling fences on some lonely hill,
> The air, their fragrance with pure beauty fill,
> By summer's breezes are their petals fanned,
> The sweet wild roses of our Maoriland. (24)

Referring to the turn-of-the-century English poets—Kipling and Newbolt, for example—the New Zealand poet Owen Leeming (1964) notes that they were paid "fulsome homage. And of course they were slavishly imitated in the Colonies. They were literature's answer to the aspidistra", and we can see from Leeming's remark that Lottie was a child of her time (287).

In her autobiography, Frame records that Lottie talked about her favourite books: *Uncle Tom's Cabin*, *Tom Sawyer*, and American poets: Longfellow and Whittier; and the English and Scottish ballads. Frame's father sang war-time songs and the popular songs of the era; he and Lottie were active in keeping up their Scottish culture of dance, music and song. He valued books, and brought home a copy of Oscar Wilde's *Fairy Tales* which he had found among some rubbish, (*CA*, 19) though his own taste ran to the stories of Zane Grey and Sexton Blake (101). On Sunday evenings Lottie held Bible readings when they "pored over the red-letter Bible" (34), and Lottie, a Christadelphian who believed in the Day of Judgement and the Second Coming, encouraged her children not to laugh at people thought odd, as they "might be angels in disguise" (28). Lottie tended to stress the doom-laden Bible stories of The Garden of Eden and The Flood and she fed Frame's youthful imagination with biblical images and stories she would transform in her own writing as an adult.

An important source of reading material for the Frame children was the weekly children's page in the *Otago Daily Times*: "Dot's Little Folk". It was inaugurated in July 1886 by the *Otago Witness*, and taken over in 1932 by the *Otago Daily Times* when the *Otago Witness* ceased publication. The historian Keith Scott (2011) bases his survey of New Zealand childhood on this children's page, focusing his attention on the experience of childhood of the generations of children who wrote to "Dot" from the page's inception until just after the end of the First World War. He mentions that Janet Frame was "the most famous literary DLF" but "does not belong to this time" (306). This study takes up the story from the mid-1930s, when the Frame sisters became contributors to "Dot's Little Folk", until the page ceased publication in 1941.

At its height in the early years of the 20th century Dot's page was extremely popular, to the extent that the children's letters "were taking up no less than three pages of the smallest type, when it was found necessary as noted on 19 April 1900 to restrict the space to eight columns". The importance of the column was both social and educational, and became a valued reading community, as illustrated by a "Farewell Letter" from Reta, who had reached the page's retiring age of 21 in 1906, and wrote on March 21 of her "many true D.L.F. friends, of whom not a few are correspondents with me" and adding that the page "has been in some ways like a second education to me". Tom L. Mills (1943), who edited a selection of New Zealand children's verse, makes a similar point when he comments that "one cannot speak too highly of the tremendous encouragement given by the Press of New Zealand to child contributors" (10). Reports of social gatherings and the weekly meetings of the *Dunedin D.L.F. Literary and Debating Club* attest to its community importance for town-dwelling readers during the early part of the 20th century.

The identity of the successive "Dots" was largely kept anonymous, but the very first "Dot" was the journalist and novelist Louisa Baker, who very much set the tone of the page and had a keen interest in both creative writing and in children. On July 16, 1886 in the *Otago Witness* Baker promised that "Dot will never find any matter that interests the children too trivial to attend to, and hopes before long to be regarded as their friend". Baker returned to England by 1894, to pursue a career as a novelist, but her influence on the page endured. Baker invited the children to choose pseudonyms. Some of these names were patriotic: "Young Newzealander" and "Scotch Lad", but most children chose names from stories or fairy-tales and Frame was "Amber Butterfly". In later years, Dot would select and print a "Letter of the Week" by way of praise and encouragement.

The continuing social significance of "Dot's Little Folk" as a reading community was also evident in a letter from Janet Frame's younger sister June ("Dancing Fairy") who wrote to say "Double Daffodil sits in front of me [. . .] Willow Blossom's Sister sits three seats at the back of me" (*ODT* October 23, 1939). Janet Frame ("Amber Butterfly") would mention her favourite correspondents in her letters: Fairey Fox, Quilp and Lady Canterbury Bell. The correspondents all had birthday greetings from Dot, and the deaths of Little Folk were also reported on Dot's Page, prompting letters of reminiscence and condolence. A nine-year old June Frame wrote of their sister Myrtle's death, announcing that "I am sorry to say that we lost our sister, Good Queen Charlotte, in March. We do miss her so much. But we are going to see her when she wakes again" (*ODT* August 2, 1937), a reference to the faith of her mother Lottie, a Christadelphian who believed in the Day of Resurrection, when she would be reunited with her dead daughter—Myrtle Frame drowned in a swimming pool, apparently as a result of an undiagnosed heart condition.

When Baker left in 1894, the editor William Fenwick took over the page himself, so that for a time, Dot was actually a middle-aged man, maintaining the standards set by Baker until he retired as editor in 1909. Most of the page's correspondents were from lower South Island, but a few letters came from further afield and occasionally from Canada: there were pen-friend arrangements with children in India, Ceylon, and Canada. Frame had her first letter published in 1935, and by 1936 was a regular correspondent. Her sisters also wrote in and occasionally had letters or poems published. By this time, Dot was Eileen Soper, who took over the page when the *Otago Witness* closed in 1932, and remained as Dot until 1938, resigning when she married. Like Louisa Baker, Soper was a journalist and after World War II she wrote novels for young readers and an autobiography. The table below shows Frame's contributions and is as accurate as possible within the limits of the completeness of the *Otago Daily Times*.

Year	Letters	Poems
1935	1	0
1936	1	0
1937	4	2
1938	5	4
1939	3	6
1940	0	8
1941	0	8

Table 1: Janet Frame's Letters and Poems to the *Otago Daily Times*.

From the early 1900s, young readers wrote to "Dot" under their pseudonyms, and got a brief, positive response. In later years, "Dot" would select and print a "Letter of the Week" by way of praise and encouragement. Each Monday, there was a poem, an article of interest, part of a serialised story and then a selection of readers' letters. The reading material was aimed at a range of ages and included re-writings of classic literature and poetry from the English canon, as well as stories and poems aimed at younger children. In 1934, Dot's page was serialising the story of Beowulf, pairing the Death of Beowulf with Walt Whitman's "O Captain! My Captain!". In 1935, the paper serialised "Thor and the Giants", the Norse Sagas of Thor, Loki, and Freya, and classical Greek myths and legends appeared at various times. There appear to have been no retellings of Māori myths, or Māori correspondents, though in a letter about ancient monsters and tuatara Frame makes mention of the Māori legend of Taniwha, "an old legend which you will probably know about a number of Māoris being eaten by a huge Taniwha" (*ODT* December 5, 1938).

The fiction and non-fiction items catered for a wide range of ages and interests. In amongst the children's adventure stories there were more sophisticated items about the wider world, and fiction which required at least a degree of maturity. For example, one piece muses on shadows in relation to the coming of summer, links the beauties of the natural world, a story from ancient Greece, and a reference to philosophers and poets. The final paragraph begins, "Plato speaks of human beings living in a kind of cave in which they do not see the actual shape of things but only their shadows" (*ODT*,

December 5, 1938) and briefly links further shadows imagery from Thomas de Quincey, Shakespeare, Chaucer, Edmund Burke and the Bible. In spite of its often sentimental tone, the successive editors of Dot's page took their responsibilities to the children seriously, both in responding positively to the children's views and interests and in supporting their developing literacy and literary skills.

The weekly poem, with which the page usually began, drew on a mix of poems written for children, sometimes by "Anon", but generally by well-known poets who wrote for children; poems from the literary canon; and occasionally poems from the correspondents. Poems included Edward Lear's "The Owl and the Pussycat", John Drinkwater's "Moonlit Apples", Rudyard Kipling's "If", three poems by James Joyce : "Noise of Many Waters", "Strings in the Earth" and "Air and Goldenhair"; poems by Walter de la Mare and Robert Graves, G.K. Chesterton, A. E. Housman; Francis Thompson's "The Daisy", W. H. Davies's "Summer", Blake's "The Tyger" and "Happy Piper", and Cowper's "Snail". There are poems by Charles Kingsley, R. W. Emerson, Wordsworth's "Daffodils", Browning's "Home Thoughts from Abroad", Robert Bridges, Tennyson, Lawrence Binyon, Edmund Blunden and W.B. Yeats's "Lake Isle of Innisfree". This was a resolutely British diet of poetry, with the occasional Irish and American poem.

Just occasionally, the poet was not British. When Dot printed a poem from the southern hemisphere, there was a note to that effect. There were a few Australian poems, for example "Cradle Song" by Louis Esson (*ODT* February 7, 1938), with a reminder from Dot that "our own land is full of subjects around which poems could be made" (15). Twice during this period, Dot (*ODT* June 6, 1938) printed a children's poem by Katherine Mansfield, described as "one of New Zealand's own daughters, and while she was alive, one of the finest writers of short stories in the world" (15). The poem on this occasion was "The Town Between the Hills"; and the following year Dot (*ODT* August 14, 1939) printed Mansfield's "Opposites", a children's poem, and wrote of Mansfield as "a New Zealand writer of whom we should all be proud" (15), giving the impression that Mansfield was the only New Zealand writer of any literary worth.

There is a distinct absence on Dot's page of any New Zealand poems of the calibre of the British and American favourites, and apart from Mansfield's, the only other New Zealand poems printed came from the columns' readers. Earlier collections of New Zealand poetry, a *Treasury of New Zealand Verse* (1906 and revised 1926) and *Kowhai Gold* (1930), attracted widespread disdain and derision from New Zealand critics and poets. In his introduction to his 1945 anthology, *A Book of New Zealand Verse*, the poet Allen Curnow (1951) describes *Kowhai Gold* as "trivial if sincere" and exhibiting a "lack of any vital relation to experience, a fanciful aimlessness" (15). Charles Brasch (1980), poet and editor of New Zealand's literary quarterly, *Landfall*, was considerably harsher: "It shamed us in the eyes of the world. It set literature in a pretentious vacuum" (186).

There was a lot of encouragement on Dot's pages for readers to send in their own poems, with frequent advice. For example, Dot (*ODT* July 25, 1938) advised that poems should rhyme, and used Drinkwater's "Moonlit Apples" as an example:

> Each verse follows the pattern set by the first verse – five beats in the first three lines, four beats in the fourth; the first three lines rhyming with themselves, the fourth line rhyming with the fourth line in the next verse. Then read it aloud and see how full of music its words are. (15)

Children were exhorted to learn poems by heart and to relish the sound of them. Writing about Blake's "The Tyger", Dot (*ODT* October 10, 1938) urged that: "This famous poem is one you should all know [...]. Learn the poem if you can, for to say it aloud is to receive a thrill of excitement up and down your spine" (19).

Dot made it clear that she did not expect free verse— pointedly to Fairey Fox, one of her young contributors, who sent in such an offering. Poems had to have a rhyme scheme. Poems using "poetic diction" and the kind of sentimentality of the time were praised for being "charming". Fairey Fox (*ODT* March 7, 1938) did not take the criticism kindly and responded with "You told me the rhyme could be improved. You surprised me, for the poem was not supposed to rhyme" (17). "Dot's Little Folk" was a distinctly interactive page, fulfilling some of the functions of present-day social media. Dot's feedback was a significant part of the page's success, and the children's letters, poems and points of view were always taken seriously: the successive and often anonymous Dots responded to the letters as a good teacher might. Although comments were often made in hackneyed terms—"charming", "pleasing" and so on—Dot (*ODT* February 15, 1937) was often more specific, and "pleasing poem" was tempered by a comment such as this one, that "There is something wrong with the last two lines of the first verse, but probably you will be able to discover what it is for yourself" (13).

This was one of Dot's earlier responses to Frame's poems, "A Treasure", but Dot's praise increased as Frame's poems became more skilful and confident, and Dot (*ODT* November 13, 1939) wrote of "Down by the Corner" that: "It shows some originality of thought, and the rhyme and rhythm are both good" (11). Frame kept a notebook recording her poems, which was later uncovered when her home in Eden Street Oamaru was renovated, and can now be seen at the Waitaki District Archives, Oamaru.

The comment Frame treasured and remarked on in her autobiography came for a poem called "Blossoms", about an orchard, which prompted Dot's (*ODT* October 2, 1939) praise for its "poetic insight and imagination" (13). Reflecting in her autobiography on this comment made during her sixth-form years at school, Frame wrote: "But, oh, how sweet were the words, 'poetic insight and *imagination*'. This was the first time anyone had told me, directly, that I had *imagination*" (Frame's emphasis). Frame ended this reflection by referring to a note in her diary of the time, "They think I'm going to be a schoolteacher, but I'm going to be a *poet*" (*CA*, 132; Frame's emphasis). Very occasionally, Dot was so impressed with a reader's poem, that it was printed along with one from a published poet, the ultimate accolade for the children who sent in their own poems;

Frame achieved this distinction twice, with "Spring Colours" on September 5, 1938 and "Autumn Rain" on April 25, 1939.

Some of the children's letters led to brief debates, mostly about gender-based rivalries and the challenges of childhood, but the impending war provoked a number of comments about the causes and ethics of the situation, as children tried to make sense of what was happening in the news. "Why do people fight with one another?" asked Frame (*ODT* March 28, 1938), "Simply because they have been hurt, and must hurt someone else". Dot's response aimed to engage with the correspondent and encourage further thought: "So you think war is a hitting back, Amber Butterfly? It is an interesting point of view. How would you prevent hurt in the first place?" (17). Frame followed this up the following week (*ODT* April 11, 1938) with a comment that Chamberlain and Eden should unite in spite of their differences, but that "these two men do not appear to have any idea of coming together, possibly because their feelings are hurt and they do not wish to 'grin and bear it'". Dot's response, perhaps feeling the correspondent was a little out of her depth, was that "such a joining sometimes results in disaster" (17).

Following the outbreak of war, Fairey Fox (*ODT* November 20, 1939), who had sent in the free verse poem, wrote a letter in which she condemned all war on the basis of the Sixth Commandment, adding "What men receive the Victoria Cross for in war time they are hung for in peace time". Fairey Fox's views on pacifism appear to be as advanced as her approach to rhyme and free verse. Just two months after Britain's declaration of war with Germany, it is surprising that such a letter was published, but Dot replied at some length, sounding disturbed by the viewpoint expressed, and terminating the debate. Dot acknowledged the rightness of the sentiment, but justified killing in self-defence, advising that Fairey Fox would understand better as she matured, and adding finally: "However, I do not think it would serve any good purpose to discuss the matter further" (15).

Frame's letters were usually less controversial, describing what she saw and heard around her, and they could receive high praise from Dot (*ODT*, May 23, 1938), for example, "an excellent example of what a best letter can be, Amber Butterfly—one subject treated as fully as possible, and interesting all the way through" (15). A year later, Frame's style was becoming more individual and less conventional, and Dot (*ODT*, September 11, 1939) was delighted with a lively letter describing what Frame could see "seated in a rather uncomfortable position in the hedge". Dot responded with "I have enjoyed your letter immensely, Amber Butterfly. It is very well written, and describes in a vivid and entertaining fashion the life of the street as seen by you from your seat in the hedge" (13). Frame's poems to Dot's page increased in length and became more complex during 1940 and 1941; and Dot (*ODT*, February 24, 1941) responded by repeating her appreciation of Frame's imagination, and adding: "I hope you will persevere with your writing of poetry. If you will study the works of the great poets, noting their choice of language and the smoothness of their verse, you will find this a great help" (8).

During 1940 and 1941, Frame was submitting poems to Dot's page, and to the children's section of another local newspaper, the *Oamaru Mail*, occasionally sending the same poem to both. For the most part, these poems may now only exist in the remaining archive copies of these newspapers, as Frame tells us that when she left school, she burnt her diaries and her childhood poems (*CA*, 140). The poems show a reluctance to depart from the clichéd "poetic diction" which Frame felt was expected of her: violets are always *shy*; mist is *silver*; and lakes are *crystal*; and the praise she received for her efforts caused her "to feel trapped by the opinion of others" (*CA*, 115). One of Frame's poems from 1938, "Winter Mornings", which she disparagingly described as her "usual factual account of the natural world", was accepted by *The New Zealand Railways Magazine* and Frame received one guinea for it. The poem was later included in Tom L. Mills's *Verse by New Zealand Children*, published in 1943. The pressure to conform to the much-praised derivative style influenced by the poets studied at school was considerable, and the very positive tone often sounds like Lottie Frame, for example in the final stanza of "At Evening" (*ODT* September 4, 1939):

> Make things happy, golden moon, just
>   for this night of spring,
> Let the sleeping daffodils their evening
>   gowns retrieve. (13)

By 1940, however, when Frame was 16, there are signs of an increasingly personal voice and of images and themes which Frame would develop as an adult. Finding poetry in unlikely places was one way of establishing an individual voice, as Frame says of her young self, "out of a desire to be myself, not to follow the ever-dominant personalities around me, I had formed the habit of focusing on places not glanced at by others" (*CA*, 115). In her poem "Dandelions" (*ODT* February 5, 1940), she sees these commonplace flowers as "a thousand marionettes of joy", an individualistic choice noted by Dot, who comments that "most people rather despise dandelions, but you have shown that, like many other common things, they possess a beauty of their own" (13). Frame (*ODT* May 30, 1938) showed the same tendency in a letter in which she describes a fascinating pattern of colours and pictures in a rock found in a nearby creek and declares "I do think it is marvellous that they resemble little pictures painted by the most famous artist" (15), an early indication of the significance Frame attached to the artist's perception. More individual ideas appear, for example the opening lines of "The Awakening of Autumn" (*ODT* April 1, 1940): "Autumn is resting to-night/Resting at peace in the glade", before a return to the clichés of

> Days will be happy and free,
> Skies will be powdered in blue
> When dear autumn wakes. (11)

Frame sent her poems to the *Oamaru Mail* under the pen-name "Amera", and the editor praised her as "an accomplished writer" for her poem "City Flowers" on June 14, 1940. This long poem anticipates some of the themes of Frame's novels, of urban decay and destruction, isolation and entrapment, and begins:

There are thin flowers in dark city places
Huddled away from the world and her dreams,
Pitifully pressing their pain-shadowed faces
For quiet of mornings and ripple of streams.

Commenting on these poems, Patrick Evans (1977) notes that "most of these suffer from rather precious subject matter and overlush imagery, but are remarkable for their metrical control and general confidence" (25–26), and quotes in full "Anzac Evening" from the *Oamaru Mail*'s *Mail Minor* on March 29, 1940. "City Flowers", published in the *Mail Minor* on June 14, 1940, is a good example of the qualities Evans notes, and owes more to Frame's reading of the early Yeats than the influence of Victorian and Georgian nature poems.

In later years, Frame would be drawn especially to the visionary poets: Blake, Hopkins, Dylan Thomas and Yeats. Yeats's concern with mythology and folklore, spirituality and death, the agrarian landscape and the natural world appear to have made an appeal to Frame's sensibilities in her school-days. The first stanza of "City Flowers" takes up Yeats's rose imagery and continues: "Will she have roses upon her pale feet/Dew-roses, warm roses, the roses of love" (*Mail Minor*, June 14, 1940). One of the poems Frame sent to Dot's page was "Kittenhood" (*ODT*, February 19, 1940), a poem which Dot found "a little involved in places" (13). It reappeared four days later in the *Oamaru Mail Minor* with a few very minor amendments, to regularise key repetitions and clarify the sense.

The themes of silence and blindness which Frame developed as an adult find early expression in Frame's poem, "Empty Houses" (*ODT*, February 17, 1941) which begins: "You sad homes of silence, you little blind houses, awake!/Let the wind blow your cobwebs away" (8). Isolation and silence are the theme of the poem Frame (*ODT* February 24, 1941) sent in the following week, "Wind Flowers" where the only sound is "eternal bird song", and "the only light is the light of sun and star", and where, "There is something felt in the silences up/in the wild, pure places" (8). As an adult, Frame would develop a strong affinity with the landscape poetry of her South Island contemporaries, and the "wild, pure places" would become a notable feature of the novels, contrasting with the man-made environment and its materialistic culture.

A year earlier, Frame had written a poem for the *Oamaru Mail*, "When Soldiers March". She quotes some stanzas in her autobiography, in which she writes of her inability to face the reality of war, and so

> turned to the shallow acceptance of glorifying the dead, with Rupert Brooke as my hero [. . .] and I did not realise until I had spent a few more years growing and observing that the kingdom that glorified those words was as much a prison as my grey school serge tunic. (*CA*, 123–24)

As 1941 progresses, however, there is an increasing use of more direct, freer, colloquial language amongst the "poetic diction" and naive patriotism; and further signs that Frame was developing her life-long love of Yeats. Frame's (*ODT* June 2, 1941) poem, "The Aeroplane", was perhaps prompted by "An Irish Airman Foresees his Death", and begins.

> We fancied that the pilot looked admiring, laughing down
> From out a sea of sky on waves of light

concluding in a shift of mood and point of view,

> And yet he did not really laugh. He fancied other things,
> Our little town was London to him then,
> And we who laughed were laughing to subdue a pain that sings
> In its intensity; (8)

There is a feel of Yeats's poem "He Wishes for the Cloths of Heaven" in the opening of Frame's poem about a poplar, written a month earlier (*ODT* May 12, 1941):

> Had I a poplar tree as gold as light
> To sing in my laughing garden, I should be
> In love with my tree. (8)

Yeats's poem was included in *The Golden Book of Modern English Poetry*, another of Frame's school prizes. In the course of the poem, Frame comes to understand that the poplar is a free spirit, "poplar trees belong to winds and/stars", and cannot be possessed by anyone: "I cannot have my tree". If the tree – and its composting leaves – form one of Frame's characteristic images in the novels, the world of fairy tales is another common topic, especially in the later novels with their use of myth and legend. Fairies, the themes of folk-tales and the spirit world, and stolen children make their presence felt in the nature poems, for example "The Crocus" (*ODT* September 5, 1941), which begins, "The spirit of the moon has hungry, starv-/ing eyes,/He would steal my yellow crocus for his/own" (8). Frame (*ODT* July 28, 1941) uses the same language of fairy tale, of cobwebs and silken threads, lace and little blue sleeves, will-o'-the-wisp and wa-ter-sheevie in "A Mimihau Lullaby"—the Mimihau is a local South Island river—for "a mortal child": "Sleep on, brown Meri-girl! A fairy's/flown/To shining Mimihau—and all for you" (2).

The freedom that comes from reading, the fairies, magic, and the companionship of books all come together in a poem which reads like a personal manifesto and is called simply, "Books". Frame (*ODT* November 25, 1940) writes of a passionate love of reading, the sense of books as personal friends and the links with writers of the past, all themes which became central to her in her adult life and her novels. Simple direct statements cut through "poetic" diction in the opening line celebrating the joy Frame feels: "I love my faithful, friendly books,/especially in the twilight". She writes of the time "When every prisoned little bird soars/gladly from its cage", free from the sense of entrapment Frame felt in conforming to adult expectations, able to fly away. Even as a school-girl, Frame has a sense of the way in which books speak to their readers from another age, from time immemorial, "And unknown voices calling from the/ageless past it seems". In her novels this is the perception that would inform her of the importance of poetry and of story-telling of all ages. The final stanza ends with a repetition of the line which begins the poem, emphasising the escape, the friendship and the timelessness:

> I love my faithful, friendly books, esspecially in the twilight
> In twilight books awaken; they grow young instead of old,
> Their crinkled covers glow with warmth and cast away the cold,
> And through the cleanly pages glitter shining hearts of gold.
> (8)

On July 7, 1941, the outgoing Dot exhorted the readers to read the great classics of the language: The Bible, Shakespeare, or Lamb's *Tales from Shakespeare*, Palgrave's *Golden Treasury*, *Treasure Island*, *Alice in Wonderland*, Dickens, etc., and that "if you read only a few of these this winter you will feel your time has not been wasted". Sadly, this piece was something of a swansong, both for the outgoing Dot and "Dot's Little Folk". In August, Dot's page underwent some changes, aiming to entertain younger children with puzzles and competitions with very few poems, no "best letter" and no feedback. The page finally closed on December 30, 1941 with a note from "Your loving friend, Dot", citing wartime paper shortage.

Frame's final poem for "Dot's Little Folk", 'The Dead Tree" (*ODT* December 8, 1941), conveys a sense of loss in its opening lines: "Only the moon will know I came/Walking alone in her gracious light", and concluding: "A little lost wind began to cry/Under the staring stars in the sky" (8). The adult Frame makes rueful reference to the closure of "Dot's Little Folk" in her short story "Dot", in which she fictionalises the page and its editor: "The war came [. . .] the confidences of children are not essential to the national economy" (*GP*, 67). The fictional male editor is revealed to be a paedophile, in a story which may reflect a sense of loss and betrayal felt by the real "Little Folk" of the time at the downgrading and then final loss of their page. Frame's sense of loss was also shared, perhaps, by the writer of July's valedictory advice about reading.

The wartime closure of Dot's page ended well over half a century of service to children, in which "Dot's Little Folk" had given rise to a community of readers, creating friendships and sharing lives, thoughts, feelings, poems and stories. As an outlet for Frame's expression of her early enthusiasms it was invaluable, and marks the beginning of the literary community Frame developed for herself as an adult writer. She found friends in books and a family of writers, about which she writes with such feeling in later life.

School Days

At school, books for beginning readers celebrated the heroes and heroines of the British Empire and colonial values, much as they did in Britain, and poems often reflected those printed in "Dot's Little Folk": poems by Walter de la Mare and John Drinkwater, for example. But Frame found a new favourite and life-long friend in Keats's "Meg Merrilees", and a taste for adventure in stories. At home, comics, newspapers and magazines—titles Frame's father referred to as "the books"—provided the light reading (*CA*, 53).

Real books came as school books and school prizes. *A Midsummer Night's Dream* and *The Merchant of Venice* were an early introduction to Shakespeare. Frame's first contact with French literature was *Contes et Légendes*, a collection of traditional tales and fairy stories which she clearly cherished (*CA*, 88). A number of books came into the household as school prizes: *Silas Marner*, *Emma* and the *Oxford Book of Light Verse*; Longfellow's *Complete Works*; and *Girls and Boys Who became Famous*, the last of these including the story of the Brontës (*CA*, 95). In a 1971 letter to Charles Brasch, Frame (Harold and Gordon 2012) wrote "I loved the Mill on the Floss. We used to have a copy at home" (44). The importance of these books for Frame was documented much earlier in her poem in the *Otago Daily Times*, "Books", quoted earlier, in which the 16-year-old Frame wrote of her books that "their crinkled covers glow with warmth and cast away the cold".

Frame's school poetry book was *Mount Helicon*, first published as an anthology for schools in 1922, in London, and seemingly aimed at the colonies. It contained much of the British canon from Shakespeare onwards, with some American and Australian poets; and one New Zealander, William Pember Reeves, represented by his poem, "New Zealand": "God girt her about with the surges/And winds of the masterless deep" (*Mount Helicon*, 252). Thematic sections included "The Empire", "Love of England", "Patriotism", "Loyalty" and "Praise of Famous Men" (x–xi). It was a poetry book Frame returned to repeatedly after her sister Myrtle's death, searching for solace and answers in Walt Whitman's "The Lost Mate" and Poe's "Annabel Lee", poems which "told everything I was feeling [. . .] I understood all the deceptions of thought and feeling which tried to persuade the mourning bird that there's been no loss" (*CA*, 89).

The prose fiction Frame loved most as a school-child was *Grimms' Fairy Tales*, borrowed from her friend Poppy, for whom it was also a "special book". As Frame began to read it, "suddenly the world of living and the world of reading became linked in a way I had not noticed before" (*CA*, 43). Reading aloud to her sisters, Frame entered the world of "The Twelve Dancing Princesses" and the girls became dancing princesses themselves: "*Grimm's Fairy Tales* was everybody's story seen in a special way with something new added to the ordinary rules of observation" (*CA*, 44). This encounter established a lifelong importance for Frame of folklore and tradition in literature, as her childhood poems show. When in 1975 Frame (2011) was asked to write an article for an education journal about a special book from childhood, she told of her delight in Poppy's book of *Grimms' Fairy Tales*, "in finding all the stories, old and new, together, and in tasting again and again the thrilling plunge of each first sentence". She again makes clear how important books were to her as companions, and concludes by saying that "when you read a book the words come to meet you and if you offer them the right hospitality, 'Table, bring meat', they stay" (56).

At High School, Frame read poetry from W.F.H. Whitmarsh's *Ils Ont Chanté*, published in 1937. As an adult she remembered it as her first encounter with the poems of Paul Valéry, writing to her close friend Bill Brown (Frame 2016) that "it is strange to look back at myself as a schoolgirl and remember the pale green book, Ils Ont Chanté, which I loved and read over and over, especially the poem by Valéry, Le Cimetière Marin" (41). In his introduction to *Ils Ont Chanté*, the editor, Whitmarsh, outlines some of the differences in structure of French and English poetry and the conventions of French rhyme schemes, and recommends pupils making a *version*, "a most pleasurable and profitable exercise", a view with which Frame probably agreed (v). *Ils Ont Chanté* contains several poems by Hugo, some poems by de Musset, Lamartine, and Baudelaire; as well as a few La Fontaine fables and some lesser known simpler descriptive verse.

Frame's introduction to French prose literature was another book of fairy stories, A.H. Guerber's (1912) *Contes et Légendes*, a retelling in simple French of folk tales from all over Europe and beyond, "intended merely as an introduction to general French reading" (v). It was a varied collection. A number of the tales were Slavonic, a few Arabian, and one was about Buddha. There were stories retold from tales recorded by Charles Perrault, Edouard Laboulaye and A.H. Wratislaw, and other collectors of folk tales to which Guerber added notes about different versions in French, German or Slavonic languages. The variety of stories had a value well beyond Guerber's aim, however, and illustrated the way in which the folklore traditions were pan-European, with variations of the same tales known in a variety of languages and cultures, as she indicates in her editorial comments on particular stories. Typical of Guerber's notes is the one on "Les Quatre Saisons" where she observes that "this is one of the most popular of the Bohemian folk stories. It has been translated into many languages, and an elaborate version can be found in Laboulaye's 'Fairy Book'" (6). Of "L'Amour d'une Mère" she similarly notes that "this is merely the French version of a tale told by every nation, and has innumerable counterparts" (115).

The source of some of Guerber's tales, A.H. Wratislaw, was a linguist, like the brothers Grimm. Wratislaw (1977) was a British Slavonic scholar of Czech parentage, who had looked at eastern European folktales to learn more of their dialects, "but found myself tempted, by the extreme beauty of some of the stories to translate the major portion of them" (v). He echoes Guerber's comment about the number of variants from different countries, and that "incidents belonging to one tale will sometimes start up at a distance in another apparently entirely unconnected with it" (101). More recently, Marina Warner (2014) makes the same point, noting of fairy tales that "stories slipped across frontiers of culture and language as freely as birds in the air" (xv).

Frame's imagination and aspirations, and perhaps the sense of justice apparent in her letters to Dot, were fed by these fairy tales which "report from imaginary territory – a magical elsewhere of possibility" (xxii). They offer fictional miracles of hope, nearly always with a just and happy ending: "Fairy tales evoke every kind of violence, injustice, and mischance, but in order to declare it need not continue" (xxiii). Frame's lifelong interest in this traditional, transnational literature is evident in her novels; in her sense of the connection between a mythological past and the realities of the present day; and the understanding she gained from folk tales that "any act was possible. Anything could happen. Nothing was forbidden" (Frame 2011, 56).

Frame's last meeting with Poppy, who had lent her the book of *Grimms' Fairy Stories*, came when the two girls were preparing to take different routes through the end of school-days. Poppy was entering the commercial class, and introduced Frame to Keats's "Ode to a Nightingale", which Poppy had learnt for a school presentation, reciting the poem "with a passionate intimacy as if the poem were directly related to her, "as if this were a farewell to childhood, to "faery lands forlorn". Frame watched and listened in amazement as "the words swept out of Poppy like a cry of panic" (*CA*, 97). Poppy had loved Grimms' *Fairy Stories* as much as Frame had, and seems to have felt she was about to be cut off from the world of poetry and imagination, just as Daphne's sister Francie would be in *Owls Do Cry* when her father suddenly announced that she would be going to work at the woollen mill.

Another school prize was *The Golden Book of Modern English Poetry*, first published in 1922; and updated in 1935 to include poems by Roy Campbell and T.S. Eliot, and to give greater representation to D.H. Lawrence, Wilfred Owen and G.M. Hopkins. The Māori writer Alan Duff (1999) recalls that when he was preparing his memoirs in the late 1990s he visited Janet Frame and "we sat in her living-room and together quoted one of our mutually favourite poets, Gerard Manley Hopkins" (25). The 1922 volume included a few of the poets of the First World War as well as poems by W.B. Yeats, the greater part of the poetry belonging to the late 19th century. It was where Frame found more poems by Francis Thompson, whose poetry she gave a talk on at school and felt she had "discovered" for herself. This volume, like *Mount Helicon*, and from the same publisher, J.M. Dent, aimed to include the best of English (and Irish) poetry from 1870 and dwelt on the Englishness of English verse in a preface to the 1922 edition by Lord Dunsany claiming that "here we have England all spread out before us" (xiv).

Frame's reading was prolific. The "heroes" of her school-days included the French poets Victor Hugo and Alphonse Daudet; the novelists Dostoevsky, Hardy, the Brontës, George Eliot, Jane Austen, Thackeray, and Washington Irving; the English Romantic poets; W.B. Yeats and Rupert Brooke. "And Shakespeare" (*CA*,128). To underline Shakespeare's pre-eminence, this two-word minor sentence in the *Complete Autobiography* is a two-word paragraph. At this stage, however, Frame had little knowledge of New Zealand writers, as the New Zealand school curriculum was essentially British, using school text books which were usually published in Britain and shipped out to the colonies. She associated the few whose names she knew with her mother, who had been in service with Katherine Mansfield's family, the Beauchamps, and felt no affinity with them. Towards the end of her school years, choosing to give her presentation on Francis Thompson, Frame was surprised to find a class-mate praised for giving a talk about Katherine Mansfield, "when none of our English studies even supposed that a New Zealand writer or New Zealand existed" (128).

At College and In Hospital

Frame continued making literary discoveries at college in Dunedin. As a student at Dunedin Training College, Frame was also able to enrol in addition for classes in English and French at the University of Otago. Frame's friend, Sheila Traill (2004), later Natusch, tells how Joan Stevens, then principal of the Training College, "soon kicked Jean [as Janet was then called] and me up the road to Professor Ramsay", the university's inspiring Professor of English (3). University set books for English in Frame's first year included *Wuthering Heights*, *Villette*, *Antony and Cleopatra*, *King Lear* and *Measure for Measure*, *English Parnassus*, an anthology of chiefly longer poems arranged chronologically from Chaucer's *Prologue* to Edward Fitzgerald's *Rubáiyát of Omar Khayyám*, Coleridge's *Biographia Literaria*, Wyatt's *Anglo-Saxon Reader*, and some Middle English texts. In Frame's second year, 1944, the Shakespeare set plays were *The Tempest*, *Macbeth* and *Troilus and Cressida* (University of Otago Calendar 1943–44). Frame clearly enjoyed the Anglo-Saxon classes, and makes reference to the Old English elegies, "The Wanderer" and "The Seafarer", in *The Adaptable Man*. In 1965 she gave a copy of the novel to one of her lecturers, G.M. Cameron, with the following inscription:

> With gratitude for memorable lectures that inspired the preoccupation in this book, with St Cuthbert & Old English language; and with the (human) request that once again the printer, not the author, may bear the responsibility for errors in quotation.

The inscribed copy remains in the collection of the English Department at the University of Otago.

In the French BA syllabus for 1943, the prescribed period of literature was 1700–1789, the period which included Voltaire, Rousseau and Beaumarchais, whose *Barber of Seville* was a set text. Other set texts for 1943 were *Knock*, by Jules Romains, and Pierre Loti's *Pecheur d'Islande*. The French literature text-book for this and all other years during the 1940s was René Canat's monumental survey,

La Littérature française par les textes, published in 1906. Canat reviews French literature from 1000 AD to the end of the 19th century, with commentary and examples from texts. In 1944, BA French set texts were Mérimée's *Carmen and Other Stories*, Molière's *Les Femmes savantes*, and Daudet's *Tartarin sur les Alpes*. Although Frame was not required to sit exams, the examination papers for 1944 indicate that a wider range of reading is expected, with questions on Balzac, Victor Hugo's drama, *Hernani*, and de Musset's poems as well as Mérimée. Michael King (2000) quotes from Frame's university records that she was "a brilliant scholar in languages" (61) and Frame pursued her interest in French long after her university days.

Both the English and the French schedules at university were solidly traditional, and the English programme as completely anglocentric as Frame's school syllabus had been. As skilful a linguist as she was, Frame's focus in her autobiography is nevertheless almost entirely on her love of English literature. She reveals how dazzled she was by *Biographia Literaria* and wrote that "the most magical word to me was still *Imagination*, a glittering noble word, never failing to create its own inner light" (*CA*, 163). She was especially drawn to the visionary poets, as Sargeson (2012) noted: "I got out of her that she likes very much Blake's visionary poems, the Book of Revelations, Dylan Thomas etc" (198). And Yeats, of course.

At university, Frame discovered more 20th-century poets: Louis MacNeice, George Barker, Dylan Thomas, T.S. Eliot and W.H. Auden; and the novels and critical works of Virginia Woolf (*CA*, 165). "Few experiences", she wrote, "could have equalled the joy given by being at a University, perceived by me almost entirely through English literature" (161). This joy came especially in the study of Shakespeare's plays, in particular *The Tempest, King Lear,* and *Macbeth,* all of which suffuse the novels. Frame tells how when she read *Measure for Measure* for the first time at university "the deeply reasoned play crammed with violations of innocence, with sexual struggle and comment, with long discussions on life, death and immortality, won my heart and persisted in my memory, *accompanied* me in daily life" (*CA*, 158; Frame's italics).

From the autumn of 1945, however, Frame was no longer able to continue studying, being admitted to the first of a number of mental hospital wards, "the University of Hard Knocks" as her friend and fellow student Sheila Natusch ruefully notes in her memoir. Frame returned to the University of Otago in some triumph in later years, however, first as a Burns Fellow, and then as an Honorary Doctor of Literature. Meanwhile, the books Frame read during her school and college years and in the hospitals helped to sustain her, continuing to offer her friendship, comfort and inspiration. During the years between 1945 and 1954 when Frame was in and out of mental hospitals, either committed or as a voluntary patient, she read extensively. She found James K. Baxter's poems; Alan Curnow's *A Book of New Zealand Verse*, published in 1951, which became her "primer of New Zealand Literature" (*CA*, 234); and she devoured Frank Sargeson's *Speaking for Ourselves*, a collection of short stories by New Zealand writers, published in 1945. Frame came to a realisation that there was such a thing as New Zealand Literature and that there was no need "to borrow from a northern Shakespearean wallet" (192).

As usual, she writes about the books she discovered as though they were people, drawing a comparison from Grimms' tales when she says "it was almost a feeling of having been an orphan who discovers that her parents are alive and living in the most desirable home" (*CA*, 193). In a letter to her friend John Money in 1948, Frame (King 2000) wrote of Dostoevsky and Rilke as her friends, saying that "I do not live here with these people, yet I do" (98). In hospital she kept by her a copy of Shakespeare's plays and Rilke's *Sonnets to Orpheus* in translation which she treasured almost as talismans, "when I clung to my copy of Shakespeare, hiding it under straw mattresses [. . .] not often reading it but turning the tissue-paper-thin pages, which somehow conveyed the words to me" (*CA*, 239). In a reply to Patrick Evans' enquiry in 1975 Sargeson (2012) confirmed that:

> Indeed Miss J did read The Godwits Fly – it was probably among the thousands of books she read when she was (so far as leisure went) a Hospital lady at large. I knew she read a good deal more Enzed lit. than I did (544).

While she was out of hospital in 1953, Frame also discovered Faulkner and Kafka at the Oamaru Public Library, and between December 1953 and January 1955, she had poems and stories published in the *New Zealand Listener*. One of these poems, on January 28, 1955 was "The Transformation", signed only "J.F.", written in response to Kafka's novella *Die Verwandlung* [The Metamorphosis]. In the poem she tells how Kafka "created his own music" and "He became the dream the dungbeetle/sucking feeding upon the excrement of word". In 1955 Frame (2011) wrote a review of Faulkner's *A Fable* for *Parson's Packet* in which she reaffirms her view of the value of artists and poets, commenting that "perhaps one may doubt whether William Faulkner is a novelist, but never that he is an artist who can take and transform, and never that he is a poet" (29). At the time when Frame began her stay with Sargeson in 1955, her world had been peopled by poets and story-tellers. Frame knew little of what had been happening in the outside world, saying of herself that "I knew only of Prospero, Caliban, King Lear, and Rilke in translation, these, for me, being the occasions of the past decade" (*CA*, 244). Like Istina Mavet in *Faces in the Water*, she had used books as "a reserve of warmth from which I could help myself" (*FW*, 214).

Later Reading

As Janet Frame was such a voracious reader, any investigation of her extensive reading in later life can only be very selective, and will focus on the writers who are the most visible in Frame's writing. Frame had the good fortune to meet Frank Sargeson in 1955, when he offered her a home in the army hut in his garden where she could write, and learn to be a full-time writer. As Kevin Ireland (2005), one of Sargeson's circle of literary friends, notes, Sargeson "ran the best literary oasis in the desert" (8) at the time, and as Sargeson's lodger,

Frame became part of the "literary world that he had created as an alternative to the family" (13).

Sargeson introduced her to Proust's *A la recherche du temps perdu* and to Tolstoy, and together they read *War and Peace, Anna Karenina, Resurrection* and Tolstoy's short stories, the characters from all these stories inhabiting Sargeson's hut with them (*CA*, 253–55). Sargeson was of the opinion that reading very long books such as *A la recherche du temps perdu* and *War and Peace* helped give a writer staying power and would build up Frame's writerly stamina, as well as providing other literary benefits (Ireland, personal communication). Sargeson discussed Milton and Shakespeare with all his callers, and would often quote from his copy of the King James Bible. Frame would almost certainly have borrowed and read Sargeson's copy of Christmas Humphreys' *Buddhism: An Introduction and Guide*, published in 1951, one of the new wave of Penguins and Pelican paperback editions of the classics, and Frame pursued an interest in Buddhist spiritual philosophy during the following years. Sargeson read and discussed Kafka's novellas, along with other modern writers. He "was devoted to his comprehensive collection of *Penguin New Writing* and to John Lehmann's *London Magazine*, and every issue of Charles Brasch's *Landfall* would have been eagerly devoured" (Ireland, personal communication).

In London, Frame continued to read 20th-century French novelists: Albert Camus, Marguerite Duras, Alain Robbe-Grillet, Nathalie Sarraute and Jean-Paul Sartre, these last two also published by Braziller, Frame's American publisher. In 1970, George Braziller arranged for Frame to meet Sarraute in New York, and Frame conveyed her excitement to Peter [E.P.] Dawson, a literary friend she had met through Frank Sargeson. In her letter to Dawson, cited by Michael King (2000), Frame wrote of her delight at being able to discuss the problems of writing with Sarraute, one of the foremost practitioners at the time of the *nouveau roman* (316).

Frame had read Sarraute's novel, *The Planetarium* (published in 1959) and was excited about Sarraute's titular metaphor of the planets and stars for characters who pursue their own orbits, circling one another, each with their own interior monologues. In an interview on "The Art of Fiction" for the *Paris Review*, Sarraute (1990) explained that these are "false stars" (162), using the image of the planetarium to illustrate her views. In this interview she discusses characterisation in the traditional "Balzacian" (155) novel which she had rejected: "we are always for each other a star like those we see in a planetarium, diminished, reduced" (162). Sarraute had found Proust, Joyce and Virginia Woolf "a revelation" (155). She wanted to break new ground and come closer to the reality of people's perceptions, rather than the external reality of the traditional novel which "seemed to have no access to what we experienced" (156).

In *In the Memorial Room*, Frame has Harry Gill grapple with this issue as he tries to write his novel in Menton. "How can one begin to *know*", Harry asks himself, "and to *say what one knows*, to say what one feels and thinks, and, in the case of a novelist, what others feel, see and think?" (*MR*, 75; Frame's italics). Sarraute's primary interest was in ideas, she confirmed, and "it's words that interest me. Inevitably. It's the very substance of my work. As a painter is interested in color and form" (1990, 163). In Sarraute's (1959) novel *The Planetarium*, the novelist Madame Lemaire is stunned by reference to her as Madame Tussaud, the maker of death-masks. This is Madame Lemaire contemplating her life's work:

> Comme c'est inerte. [. . .] Une mince couche de vernis luisant sur du carton. Des masques en cire peinte. [. . .] Ce sont des moulages de plâtre. Des copies. [. . .] Tout est creux. Vide. Vide. Vide. Entièrement vide. Du néant. Un vide a l'intérieur d'un moule de cire peinte. [. . .] La vie est ailleurs. [. . .] (191–92). [How lifeless everything is. A thin layer of shiny varnish on cardboard. Masks of painted wax. [. . .] They are plaster casts. Copies. [. . .] It's all empty. Hollow. Hollow. Hollow. Completely hollow. Nothingness. The hollowness inside a painted wax mould. [. . .] Life is elsewhere. [. . .].

We see this trope of replicas, and hollow, lifeless masks used pointedly in *Living in the Maniototo* in the Baltimore home of Irving and Trinity Garratt. They pay a kind of empty homage to Shakespeare and have reduced him to a hollow mask, like those created by Madame Lemaire. The Garratt's mask is "toothless, eyeless" but they describe it as "the usual likeness" (*LM*, 16). In their house of replicas, Shakespeare is just part of the furnishings and Irving Garratt speak of him familiarly "as people do of Shakespeare who keeps open house and is therefore everybody's prized relative" (*LM*, 16). Frame's conversation with Sarraute seems to have been very much a meeting of like minds. King (2000) comments that Frame "drank every word she said" and reports Sarraute's response to her conversation with Frame: "it's so gratifying to find someone who understands what one is trying to say" (316). This understanding is reflected in Charles Brasch's comment in his journal on *The Edge of the Alphabet*, when he remarks on Frame's "exposure of the gulfs, abysses, that underlie all our lives, of the constant attempt to conceal reality from our gaze which nearly all our activity represents" (CBH February 24, 1963).

In the 1970s, Frame's novels *Intensive Care* (1970), *Daughter Buffalo* (1972) and *Living in the Maniototo* (1979) became significantly more experimental in form, encouraged perhaps by her reading of the *nouveaux romans*. Her typographical idiosyncrasies did not find favour with the Braziller copy editors, who made substantial changes to Frame's formatting and punctuation in her 1960s novels. Frame favoured the French system of punctuating dialogue, with a long dash rather than quotation marks, seeing it as a more effective means of eliding speech with unspoken thought. The Braziller copy-editor changed Frame's often idiosyncratic formatting to their house style, adding quotation marks and capital letters where Frame begins a fragment or minor sentence in lower case. A brief section from *The Edge of the Alphabet* serves as an illustration. The most recent Random House edition (2005) has this:

> You witch-octopus whom I loved, who in the dark distressful ocean manoeuvred for me with your bright tentacles of comfort: (Are you all right, Toby?)
> [...]
> the dictionary epicentrum the point at which the earthquake breaks out, do we live there, is that the disturbance or epiphanym epiphyte
> hands out of your pockets, Toby. (292)

The Braziller editing (1962) loses subtlety, in its more conventional formatting, and is as follows:

> You witch-octopus whom I loved, who in the dark distressful ocean manoeuvred for me with your bright tentacles of comfort.
> "Are you all right Toby?"
> [...]
> The dictionary epicentrum the point at which the earthquake breaks out, do we live there, is that the distance or epiphanym, epiphyte?
> Hands out of your pockets, Toby. (48)

Frame's punctuation in the Random House edition is closer to free indirect discourse and elides the character, Toby, and the narrator more successfully than the Braziller punctuation.

The issue of formatting and punctuation was not a new problem. Frank Sargeson, left in charge of the proofs for *Owls Do Cry*, found himself having to defend Frame's innovative and idiosyncratic style against over-zealous copy-editors who wanted to make her style conform to the publishing conventions of the time, and produced first proofs which Sargeson described in a letter to Dan Davin as "a terrible balled-up job" (FSH July 20, 1956). Frame might have expected American publishers of Sarraute's *nouveaux romans* to be more flexible. She enjoyed reading contemporary French fiction, she said in an interview for the University of Otago's *Critic* on March 19,

1965, as French novels "are concerned with things as against people [. . .]. French novels are more adventurous than English and their novel form more elastic".

Frame had always enjoyed French literature. French short stories were also a life-long interest, and Frame gave her English copies of stories by Maupassant (*Selected Short Stories*) in 2000, and Camus (*The Fall* and *Exile and the Kingdom*) in 1969 to her psychologist friend John Money. Frame (2016) tells Bill Brown she is reading Camus's *Carnets* in English, after her return from Yaddo to Dunedin, making use of the library there, though she has a French edition as well (111). After her return to Dunedin, Frame continues to enjoy a book of Mallarmé's poems ("some beautiful things in it"), amongst other modern French poetry (128). Later, when Bill Brown sends her Rilke's *Vergers*, with some of his translations, she assures him that "I have a fairly good French dictionary as well as an excellent book of French idioms and figurative phrases full of interesting things, goodies, and I'm going to work in between other work on a translation or two" (142).

There is reference to one of Camus's stories in *A State of Siege*. Frame quotes from Camus's "La Femme adultère", one of the stories from *Exile and the Kingdom*, the story of Janine, whose journey with her husband across the southern Algerian desert leads to a transforming night-time experience as she visits an Arab fort while her husband remains asleep at their hotel. Her experience of the alien desert and its Arab communities forces Janine to acknowledge her loneliness and isolation in her marriage to the unimaginative Marcel, and her solitary escape to the fort is narrated in the language of a woman escaping to meet her lover. Janine abandons herself to the night sky and the moving stars, allowing herself to be possessed by the moment and the experience. Frame chooses not to translate this very moving moment and quotes a fragment of it in French: "Devant elle, les étoiles tombaient, une à une, puis s'éteignaient parmi les pierres du desert, et à chaque fois Janine s'ouvrait un peu plus à la nuit" (*SS*, 238). [Before her the stars were falling, one by one, extinguished among the desert stones, and with each one Janine opened herself a little more to the night.] Like Malfred, Janine had chosen a life of security rather than freedom and risk and experiences a conflict between her desire for independence and a sense of guilt. Janine engages in an odd sort of adultery, as Malfred remarks of herself, that she "may be regarded as a promiscuous woman, even an adulterous woman, to lie so with the landscape of my country" (*SS*, 238). Frame makes a further link with the same theme from Charles Brasch's poem "The Silent Land", where "Man must lie with the gaunt hills like a lover".

    The character of Alwyn in *The Adaptable Man* may owe something to Camus's (2004) apparently motiveless assassin, Mersault, in *L'Étranger*, who initially appears to lack human feeling. This emotional detachment is established in the novel's opening lines, "Aujourd'hui, maman est morte. Ou peut-être hier, je ne sais pas" (65). [Mother died today. Or maybe yesterday, I don't know.] Camus carefully avoids attributing responsibility to Mersault for firing on an Arab labourer, whose lack of consequence is signified by the absence of a name, just the detail of his blue overalls, "en bleu de chauffe" (103). Alwyn's victim is also just a labourer, a foreigner, another person of no consequence. For Mersault, "la gâchette a cédé" (108), [the trigger yielded] and Frame similarly appears to separate the seemingly unfeeling Alwyn's brain from his hands: "But Alwyn hadn't used an axe to kill the Italian. His hands had been strong enough" (*AM*, 66). Alwyn's lack of empathy reveals itself further in conversation with his girlfriend Jenny. He tells her he wishes he "had a motive", and when Jenny asks "For what? Marriage or murder?" Alwyn replies: "Both" (74). Later, when Jenny proposes, he fails to reply: "He looked surprised, frowned, laughed" (76). Mersault came to a sense of the world's "tendre indifference" (Camus 2004, 157) [benign indifference] the indifference of nature to human mortality, as he prepared for his execution; Alwyn seems to have entertained something of this concept from the outset, as he adapts to the way in which he sees the world moving. He is of the opinion that his uncle and father are "poking around in yesterdays numbed by toothache or Godache" and "are like infants in this modern age" (*AM*, 62).

Frame read French poetry as well as French fiction. She had always enjoyed Victor Hugo's poems, and as an adult tried writing poems in French herself. Paul Valéry's "Le Cimetière marin" was a favourite from her schooldays and Frame was intrigued to learn Rilke was excited by Valéry's poem when he came across it in the 1920s; and that Rilke had felt he had a lot in common with Valéry (Frame 2016, 40). In the same letter, she told Bill Brown she was trying to locate a copy of Rilke's French poems. She had read Rilke's *Sonnets to Orpheus* in hospital in J.B. Leishman's bilingual English-German edition. Frame had also been reading about Rilke's time in Paris, where he moved in French literary and artistic circles, probably when she came to Europe. Later, Frame and Brown translated some of Rilke's French poetry, most notably the lines from "Vergers" [Orchards] which provide the epigraph and title to the second volume of Frame's *Complete Autobiography, An Angel at My Table*.

Frame was an avid listener to music and poetry programmes on the radio. While she was living in England, between late 1957 and mid-1964, the poetry programmes which she heard were carried on the BBC Third Programme, inaugurated in September 1946. The edition of the *Radio Times* which introduced The Third Programme in 1946 asserted that it was designed to have "no fixed points. It will devote to the great works the time they require. It will seek every evening to do something that is culturally satisfying and significant". The illustration below is for the evening of September 3, 1956. The focus in poetry programmes was often on contemporary poets, seen in titles such as "New Poetry", 'The Living Poet", "Poetry Today", and "The Poet's Voice", in which poets read from their own recent and often unpublished poems. The evening illustrated ends with an item about the traditional ballad, in which there was a notable revival of interest in the 1950s and 1960s. Frame would refer to lines from the traditional ballads in her novels, notably *The Adaptable Man* and *Intensive Care*.

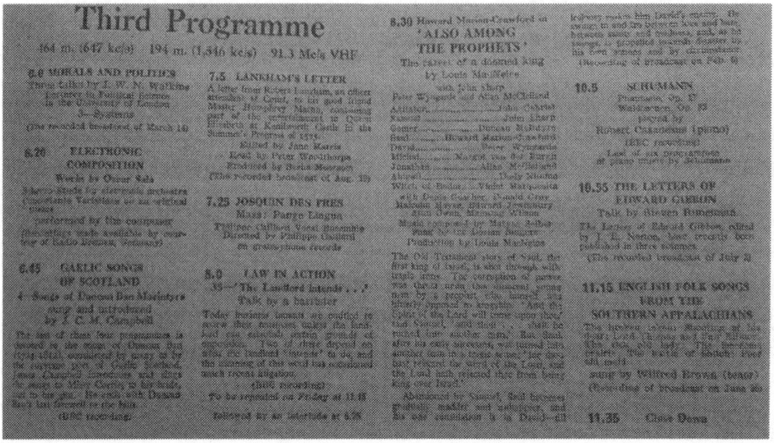
Third Programme

6.20 ELECTRONIC COMPOSITION

6.45 GAELIC SONGS OF SCOTLAND

7.25 JOSQUIN DES PRES

8.0 LAW IN ACTION

8.30 Howard Marion-Crawford in 'ALSO AMONG THE PROPHETS'

10.5 SCHUMANN

10.55 THE LETTERS OF EDWARD GIBBON

11.15 ENGLISH FOLK SONGS FROM THE SOUTHERN APPALACHIANS

11.35 Close Down

Figure 1: BBC Third Programme, September 3, 1956. Courtesy of the Radio Times

One of the regular contributors to the BBC's poetry programmes on the Third Programme was Sylvia Plath, reading her own new poems on editions of "New Poetry", "The Living Poet" and "The Poet's Voice", and providing her own commentary on these poems. Between late 1960 and the beginning of 1963, she was regularly invited by BBC producers to contribute to poetry and review programmes, especially on American poetry. The BBC commissioned Plath's verse play, "Three Women", first broadcast on August 19, 1962, and repeated on September 13 the same year, "soliloquies of three women in a maternity ward", in which three women recall their very different experiences of childbirth, their joys and sorrows.

Plath died on February 11, 1963. Her final broadcast had been on January 16, reviewing contemporary American poetry, and subsequent editions of "The Critics" in which Plath was a participant were cancelled for a few months afterwards. After her death, the poet and critic Al Alvarez, who had promoted Plath's work in the *Observer*, was given a free hand in making a programme in her honour, originally planned for May 3, 1963 but not broadcast until September 23. It would include excerpts from interviews with Plath, an unused script Plath wrote just before her death for the cancelled "The Critics" series, and a selection of her own recordings of her poems. The unused script was a piece Plath had written about her childhood, and Leonie Cohn, a producer at the BBC talks department, wrote to Al Alvarez to commend it. It was published in *The Listener* on August 24, 1963 as part of "The Writer and His Background" series.

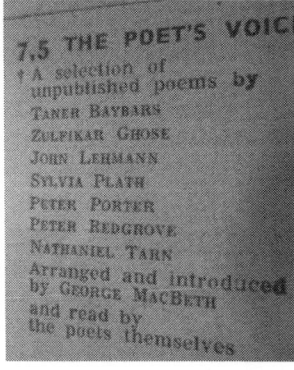

Figure 2: BBC Third Programme, November 17, 1962. Courtesy of the Radio Times

Frame was reading and almost certainly listening to the poetry of Sylvia Plath on the BBC's Third programme. Plath was living in Britain at this time and was a regular radio broadcaster, reading her own poetry and commenting on the American literary scene. It is clear from the heart-stopping lines echoing Plath's poetry in *Towards Another Summer*, that Plath's death caused Frame considerable distress. Frame began writing *Towards Another Summer* a few days after Plath's death, names one of the novella's minor characters "Sylvia", and writes of her grief:

> Since you came to me last night,
> and said
> what you said
> I rode on a red bus
> inside a clot of blood
> I rode in grief over London. (*TS*, 48–49)

Frame's line: "You came to me; you said", suggests that Frame, living in London at this time, listened to Plath's broadcasts, including "The Poet's Voice", broadcast on November 17, 1962 in which Plath took part, and which was "a selection of unpublished poems [. . .] read by the poets themselves". The programme was rebroadcast in Plath's honour on February 17, 1963, six days after her death, and a few days after Frame had begun writing *Towards Another Summer*. Ted Hughes (1989) notes that Plath was preparing "Lady Lazarus", "Daddy", "Fever 103°" and "Death & Co" for the programme. These poems were published in journals during her lifetime and posthumously in *Ariel* in 1965 (293–9). Frame would draw on Plath's poetry again in parts of *Intensive Care* (1970), and this will be discussed later, in Chapter 3.

Frame was interested in writing from all over the anglophone world and beyond. Sargeson had given her a copy of Olive Schreiner's *Story of An African Farm*, and a novel of Doris Lessing's, presumably *The Grass is Singing*, published in 1950 (*CA*, 255). Later, Frame enjoyed the work of other writers from southern Africa: Dan Jacobson, Alan Paton and Nadine Gordimer. She was intrigued by the point of view of these other "colonials", aware that these gifted and high-minded white southern Africans, "despite their imagination and empathy were not writing from the unique point of view of native Africans" (*CA*, 311). In London, Frame joined the local library "and greedily accepted the rule—'as many books as you wish'" (*CA*, 308). Among the novelists she admired were Margaret Atwood, one of the "stars of the evening" at a Toronto literary festival in 1984, and Joseph Heller.

Frame (2011) also admired an earlier generation of writers and singles out Joseph Conrad and Thomas Hardy for their evocation of the natural world. Of Conrad's *The Secret Sharer* she remarked that although he writes about "a world that clearly manages better without women [...] he uses a special tenderness to describe the sea, and one feels included, then" (124). Hardy's landscape is timeless: he is "the supreme describer of the countryside and the weather and climate of the land, and its inhabitants all under the sky that is forever the sky above the heath in King Lear" (137).

Frame had a passion for indigenous and local varieties of language, and a high regard for the value of spoken language. In the 1970s Frame expressed her frustration with the practice of publishers who anglicize or americanize New Zealand English "often destroying the meaning and rhythm of the sentence", and her hope that New Zealand publishers would refrain from translating Māori words into English: "We want our words. If I write of a *bach* by the sea I do not want it to be turned into a bungalow or cottage or mansion. If we write of a *tangi*, we mean just that: a *tangi*" (64). Frame made further comments on her interest in the revival of the Māori language in an interview for the *New Zealand Listener* of September 24, 1988, with Marion McLeod, delighted that after years of linguistic neglect that Māori were "speaking and writing their own language" and, more to the point, "sharing its riches". In a discussion about her final novel, *The Carpathians*, she went on to tell McLeod about her visit to a marae, where "there was a wonderful old woman who had extraordinary mana, like Rua, the flax weaver in the novel", whose tangi Frame later attended.

Frame wrote appreciatively of the work of the Māori writer Patricia Grace. While Frame was chair of PEN NZ in 1975, she awarded first prize for a "first work of fiction to a new writer" to Grace for *Waiariki*, and commented in a letter to Bill Brown, March 1, 1976, that Grace was "a genuine writer" (King 2000, 402). Grace (Alley, 1994) expressed her admiration for Frame with a contribution to Frame's 70th birthday festschrift, appropriately a version of a Māori myth, *Sun's Marbles*, Grace has suggested (Grace, personal communication) that Frame was more likely influenced by people she had met and knew, but the stories in *Waiariki*, show that Frame felt a real sense of affinity with Grace's writing, a sense of kinship with the characters in Grace's Māori stories.

Frame developed a long-term friendship with Māori poet and short story writer Jacqueline Sturm, who married the poet, James Baxter. The relationship was noted in a letter to H. Winston Rhodes by Frank Sargeson (2012), who thought that "a curious sight is to see Janet in company with Jacquie Baxter, they are like two superior peasant women who communicate by having nothing to say to each other–meaning of course they get on famously" (510). There is further evidence of their close friendship in the poems Jacqueline Sturm (2003) wrote "for Janet", such as these lines:

> Last year you sent me a photo
> Of your blossom tree in bloom.
> This, you wrote on the back,
> Is a poem.
> May your next spring be
> A revelation like the first,
> As poignant as the last. (24)

Frame's (2011) sense of the importance of indigenous forms of language is evident in her dismay at the capacity of dominant cultures to "almost vacuum-clean, overnight, another culture and language", but this cleaning-up and disposal was tempered in Britain by the "counter-invasion of culture" of the Windrush generation of West Indian writers as well as writers and their English from other parts of the Commonwealth (64). She read Samuel Selvon, as an example of those writers: "who, living and working and writing of another land, in their English, yet seem to record, as if it were an underground stream flowing through their writing, the life of the West Indies" (60). In later years Frame's reading chiefly centred on her interest in poetry, and in short stories taken from a wide variety of cultures, including French and Russian.

If Frame's poem, "Books", published in Dot's page, was her childhood manifesto on the value of language and reading, her adult one was the article she wrote for the *Times Literary Supplement* of June 4, 1964. In this piece Frame recalls her own "gateway" into literature through her reading, and her interests as a novelist. "I was lured" she says "through the gateway of doom by the poems and ballads my mother used to recite to us", and she urges that the writer should not stay in a "favourite city" of literature but to "go alone through the gateway entered or arrived at, out into the other 'world', with no luggage but memory and a pocketful of words". She affirms that her central concern is with "English *words* and the way writers, chiefly the poets, have chosen, grouped, shaped them" (Frame's italics). The following chapters consider how Frame set about shaping those words, reworking texts—prose, poetry, mythology and folklore—into a richly layered œuvre of her own.

Chapter Two: Poets and Poetry

The Importance of Poetry

Janet Frame embraced poetry as the highest of all art forms, for as she tells us in her "Beginnings" essay for *Landfall* in 1965 she had been born into a "pocket" of poetry: "In my family words were revered as instruments of magic" (2011, 42). She told Elizabeth Alley (Alley and Williams 1992) in a New Zealand radio interview on October 19, 1988, that she viewed poetry as "the highest form of literature because you can have no dead wood in a poem" (52). Although Frame (2011) did not rate her own poetry very highly, and described herself as "a moth-hole poet" (258), she wrote poetry all her life, including substantial sections of verse in her novels. Frame's early poems for "Dot's Little Folk" in *The Otago Daily Times* and the *Oamaru Mail Minor* show how much she learned from the range of poetry "Dot" included in her page, and from Dot's feedback on her own letters and poems. Even more influential were the poets of her school anthologies, to which she refers frequently in her novels, as well as the poetry reading of her more mature years studying in Dunedin and in her later adult reading.

Frame's sense of the use of poetry extends beyond verse forms and includes poeticized prose such as we find in the King James Bible, and in the work of William Faulkner, a novelist she considered to be a poet. For Frame, "Poets are not afraid to drown" (*PM*, 56). As a child, Frame had begun "to collect other words labelled "poetic" [. . .] because poetry emphasized what was romantic" (*CA*, 93). She had argued with her sister about which was the more poetic word "tint" or "touch", following the examples set by her mother, Lottie, and by "Dot's" view of the poetic. Dot had praised and published Frame's poem about a blackbird, changing one of Frame's chosen words, and Frame later wrote that she was annoyed that she changed 'gay' blackbird to 'blythe' blackbird, for I thought blithe too clumsy. Over the years I remember my irritation over the change of my chosen word, just as I remember Myrtle's pressure to change 'touch' to 'tint'. (*CA*, 119)

As an adult, Frame might have agreed with Charles Brasch's view that "every good poet in his own way creates a new world & remakes this one, modestly or magnificently" (CBH February 8, 1952). She regarded risk-taking as an inherent feature of good writing, and asks:

> What is that tide flowing out of the room and into the street?
> Somebody's best-kept words have got out.
> We are in danger of wet feet! (*PM*, 56).

Frame read Stéphane Mallarmé at Yaddo. As she wrote to Bill Brown, "I have Mallarmé's poems from the library and a collection of modern French poetry" (2016, 128). Her reading would have shown her the French poet's departures from conventional poetry forms and typography, as in this example from Mallarmé's "Un Coup de Dès":

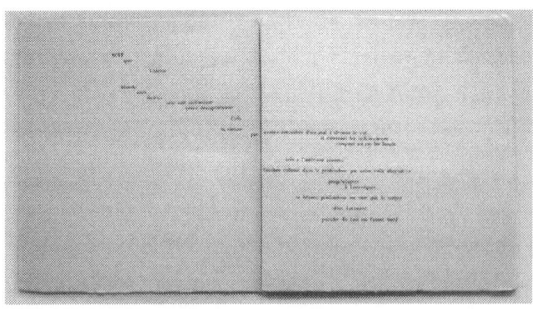

Figure 3:
Stéphane Mallarmé:
Un Coup de Dès

Frame's adult poetry is no longer restricted by notions of "poetic diction", traditional verse-forms or poetic subject matter, as in her poem about Kafka's beetle, printed on January 28, 1955 in the *New Zealand Listener*, with its evident debt to Rilke, and its distinctly unpoetic diction. Gregor Samsa, who lived a totally conventional life,

> Anchored always
> With featherweight balloon and mock of silent promise
> He chose the transformation ...
> .... He became the dream the dungbeetle
> Sucking feeding upon the excrement of word. (17)

Frame chooses to call this poem 'The Transformation" [*Die Wandlung* in German] rather than "The Metamorphosis", the usual translation of the title of Kafka's novella, *Die Verwandlung*, in an apparent echo of Rilke's line "Choose to be changed" ("Wolle die Wandlung") from the *Sonnets to Orpheus*. Frame viewed the "featherweight balloon" of Gregor Samsa's conventional life as a trap to avoid and was aware, as she says in her autobiography, that "much of my life would be spent trying to escape from a prison", and added that she did not want to use poetry "to put myself in human danger and to try to force a flow of love towards me. I was learning that the uses of poetry are endless but not always harmless" (*CA*, 361).

Frame employs the characteristic literary features of verse-writing in her prose: metaphor, rhythm, a marked use of alliteration, and a strong sense of sound. As Marc Delrez notes in his 2012 unpublished conference paper, "Rilke in Frame", "her intertextual intrusions almost invariably take the form of a gesturing towards the realm of poetry". She exploits the quintessence of the Anglo-Saxon roots of the language, largely monosyllabic and alliterative—the language of home, landscape and feelings—in her densely metaphorical prose with its layers of voices and allusions. Some early reviewers found the overtly poetical style of her novels disconcerting. Owen Leeming (1963) criticised Frame's "decided weakness for metaphor" in his *Landfall* review of *Scented Gardens for the Blind*, but was pleased to find there were "no irruptions of poetry" (388).

The New Zealand poet James K. Baxter, however, took a more expansive view of the function of metaphor within poetry which applies equally to Frame's prose: "In a good poem inward and outward knowledge are perceived, as it were, in the same instant, by a single intellectual act, and the natural form to enclose the moment of perception is the metaphor" (Baxter 1967, 12). As Frame said of herself to Charles Brasch, responding to Leeming's criticism, "but isn't the need to compare, to perceive relationships the source of all art? [...] I'm afraid I breathe metaphors, mostly bad or indifferent; it is the obsession with images that prompts me to write" (2010, 11). She found support for her style from Brasch, who said he thought that "Janet shares my interest in moulding language to greater intensity and richness" (CBH July 13, 1965).

Frame (2011) also had a poet's concern for the importance of sound in her prose-writing. Undated notes on Maurice Gee's *A Special Flower*, published in 1965, show that she was critical of Gee for using words which "were not made to work as instruments", and noted that the "author has not a fastidious ear" (223). Frank Sargeson remarks a number of times on Frame's habit of composing pieces in her head, and in a letter to Charles Brasch describes how she then writes them up "as fast as she can make her pen move or her typewriter type" (FSH October 3, 1956). In other words, she composes by ear and not by eye: Frame is a musical writer rather than a painterly one. She was an avid listener to music as well as poetry on the radio, sharing news of the music she enjoyed, especially Bach, Beethoven and Schubert, with her friend Sheila Natusch. In her review of Frame's 1952 prize-winning short stories, *The Lagoon and Other Stories*, Dorothy Ballantyne writes that Frame

> belongs with the listeners of this world, not the watchers. She is not the first writer to weave everyday speech into her prose, but she is a pioneer in this respect. No New Zealander before her has used this speech so poetically, for what is really a lyric purpose. (HMH June, 1952)

The importance of music to Frame may have lain partly in its rhythms and shape, but also probably as a language in itself, conveying feelings which may be beyond words. Frame wrote to Charles Brasch from the Macdowell artists' colony in the USA that "There's a painter who's a marvellous pianist [...]. I'm still romantic enough to want to spend the rest of my life with someone who can play Beethoven sonatas to me" (King 2000, 343). The "marvellous pianist" was William Theophilus (Bill) Brown, who became a lifelong friend, and Frame made recordings of poetry to send to him. Brown had given her a tape-recorder so that he could send her recordings of his playing that her sent her, and which she so much enjoyed, and she taped poems from Brasch's *Home Ground* collection, to send to Brown.

As an adult, Frame was especially drawn to those poets with a mystical vision of life such as Blake, Yeats, Rainer Maria Rilke, T.S. Eliot, and poets with a view of wonder and joy in the natural world, the English Romantics, Dylan Thomas, G.M. Hopkins as well as those who looked at death directly, without euphemism or avoidance, like Dylan Thomas, Sylvia Plath and Rilke. She also quotes and alludes to the poetry of people she knew or met: Stephen Spender—who she met briefly in California—and the New Zealand poets Alan Curnow, Ruth Dallas, James K. Baxter and Charles Brasch. She continued to read Rilke's poetry throughout her life, including the French poems in "Vergers" [Orchards], which she translated into English with Bill Brown in California.

One of Frame's most perceptive early critics, Jeanne Delbeare (1975), notes the way in which Frame developed a sense of being part of a family of poets and writers and that she links "herself with Rilke and Ovid and all the poets of the past whom she has assimilated and whose voice is part of her own" (35). Delbeare's comments point towards Bakhtin's observations on novelistic prose, on the writer who orchestrates and assimilates all other voices without losing his own, as Frame dissolves the borders of prose and poetry using direct quotation, pastiche, parody and allusion to create a polyphonic texture of poetic prose and links to poets present and past.

Poetry at School and College

The poems of Frame's schooldays are among the most keenly felt and she references them frequently, especially in the early fiction, and they surface again in the later novels. The children's poems of John Drinkwater, Walter de la Mare, Edward Lear, Lewis Carroll,

W.H. Davies, R.L. Stevenson, and Eleanor Farjeon featured regularly on the "Dot's Little Folk" pages of the *Otago Daily Times*, as did poems by William Wordsworth, Walt Whitman and William Blake. Drinkwater's "Moonlit Apples" was a regular, and "Dot" used it as the basis of her lesson in prosody. Whitman's "O Captain! My Captain!", Blake's "The Tyger" and poems from Blake's *Songs of Innocence & Experience* also made a number of appearances over the years along with Victorian nature poems and the children's verse. The reading curriculum during Frame's schooldays in Oamaru was based on the English literary tradition and included almost no literature from New Zealand.

Frame writes in her autobiography of her attachment to her school poetry anthology, *Mount Helicon*, published in London in 1937 and aimed at the colonial school market. It contained many of the best-known English poems from Shakespeare and Marlowe to those of the early 20th century, and included poems by the American poets Walt Whitman, E.A. Poe, Henry Wadsworth Longfellow and John Greenleaf Whittier, as well as poetry from the British Isles. As an adolescent, mourning the death by drowning of her older sister Myrtle following heart failure, Frame found "that the poets in *Mount Helicon* were writing the story of my feelings. I could scarcely believe their depth of understanding" and she found herself agreeing with her mother's habitual murmuring of "only the poets know, only the poets know" (*CA*, 88). Singled out particularly was Whitman's, "The Lost Mate", his poem about a bird's fruitless search for its lost love, which Frame felt seemed to understand the process of her grieving for Myrtle,

> with all the false alarms and pondered might-have-beens, the anger and regret and the desperate reasoning that enlisted the help of magic, and ending in failure to find what was lost and the letting go of all hope of finding it. (89)

In *Faces in the Water* (1961), Istina Mavet recalls using some of these childhood poems in a talismanic fashion, much as she used her Shakespeare, to keep the horrors of her impending electrotherapy at bay: "Over and over inside myself I am saying a poem which I learnt at school when I was eight. I say the poem, as I wear the grey woollen socks, to ward off Death" (*FW*, 17). The poem was Drinkwater's "Moonlit Apples", and she manages to recite three lines of it before the electrotherapy machine takes over. The magic of the poem seems to invoke the protective limits of childhood, but fails to protect Istina. Later, on a Sunday walk around the hospital grounds, Istina sees the old men, who "were dead though their mouths moved", as though they were the unresponding inhabitants of the house visited by de la Mare's "Traveller" in "The Listener" when he came "knocking at the moonlit door", another of the poems she had learnt as a very young girl at school. "A traveller", observes Istina, "could knock for years at the door of that dismal ward [...] and get no answer" (42).

Frame feels the power that poetry has to speak for us and uses it to enable the articulate or underprivileged characters to give expression to their unspoken thoughts and feelings. In *Scented Gardens for the Blind* (1963), for example, she uses poetry to provide insight into the thinking of Erlene, the imaginary daughter of Vera Glace, who as we learn only at the end of the novel is an inmate in a mental hospital. Vera is a former librarian and has been living in the hospital for 30 years. She is an elective mute or aphasic, who protects herself from the difficulties of her life behind a barrier of mutism, projects her mutism onto her "daughter", and invents an imaginary husband, Edward, in England. Erlene recalls the poems of her schooldays in her return to a childhood state, the poems of Walter de la Mare and R.L. Stevenson in the junior classes and those of E.A. Poe and Matthew Arnold in an older class. They signify an age of neatness and mathematical certainties, "Given, To Prove, Construction, Proof, Conclusion" (*SG*, 52).

Erlene, writing as an inmate of a mental hospital, recalls her schooldays in which she sought to protect herself against the frightening uncertainties of the adult world. She cites the simplicity and apparent certainties of geometry and the children's verse read at school. Stevenson's "Bright is the ring of words" forms the epigraph to *Mount Helicon*, Frame's school poetry anthology. De la Mare's "A song of enchantment" and "Someone came knocking" were regularly included in "Dot's Little Folk", as well as in Erlene's lessons at school, and "belonged among clapping games, beads, paper cut-outs" of the "Infant Room" (53). These verses contrast with the terrifying freedom of university which Erlene later contemplates, where "she was going to walk up and down the streets till late at night, thinking about Plato and Socrates, trying to solve the problems of being and not-being, hand in hand with Death" and where she finally imagines herself wandering off and drowning, like Shelley (231–32).

Even as a young girl, Erlene had her suspicions about the optimism of children's verse, finding more to feed her imagination in Mathew Arnold's "The Scholar Gypsy", a poem she returns to a number of times. Her teacher, Miss Walters, is an uncritical reader, dismissing Arnold's pessimism and despair in "Dover Beach" with an overly bright "What nonsense, really [. . .] when poets write in this way it is usually because they are ill or overstrained; the despair is part of their illness" (*SG*, 55). Erlene perceives Miss Walters' fears, and her failure to confront Arnold's nightmarish world from which the old religious certainties have gone. When Miss Walters reminds the girls of the tennis session at "Four-fifteen sharp", Erlene silently responds: "Sharp and lonely" (55).

Erlene knows that the "Arabia" of de la Mare's poem, "where the princes ride at noon", did not reflect the harsh realities of life, that "it had never been like that, there was all disease and desert and fighting and hunger" (*SG*, 58). Erlene regards with despair the futility of reciting the poems she learnt as a child, Poe's "Annabel Lee" or Keats's "Meg Merrilies", the last poem her imaginary father heard her recite before he left for England, since "nothing she uttered would ever reach anyone's ears" and nothing would remain but "the stale smell of accumulated sentences and phrases; and no trace of a human being" (227), comments which stress her desolate loneliness and isolation.

Arnold's "The Scholar Gypsy" is the poem which Erlene recalls most often, and which meets her need for a text as a source of self-referencing. It retells an old story of a boy forced through poverty to leave his studies at Oxford. He finds that the gypsies "had a traditional kind of learning among them, and could do wonders by the power of imagination" (Palgrave 1940, 426), in an apparent authorization of Vera/Erlene's state of living within her own imagination. The poem begins as a traditional pastoral elegy, but addresses Arnold's sense of the value and power of the imagination, the perils of conformity, the loss of faith, and the value of the world of learning—the Oxford towers remain within his sight—all issues of importance for Frame. Arnold's concerns with the "strange disease of modern life", the value of the natural landscape for its peace and permanence, and "the sick fatigue, the languid doubt" (432–33), are also of abiding interest to Frame, and show how Arnold anticipates Rilke and Yeats.

In her sessions in the mental hospital with Dr Clapper, Vera/Erlene recasts the psychiatrist as a character from a children's story or fairy tale—Uncle Blackbeetle—taking the image from a real beetle on the window-pane, as a way of lessening the threat from this powerful authority-figure. She asks Uncle Blackbeetle if he knows Arnold's poem, but her question remains unanswered. Later, Erlene tries to ward off her night terrors in bed by thinking about the Scholar Gypsy, her child-like thinking suggested by her fears that he would be unable to manage in New Zealand, as "he would get lost in the bush and not know how to boil the billy" (*SG*, 100).

As Erlene moves through the school system and joins the sixth form, her stock of poets expands to include Milton, Wordsworth and Shelley, but she retains her attachment to "The Scholar Gypsy", as she tries to make sense of uncertainties and dreams which "refused to be drowned, but floated accusingly within sight and sound of the dreamer" (233). She is conscious of her lack of experience of the world and of love and the limitation of her perceptions, thinking "but I don't know about love, Erlene thought. Love is the Scholar Gypsy and my mother and father and the sound of trees at night" (233). Finally, Erlene decides "there was no reason to speak any more" (237). The psychiatrist Dr Clapper's "slaughter of the fly", instinctively swatting a fly with his newspaper, leads Erlene, conscious of her own powerlessness, to recall Blake's (2004) poem:

> Little fly,
> Thy summer's play,
> My thoughtless hand
> Has brushed away. (124)

Blake's simple verse-form and child-like language belie the poem's underlying seriousness of purpose, the wanton destruction of life, and point up the unthinking power of the psychiatrist. Dr Clapper reappears with biblical images of power: "No fire would fall from the sky; no God would descend to comfort his silent people" which combine with a last glimpse of "The Scholar Gypsy" who "could wait forever now" (236–37). Erlene exercises the one power she has: the power of silence.

Poetic Visionaries: Blake, Yeats, Rilke and Dylan Thomas and their Celebration of the Natural World

Although Frame uses poetry to expose the reasons for silence in *Scented Gardens for the Blind*, she also uses the power of the Romantics and visionary poets' celebration of life to express her own sense of the paramount importance of the natural world. Her sense of affinity, for example, with the poetry of William Blake is evident from her earliest novel, *Owls Do Cry* (1957), and her interest in Yeats reveals itself in the poems of her late childhood, for example "City Flowers". As a young adult, Frame was introduced to Rilke's *Sonnets to Orpheus* in Leishman's translation, later enjoying other translations of Rilke's German poetry; and these three visionary, mystical poets, their symbolism and sense of the destructiveness of the modern world make their presence felt in the language and themes of Frame's novels.

The warmth of Blake's Christianity chimes with Lottie Frame's insistence that God was kind and her Christadelphian belief that "only God knew whether or not there was an angel inside a beggar or swagger" (*CA*, 28). Frame's novels make frequent reference to the value of the commonplace and the sense of the world as precious. They display a Blakean concern with apocalypse, and the ways in which the world falls short of its potential. Mark Williams (1990) describes Lottie's faith as a "Blakean sense that Christianity is at heart a message about transforming, not repudiating, physical existence" (33), quite different from the attitude of the dominant puritan Christianity in New Zealand at that time. Frame is inspired by Blake's independence of thought and spirit as well as his sense of the value of an artisan culture, of craftsmanship, increasingly sapped by a soulless and often cruel factory system: his "dark satanic mills". Blake took his imagery largely from the natural world, birds, trees, flowers, the land itself and the pastoral imagery of the Bible. For Frame, too, the freedom of wild life contrasts with the constraints of modern life.

Frame frequently uses references to the poetry of visionary poets to underline the shallowness of parts of modern culture. She makes particular reference in *Living in the Maniototo* (1979) to the poetry of Yeats and Dylan Thomas to highlight her view of a more desirable state of being. The novel's protagonist, Mavis, is a guest of the Garretts in Berkeley, California; a couple who have who have gone travelling and left Mavis occupying their home, where she can complete her novel. Yeats's presence in the novel is central to Frame's view of the Garratts and in Berkeley, the Garretts' book collection announces that theirs is "a house without Yeats" (*LM*, 114). In shifts of register, Frame's parody of "The Lake Isle of Innisfree" fuses echoes of Yeats with the materialist concerns of the Garretts, purchasing their conventional retirement home:

> They will sell this house and go soon, for their
> name's on the waiting list,
> and they've paid a huge deposit for the suite with a view of
> the shore. (*LM*, 114–15)

For Mavis, this is a loss, an awful failure of imagination. She invokes "Byzantium", Yeats's metaphor for his own spiritual journey to an artistic infinity:

> No rage. No towers.
> Only the Garretts' lives demanding
> I want a Shakespeare like the real Shakespeare
> I want a miraculous marble table.
> We have all, all, and "the agony of flame that cannot
> singe a sleeve". (*LM*, 115)

In *Living in the Maniototo*, Irving Garrett is a town planner in Berkeley, California, but as we learn later, has "not planned any *real* towns I can't drive you to one of my towns. They're not built. My plans are studies, exercises" (*LM*, 195; Frame's italics). Nothing is real, natural or of any practical value. By way of contrast, Tommy, the Baltimore jeweller who dies suddenly and mysteriously, is a "craftsman and artist" (33). Similarly, the Americanized New Zealand shopping mall, tellingly named "Heavenfield", in fictional Blenheim (on Auckland's north shore) is in its inappropriate scale "a huge windowless pretence" with an aviary "where canaries and lovebirds sing, and fly in flashes of blue and yellow, an arrogant costly restoration and reminder, however, of the lost noise of the sun" (23). This denial of the value of the natural world is contrasted by the protagonist in her description of a skunk in the Berkeley garden. Frame conveys the way in which the natural world re-imposes itself on a world from which it has been all but destroyed, the pride and dignity of the skunk's movements compared to those of a wealthy inhabitant with a sense of her own entitlement:

> I saw a skunk coming down the steps by the corner of the house, walking sedately step by step, like a woman in a black and white fur coat going to the opera, walking down the stairs of the circle to take her place in the front row. (*LM*, 215)

In the spiritual wastelands of Blenheim, Berkeley and Baltimore, nature is all but obliterated. With a child's innocence and eye for the unvarnished truth, Brian's nephew Lonnie, "a milk-and butter-fed child" from New Zealand, is baffled by the artificial cityscape he finds himself in, and cannot understand why there is no daylight, or why there is "no outside" (*LM*, 101). Mavis, born like Lonnie in a land of earthquakes, has a sense of herself as "a guest, as are all who live there, of the Taranaki mountain" (133). She understands and accepts the risks of living in a natural environment. This respect for the natural world is also seen in the choice of title for Mavis's novel "The Green Fuse", from Dylan Thomas's (1988) poem "The force that through the green fuse" in which nature is seen as both creator and destroyer:

> The force that through the green fuse drives the flower
> Drives my green age: that blasts the roots of trees
> Is my destroyer. (13)

Frame turns from Dylan Thomas to Yeats again in her delineation of Roger, one of a quartet of fictional guests who interrupt Mavis in her novel-writing. For the most part, Roger is a ridiculous figure, unrealistically engaged in a spiritual visit to the Californian desert, and "sounding hopelessly like a boy who's just seen a film about the desert" (*LM*, 166). He has his own unexpected moment of epiphany, however, when a hare, a real, trembling creature of the natural world, trustingly shares Roger's patch of shade:

> With the quivering hare crouched beside him, Roger progressed from loneliness to a blessed feeling of shared aloneness. He and the hare were at home together, and this was all that being at home meant, no more, no less. Just sharing a space in peace. (*LM*, 177)

The spare and unadorned simplicity of the language here and the half-rhyme of "space" and "peace" underline the importance of the incident. When the sublime moment had passed, Roger—slumped and waiting for rescue—thinks again of Yeats (2000), and the poet's lines to a friend

> whose work had
> come to nothing
> Bred to a harder thing
> than Triumph. (186)

Like Blake and Yeats, Frame frequently invokes the wild birds. For Blake, a bird is a symbol of childhood innocence as well as freedom from constraint, since a caged bird cannot sing for joy. In Yeats's "The Lake Isle of Innisfree", one of the poems of Frame's schooldays, the bees, linnets and crickets all have their freedom; and Yeats hears the lake's waters "in the deep heart's core" (*Mount Helicon* 1948, 270). Frame uses verse to break free of generic boundaries, and Mavis's use of verse in the novel, the prose poetry, pastiche and parody mirror her concern with escaping from conventional constraints. In her "Hypotenuse" poem, she reflects on the creative process, taking as an image a Scarlet Tanager, an American bird which precariously survives the winter to sing again in spring. Like the birds of Yeats and Blake, this bird sings a life affirming song:

> And then, my blood-color furled, I flew to the highest
>   bough and I sang
> in detail, without violence, a civilised version of my song.
> (*LM*, 69)

The image of a bird is a recurrent one in Frame's fiction. In the natural world a bird is free, but bound by instincts, in particular in migrating birds, the homing instinct. Frame takes the title of her novella, *Towards Another Summer*, written in 1963 but published posthumously in 2007, from Charles Brasch's (1984) poem, "The Islands". She takes the poem's final lines both as her novella's epitaph and its closing words: "and from their haunted bay/The godwits vanish towards another summer" (17). She draws on the image of the native New Zealand migratory bird, the godwit, in an extended and powerful metaphor in which the bird, though free, is easily unnerved and left in a state of fluttering panic, in a more complex and personal vision of the wild bird than the timelessness of Yeats's wild swans, or in Blake's joyous birdsong.

In *Towards Another Summer*, Frame exploits the identity of the godwit to convey the sense of displacement and belonging felt by the novella's protagonist, Grace Cleave, a New Zealand writer living and working in London. Grace has been invited to spend the weekend with a friendly journalist and his New Zealand wife. She feels that overnight she "had changed to a migratory bird" (*TS*, 14–15), a feeling so strong that she checks under the bedclothes for feathers, and is relieved to find that, unlike Kafka's Gregor Samsa, she still has her outward human form. The extended image of the wild bird expresses her vulnerability and panic-stricken helplessness after she feels her failure to shine in a literary interview at the BBC's Bush House in London, when she subsequently "ruffled her feathers, flapped her wings wildly, went hysterically out into the Strand" (*TS*, 38).

The migratory nature of the godwit also conveys Grace's bouts of homesickness, heightened by her browsing among her hosts' New Zealand book collection, especially Allen Curnow's seminal 1951 *Book of New Zealand Verse*, which left her "a migratory bird instantly in her New Zealand world" (*TS*, 133). It was a book she kept by her bedside at home, but which she appears to find too painful to read in London, and in reading poems from her host's copy, she feels herself to be exiled, "suffering from the need to return to the place I have come from before the season and sun are right for my return" (*TS*, 59). While she explores the freezing village on her lone walk, Grace muses on stories from Greek mythology about the escape through flight of deities transformed into migratory birds, a nightingale and a swallow, linking the imagery of birds and her own plight with the mythology of the ancient world: "Philomela; Procne; it was an old tradition; we must tend the myths, she thought; only in that way shall we survive" (*TS*, 98).

Critical writing has only recently taken note of Frame's affinity with the natural world and her use of it in her writing. In an article on Frame's poetry, the French academic Valérie Baisnée (2009) argues in "A Home in Language" that for Frame the natural world "provides nourishment and maternal protection, as well as 'feeding' the poet's imagination on the level of language. Images of trees further help to root language in the world" (91) and trees are a link with biblical imagery of the tree of life and the cross. The New Zealand poet Bill Manhire (2008), in his introduction to *Storms Will Tell*, a posthumous collection of Frame's poetry, notes the dominance of Frame's pastoral imagery and argues that "it would be hard to find a more fecund sense of the natural world in any recent writer" (23), a point which also holds true for Frame's novels.

Frame makes striking use of other images from natural life cycles, for example of leaf fall and composting, to convey her view of the writer's intertextual relationship to the cycle of literature, for example in the comment that "in authorship, the author is not the tree scattering his books like leaves; the books are the tree; the author is shed, blown away, dies to make compost for other leaves and other trees" (*MR*, 113). These are the words of Harry Gill, the protagonist in *In the Memorial Room* (2013), a novelist, who takes up the fictional Margaret Rose Hurndell Fellowship in Menton in the south of France. The novella was written in 1974 after Frame had spent six months as a Katherine Mansfield Fellow in Menton. A more striking and extended image, however, is the uprooting of the pear tree which links the three sections of *Intensive Care* (1970). The tree felling is presented as sacrilege, the destruction of natural life by people who have lost touch with their land and its history. Milly, the protagonist of Part Three of *Intensive Care*, is distraught, "I am robbed and betrayed", she says, when her father takes an axe to the Livingstone pear tree after a branch fell with the weight of snow. "It was like the tree speaking", Milly thought, "and it scared them". Milly feels a strong personal connection to the tree and its roots:

> Under the Livingstone pear tree is like being under some kinsiderate creature where its ribs have leaves growing on them and stretching out and waving to jostle the rain and snow off your head, keeping you dry. (*IC*, 336–38)

The image of the tree had been part of Frame's writing since the days of writing for "Dot's Little Folk" in the *Otago Daily Times*. A poem about an orchard, "Blossoms" drew the praise from Dot which Frame treasured, "poetic insight and imagination" (*ODT* October 2, 1939). Frame's final poem for Dot's page, "The Dead Tree" begins in hope: "New born it seemed like everything/—Bird, bud and blossom—", but ends in desolation:

> And my apple boughs were not aflame
> With blossoms; and only the moon
> knew why
> A little lost wind began to cry
> Under the staring stars in the sky.
> (*ODT* December 8, 1941)

The poem expresses her sorrow at the passing of "Dot's Little Folk", the children's page which became a publishing institution, and had been a significant part of her creative life.

Images of trees and orchards abound in Rilke's poetry, which Frame first encountered in 1948 through the *Sonnets to Orpheus*, in J.B. Leishman's bi-lingual edition first published in 1936, and revised in 1946. The first of Rilke's *Sonnets to Orpheus* (even in Leishman's wooden translation) appears to have struck an immediate chord with its invocation of Orpheus, the musician-poet, and the images of trees:

> A tree ascending there. O pure transcension!
> O Orpheus sings! O tall tree in the ear!
> (Da stieg ein Baum. O reine Übersteigung!
> O Orpheus singt! O hoher Baum im Ohr!) (34–35)

The image of spring as the kind of poetry-loving child may also have had a direct appeal for Frame:

> Spring has come again. Earth's a-bubble
> with all those poems she knows by heart, —
> (Frühling ist wiedergekommen. Die Erde
> ist wie ein Kind, das Gedichte weiß;) (74–75)

Frame's affinity with Rilke would prove to be life-long, a shared interest in the value of the natural world, the destructiveness of industrialisation, the loss of conventional faith, and a sense that in life we should openly acknowledge the advent of our own death. In the 1970s, Frame would read and translate Rilke's later French poetry, in particular "Vergers" [Orchards] with Bill Brown in the USA, the fecund and self-reviving orchard still a significant image for her, and especially so in her final novel, *The Carpathians* (1988).

Rilke had a huge impact on 20th-century British and American poets, on W.H. Auden, Stephen Spender, W.B. Yeats and T.S. Eliot, all poets whom Frame read and admired. Rilke's poetry has been translated or "versioned" by a very wide variety of English-speaking poets including, in Frame's time, Stephen Spender, Cecil Day Lewis, and in New Zealand James Bertram, a friend and collaborator of Charles Brasch. In the USA, Auden reviewed the first English translation of Rilke, and references him frequently in his own poetry. For example, in his *Sonnets from China* Auden (2006) refers to the composition of Rilke's *Sonnets to Orpheus*:

> Tonight in China let me think of one
> Who for ten years of drought and silence waited,
> Until in Muzot all his being spoke,
> And everything was given once for all. (144)

In an attempt to account for the appeal of Rilke amongst anglophone poets, Karen Leeder, a Professor of German from Oxford University, suggested in a Rilke-Gesellschaft conference in London in September 2015 that anglophone poets had a strong sense that Rilke was addressing them directly, inviting a response, feeling that in translating and referring to his poetry they were in conversation with him. Frame seems to have felt an affinity with Rilke because he was a poet who lived, as she did, entirely for art. Rilke was acquainted with the prominent artists of his day, including Rodin and Cézanne, and he was commissioned to write a monograph on Rodin in 1902, noting the sculptor's working method of close observation, and later became Rodin's secretary. Rilke translated poetry from French to German, and in his preface to his translations of Rilke's French poetry, A. Poulin Jnr. (Rilke 1986) notes that Rilke's French poetry was much admired by Paul Valéry and André Gide (xii). At the writer's colony at Yaddo, Frame (2016) learnt more about Rilke and his connections with French poets. She tells Bill Brown that "I've had a whole world of feeling overturned or unburied by reading in the story of Rilke in Paris – how R. was influenced by Valéry's 'Le Cimetière Marin' [. . .] Rilke liked the poem because to him it was 'a perfect poem'; I liked it because I liked it and it moved me" (41).

Frame's immediate feeling for Rilke's poetry is evidenced in a letter to John Money (King 2000) in 1948, the year she first encountered the *Sonnets to Orpheus,* when she quotes: "Be not afraid of suffering, render/Heaviness back to the earth again" (98). Rilke also made his presence felt among New Zealand poets, and in June 1949, *Landfall* included Rilke's 4th Elegy from *The Duino Elegies* in an English version rendered by James Bertram:

> O Trees of Life, o when in winter mood?
> We are not singleminded, have no instinct
> Like migratory birds.
> (O Bäume Lebens, o wann winterlich
> Wir sind nicht einig. Sind nicht wie die Zug-
> vögel verständigt.) (Rilke 2009, 22)

In these opening lines, the poet remarks on man's lack of harmony, "nicht einig", with nature—"singleminded" is an odd translation of "einig" here—but the poem rehearses the common New Zealand themes of migration and the relationship with nature. This version of the "4th Elegy" was available to Frame while she was living in Frank Sargeson's hut where she had access to past issues of *Landfall*, every copy of which Kevin Ireland says "would have been eagerly devoured" (Ireland, personal communication). This translation may have suggested to Frame the image of migratory birds, "Die Zugvögel", which she uses in *Towards Another Summer.* The *Landfall* editor Charles Brasch quotes a number of times from Rilke's poetry in his *Journals*, for example these lines on January 28, 1962 from "Archäischer Torso Apollos": "Du musst dein Leben ändern" [You must change your life] "is this not a demand that much of greatest art makes of us?" (CBH January 28, 1962). In an entry a little later on March 6, Brasch remarks of Patrick White's *Riders in the Chariot*, "what a commanding silence [...] from page after page the cry comes up: Du musst dein Leben ändern" (CBH March 6, 1962).

Frame's correspondence with both Bill Brown and Charles Brasch contains frequent reference to Rilke, and she later read more of Rilke's German poetry in a bi-lingual edition of his poetry translated by C.F. MacIntyre. When she found the apple tree in her garden at home in Dunedin had but one single blossom and one apple, Frame (2016) writes to Brown that "Rilke would have had something wise to say about this smallest tree and its one blossom" (104), and a little later tells Brown "I should have a quote from Rilke here—he's said everything" (246). After Brasch's death in 1973, Frame (2011) wrote a memorial piece for "Tributes from Friends" in *Islands* 5 about a visit from him when he brought her some anemones, and she recalled "the Rilke poem" about these flowers. She had remembered the poem's first word in German, "Blumenmuskel" [flower-muscle] and quoted it, and "Charles finished the quotation, speaking in German" (54).

Like Rilke, and writers she knew in New Zealand, Frame lived in the literary world, and believed in the exalted role of the artist in society. And like the early 20th-century writers already mentioned, she seemed to feel Rilke was addressing her directly, in spite of Leishman's stilted translation—she found better versions in later years. The friendship with Bill Brown was one in which Frame could discuss translation issues and clarify her thinking and her doubts about varying interpretations of original poems. Writing to Bill Brown in 1970, she describes the Leishman translations in a Penguin edition of Rilke as "shocking" (Frame 2016, 104), as noted earlier, and the translation of "The Swan" as "unforgivably bad" (114). Frame acknowledges the use in *Faces in the Water* (1961) of translations of Rilke's *Sonnets to Orpheus* in the 1930s by the New York translator M.D.H. Norton. Later she discovered and particularly enjoyed translations from the 1940s by C.F. MacIntyre. Her bi-lingual editions of Rilke's poetry, both Leishman's and MacIntyre's, seem to have led her to consider the German original where the English and German words are clearly related, and when the syntax is simple, as we see from her anecdote about the anemones and her occasional inclusion of Rilke's German in the text of her novels.

In *Faces in the Water*, the medical staff in the mental hospital appear to be reinterpreting Rilke's words "*Wolle die Wandlung* [. . .] Choose to be Changed" (*FW*, 141) in favour of surgery, a leucotomy, for inmates suffering from what the medical authorities perceived to be intractable mental health conditions. This interpretation of Rilke's German highlights a moment of crisis for the protagonist, Istina Mavet, in relation to the hospital doctors and nurses who hold her life in their power. Istina muses, "'Choose to be changed; with the flame with the flame be enraptured'—but in too many cases the flame was the ice-pick of a leucotomy" (141). Towards the end of the novel, however, when Istina has been allowed into the library van, and she has been given a modicum of freedom to choose books, her thoughts return to Rilke's sonnet as she wonders more positively, "cannot one exercise one's will as a living hammer to force the shape of change?" (*FW*, 215).

Frame returns to the theme of controlling one's own life-change in *Living in the Maniototo* (1979), where Rilke's lines about choosing to be changed are also a key point of reference. Zita, another of the imaginary quartet of guests staying with Mavis in the Garretts' house responds to her husband Theo's stroke with the hope that it will "force them both to realise that their changelessness was a dream and that change need not be a continued nightmare" (*LM*, 205). A refugee of the 1956 Hungarian uprising, Zita has lost her language, culture and homeland, and has embraced change as Rilke exhorts, unlike her mother, whose fearfulness has led her to embrace elective silence, or Theo who, as Zita's pun identifies, aims to control everyone around him: "Theo has a *stake* in everyone he rescued"

(*LM*, 152). Frame also shares with Rilke the sense of a need to face death as part of the natural cycle of life, as in the lines from the *Sonnets to Orpheus* she quoted in English to John Money, cited earlier:

> Be not afraid of suffering, render
> heaviness back to the earth again.
> (Fürchtet euch nicht zu leiden, die Schwere,
> gebt sie zurück an der Erde Gewicht). (1946, 40-41)

Looking back from her home in Taranaki at her time in America, Mavis had seen in another image of the natural cycle,

> how close death is to the process of "going to seed", for both are really an abundance of life which shocks and frightens by its untidiness, its lack of boundaries and the finality of its choice of a place to grow. (*LM*, 78)

Thora Patten, the narrator of *The Edge of the Alphabet* (1962), quotes the opening lines of the same sonnet, in German at first, continuing in English, as Zoe Bryce, one of the novel's protagonists, struggles between life and death: "*O ihr Zärtlichen*... Step now and then you gentle-hearted into the breath not breathed for you" (*EA*, 96). Later on, in Hyde Park, Zoe, a timid and anxious former school-teacher from New Zealand, with an overwhelming sense of her own failure, has chosen to end her own life, and returns to another Rilke sonnet, twisting her piece of silver paper—her piece of creativity—in her fingers, asking: '*Was anything real at all? Nothing*' (*EA*, 273; Frame's italics). Zoe chooses her own moment to "render heaviness back to the earth again" as she "lay down, arranged and ordered, to die" (EA, 274).

Frame returns to the theme of heaviness again in *Daughter Buffalo* (1972*)*, when the elderly New Zealand poet Turnlung, living and writing in New York, inverts Rilke's musing on life and music in his poem "The Neighbour" ("Der Nachbar") into part of his extended treatise on death. Death, he says, is "heavier than the heaviness of all things" (*DB*, 433), where Rilke (1947) was writing about life (Das Leben), not death, and his lines read:

> Life is heavier
> Than the heaviness of all things.
> (Das Leben ist schwerer
> Als die Schwere von allen Dingen). (28–29)

Turnlung, whose own poems form chapters of the book, also recalls Henry Vaughan's meditation on "beauteous death, the jewel of the just" (Gardener 1966, 275), which Turnlung once had to paraphrase for an exam. After punning reflections on dual/duel/jewel, he relates Vaughan's 17th-century metaphysical poem to his own experience, "there have been deaths in my own life which touched the pressure points of my experience, enriching it as if by fine jewels" (*DB*, 485). Turnlung returns to Vaughan later in conversation with Edelman, his American homosexual lover, adding that "jewel is a treacherous word". Turnlung's feel for the metaphysics of Rilke and Vaughan, however, is lost on Edelman, whose prosaic mind can only wonder "if he'd had an unpleasant experience with jewels or jewel investment" (*DB*, 504).

Frame's interest in Rilke was a lifelong affair. Lines from Rilke's (1986) later French poems "Vergers" [Orchards], form the title and epigraph to the second volume of her autobiography, *An Angel at My Table:*

> Reste tranquille, si soudain
> L'Ange à ta table se décide;
> Efface doucement les quelques rides
> Que fait la nappe sous ton pain. (*CA*, 144)
> (Stay still, if the Angel
> suddenly chooses your table;
> gently smooth those few wrinkles
> in the cloth beneath your bread.) (133)

The appearance of the angel forges a link with the angels of Frame's mother, Lottie, and her Christadelphian belief, and with Frame's own memories of being transported, in a large choir in Dunedin, by singing Beethoven's "Ode to Joy" from the *Ninth Symphony*. She says, "I remember the happiness and recognise it as one of the rewards of alliance with any great work of art, as if ordinary people were suddenly called upon to see the point of view of angels" (*CA*, 175). She quoted the opening lines of Rilke's poem, in French, in birthday poems she wrote for her American friends Bill Brown and Paul Wonner (*ST*, 35, 69). Frame (2016) asked a friendly French PhD student who came to visit her to record some of these French poems of Rilke for Brown and Wonner (328), and "Reste tranquille" was also a poem which Frame requested be read, in French, at her funeral (Jocelyn Harris, personal communication).

Rilke's poem sings in tune with Frame's views of art, and, as Delrez (2012) asserts, is "an evocation of the numinous moment of inspiration" (9). On his way to take up his literary fellowship in the novel *In the Memorial Room*, the novelist Harry Gill (*MR*, 28) calls on Rilke's angels as he approaches Menton: "Les Anges, sont-ils devenus discrets!" [Have the angels turned discreet!]. Harry is dazzled by the light and the shining greenery of the trees which "bathe my eyes with blessing" as he contemplates his imminent blindness and the loss of his view of the natural world:

> Et que mes rouges, mes verts, mes bleus,
> Son œil rond rejouissent.
> S'il les trouve terrestres, tant mieux
> un ciel en prémisses (*MR*, 28–29).
> (And let my reds, my greens, my blues
> Make his round eye rejoice.
> If he finds them earthy, good!
> For a paradise of premises). (Rilke 1986, 150–51)

In Frame's final novel, *The Carpathians*, the repeated phrase "ancient springtime" is her translation (or Bill Brown's) of Rilke's "printemps antique"—Poulin has the far less euphonic "antique spring"—from the title poem of Rilke's "Vergers", written, as he says, in a borrowed language ("langue prêtée") about his long held fascination with orchards:

> Peut-être que si j'ai osé t'ecrire,
> langue prêtée, c'était pour employer
> ce nom rustique dont l'unique empire
> me tourmentait depuis toujours: Verger.
> (If I dared to write you, borrowed
> tongue, perhaps it was to use
> this rustic name whose rare kingdom
> always has tormented me: Orchard).
> (Rilke 1986, 156–57)

Frame links Rilke's "ancient springtime" with the orchards around the fictional New Zealand town of Puamahara, where a memorial to the fictional legend of the Memory Flower is located and the motif of the "ancient springtime" pervades the novel. The images of orchards and spring-time renewal are a key trope in Frame's thinking and in her writing. She wrote to Frank Sargeson comparing his fertile imagination and literary achievements to the natural spring-time processes of renewal, and Michael King (1995) uses this comment as an epitaph for his biography of Sargeson:

> Do you remember the narrow channels you made, all alone, into that part of the land where everyone said nothing would grow? [. . .] You can look at all those creeks and canals that followed and see the orchard. What an orchard!
> (9)

The orchard and the renewal of its trees, fecundity and spring-time renewal, was a key image for Frame from childhood onwards and throughout her life, and she had a strongly felt connection with Rilke's imagery which she linked with her own thoughts about the natural world. Her concern with landscape, of course, was something she shared with the poets who were her New Zealand contemporaries; and with the English Romantic poets who had dazzled her as a young woman.

The English 19th Century Romantics and *A State of Siege*

The English 19th-century Romantic poets were a major part of the school poetry-reading diet in New Zealand, and Janet Frame's first encounters with Wordsworth, Keats, Coleridge and Shelley came through her reading of "Dot's Little Folk" in the *Otago Daily Times*, and through *Mount Helicon*, her school poetry anthology. The 1943 University of Otago Calendar shows that the university syllabus also relied entirely on the English canon, and Coleridge's *Biographia Literaria* was one of the first set books which Frame encountered (*CA*, 163). In Coleridge, Frame "found the feast of imagination spread almost in loving fashion, in great kindness and abundance" (164).

The Romantic poets were inspired by the natural world around them, the lake poets—Wordsworth and Coleridge—by the sublime lakes and mountains of Cumbria. In London, Frame was drawn to Hampstead Heath, near where Keats lived, where she walked as far as the pond, and "began to repeat to [her]self, naturally" lines from Keats's "La Belle Dame sans Merci", aware that she was one of thousands who had done so, "at the sight of the tall brown rushes growing at the edge of the pond" (*CA*, 307).

While she lived in England, from the summer of 1956 until the autumn of 1963, Frame went on a camping trip to the Lake District where she "roamed the Fells all day visiting places known to Wordsworth, Coleridge, Shelley" (*CA*, 417). Frame shared the Romantic poets' belief in the importance of "Imagination". She also shared their view that the artist possessed a heightened faculty of insight which tended to set him or her apart from society.

Echoes of lines from the major and occasionally minor Romantic poets are heard throughout Frame's novels, and Frame's writing is imbued with the spirit of a Romantic view of landscape and people. She often uses specific references to romantic poetry and music to point up a gulf between her characters' imagination and their more prosaic aspirations. In *Owls Do Cry* (1957), Daphne's sister Chicks, one of the four Withers siblings, is desperate to "fit in" to the respectable conventions of Waimaru, a town of conformist, conventional lives, and to conform to the codes of her perceived social superiors. She reads Brontë novels vacantly, and has vague recollections of Wordsworth's "Daffodils". She plays Beethoven's Fifth Symphony to impress the visiting Dr Bessick and his wife, her social superiors in Waimaru, since she feels "quite safe with the Fifth Symphony. I can mention about fate knocking on the door and that kind of thing" (*OC*, 101).

With rather more mature aspiration in *The Adaptable Man* (1965), Muriel, the childless second wife of Suffolk farmer Vic Baldry, unsuccessfully attempts to coerce the poets and an inherited magnificent glass chandelier into her barely understood romantic aspirations for a better life. Keats's "Ode to a Nightingale" is remembered for its "extravagant" lines about red wine, "I've heard that this was Keats's favourite wine", although she says she is "not up on poetry at all. It amazes me that poets still write" (*AM*, 176). Muriel is usually more interested in the practical activities of the Women's Institute; and beauty needs to go hand in hand with prosaic usefulness: "She was not a sly romantic who fires arrows in chosen places with skill and precision; she was honestly unable to handle the weapons that her rarely felt needs put before her from time to time" (160).

Frame makes particular use of these romantic allusions in *A State of Siege* (1966), in which Malfred Signal, retired art teacher, aims to paint the natural scenery around her from her new but isolated island home as "a new view", but consistently fails to move beyond the conventional view of landscape to an imaginative vision. As an art teacher, Malfred had been dutiful and conventional, and her paintings of the natural world "were prized for their water-colour likeness to the original scenes" (*SS*, 35). Malfred felt acutely envious and resentful of the talent of her pupil, Lettuce Bradley, "an ordinary schoolgirl" who had "found her way to the secret store" in her paintings, who "had been able to absorb, as a mindless sponge absorbs food from the sea, the myths and legends of her own country" (136). In her awareness of her own artistic shortcomings, Malfred seeks to unlock the "room two inches behind the eyes" (36), a phrase Sargeson (2012) thought Frame found in a book about the German romantic composer, Wagner, in the bach on Waiheke which she rented (486).

Malfred echoes Shelley's "Ozymandias", "Look on my works, ye Mighty, and despair", as part of a web of suggestive allusion to Romantic poetry, when she asks "Where were the people to look on the scene and know its meaning?" (*SS*, 47). Frame may have been thinking of Rodin's view of art as contemplation, from her reading about Rilke's time in Paris with Rodin (2016, 41). Malfred repeatedly uses the phrase "as I see it" and in her desire to change the way she sees and paints the world around her Malfred tells herself that "I'll stare at it, I'll see it, I'll paint it as it is" (*SS*, 53). In Rilke's description of Paris life, *The Notebooks of Malte Laurids Brigge*, the protagonist, Brigge, repeatedly says that he is "learning to see [. . .] everything penetrates more deeply into me and does not stop at the place where until now it always used to finish". Finally, Brigge decides he "ought to begin to do some work, now that I am learning to see" (1992, 26).

That Malfred fails in her aim to create a new vision seems inevitable. She is unable to free herself from the stultifying habit of subverting her individuality and personal freedom to the social and familial pressures imposed on her, and which she has lived by all her life, unlike Brigge, who experiences a measure of independence. Malfred's paintings never upset the status quo; her life has been measured in teacups: "(Yes, Miss Henderson; no, Miss Wallace; do you take sugar and milk, Miss Ford?)" (*SS*, 53). Unlike Elizabeth Barrett Browning, whose "Sonnets from the Portuguese" she reads, she does not escape. Malfred has no rescuer, and expects none. She rejects as fanciful the notion of "the dream in the human mind that some agent, some time that was never too late, would bring permanent longed-for release from imprisonment!" (68). Instead her sleep is disturbed by dreams of her rejection of her former would-be lover, Wilfred.

When she moves into her new home on Karemoana, Malfred finds a selection of books waiting for her: John Keats, Matthew Arnold and Elizabeth Barrett Browning, "that other woman who had been set free" (SS, 68), but significantly no modern poetry and no

New Zealand landscape poetry. Malfred recognizes the volumes she finds are the kind of books which are conventionally given to children and students as presents or school prizes, as she arranges her "big *Beautiful New Zealand* books" (65) among them, full of conventional paintings. Like Erlene in *Scented Gardens for the Blind*, she draws her stock of poetry almost entirely from the anthologies she read at school or as a student, though Malfred is a middle-aged woman, not a young girl. The limitations of her reading parallel those of her painting, and the stifling effects of her dutiful life which leave her unable "to explore beyond the object, beyond its shadow, to the ring of fire, the corona at its circumference" (239).

When Malfred begins reading from Keats's odes and *Sonnets from the Portuguese*, "as the pleasant indulgence of one who is at last alone, in charge, and at rest" (*SS*, 68), she is soon disappointed that her surroundings do not correspond to her understanding of the Romantic vision, to Keats's Grecian Urn: "Where is the vision of perpetual youth, where are the lovers, the frozen blooms on the Grecian Urn?" (76). Phrases from Keats's odes "To a Grecian Urn" and "To a Nightingale" merge as Malfred "wondered, this was immortality? The vision was this street, not the scene on the Grecian urn. And one could grow tired of immortality, one could plead to die because one was not doomed to do so" (76). Malfred's fundamental failure of vision is highlighted by her inability to be inspired by the English Romantics in her new surroundings. She is unable to fulfil her aim "first of all, to observe, to clean away a dusty way of looking" (37), and remains fixed and immoveable, like the lovers on the Grecian urn.

On her fifth day on Karemoana, when Malfred begins painting her seascape, the links with her past life are plentiful, and there is no sense of the promised fresh start. On the contrary, she uses the child-size tubes of paint she has found in the bach, and mixes them with the hoarded tubes of lanolin from her late mother's sick-room. The resultant stench of death distresses her, and in the painting she calls *My Last Days in Matuatangi* [. . .] "no one could make out in this foam of lanolin the arms of someone being drawn under by the waves" (*SS*, 79–80) in an echo of Stevie Smith's (1987) best-known poem, "Not waving, but drowning" (167), and which Frame would have known as it was broadcast frequently in Britain in the 1960s while Frame was living in London.

Malfred's feelings of hopelessness increase on the long final night of the storm, and her despair that the space in her life left by her mother's death was like a fruitless, barren spot "where it was too late for any other object to grow" (*SS*, 180). She longs for the child-like simplicity and comfort expressed in "I Am" by John Clare: "*untroubling and untroubled here I lie/the grass beneath, above the vaulted sky*" (181; Frame's italics). The novel's concluding sentence draws on Matthew Arnold's "Dover Beach". In *Scented Gardens for the Blind*, Erlene's teacher, Miss Walters had dismissed Arnold's despair at the world's sufferings:

> To lie before us like a land of dreams,
> So various, so beautiful, so new,
> Hath really neither joy, not love, not light,
> Nor certitude, nor peace, nor help for pain. (Hayward 1958, 344)

She briskly describes the feelings expressed in this poem as "nonsense, really [. . .]. Why the world is full of hope and joy!" (*SG*, 55). Neither Erlene nor Malfred experience "hope and joy". Malfred's hopes of "a land of dreams" bring her neither light nor peace and she finds none of Coleridge's "feast of the imagination". Arnold's opening lines are a prelude to the tumult which follows them,

> The sea is calm tonight.
> The tide is full, the moon lies fair
> Upon the Straits. (344)

The quiet echo of these lines at the close of Frame's novel—"and the sea lay calm at last" (*SS*, 244)—concludes the turmoil of Malfred's final tempestuous night.

New Zealand Poets

Janet Frame's appreciation of poetry in English was not confined to British poets: she had been introduced as a schoolgirl to the American poetry of Walt Whitman, Edgar Allan Poe, John Greenleaf Whittier and Henry Wadsworth Longfellow—all found in the pages of her school anthology, *Mount Helicon*. Furthermore, her mother Lottie had a great love of Longfellow and Whittier. Frame also formed lasting friendships with New Zealand poets she read, among them Charles Brasch, Ruth Dallas, and James K. Baxter, and was pleased to meet other poets whose work she had read. At a reception in New Zealand House in London in 1984, on her way home from a writers' conference in Toronto, Frame (2011) says "I met for the first time, Fleur Adcock, our fine poet", claiming her as a fellow New Zealander despite Adcock's permanent home being in London, and at the same reception she was similarly pleased to see again another London-based New Zealand poet, Kevin Ireland, whom she had last seen as a visitor to Frank Sargeson's bach in Takapuna in the mid 1950s (192–93).

Looking back in her autobiography at the year 1945, Frame notes the determination of Allen Curnow to publish an essentially New Zealand poetry anthology, *A Book of New Zealand Verse*; Frank Sargeson's aim in editing the New Zealand short-story collection, *Speaking for Ourselves*; and James K. Baxter's first published book of poems, *Beyond the Palisade* (*CA*, 192). In March 1947, Brasch established the New Zealand literary quarterly, *Landfall*, and in its first edition wrote of his desire "to reincarnate the tradition in local form" (6). Baxter, who was at school in England for three years as an adolescent, makes clear in a letter to Curnow that he values both British and New Zealand influences: "There was no conflict, but both armies were real; tradition was not alien nor shadowy, N. Z. Landscape and life was immediate [. . .]. I think I can make something out of N. Z. for myself. Her people" (JBH July 7, 1945).

These publications mark the moment of Frame's realization "of New Zealand as a place of writers who understood how I had felt when I imported J.C. Squire to describe my beloved South Island rivers" and she delighted in "our land having a share of time and not having to borrow from a northern Shakespearian wallet" (*CA*, 192). The establishment of a New Zealand tradition was not always uncontested, however. Curnow's selection of poems for his New Zealand anthology was mostly welcomed by James K. Baxter, who told Curnow in the same July 1945 letter that "You have indeed created something sturdy and lasting; something long-needed; something of a classic nature". He offered, however, criticism of some of Curnow's choices. He thought Arnold Wall "has for me too great a tang of the *Kowhai Gold* insipidity"; and he disliked Ursula Bethell's Latinisms, though he admired "her strength". These criticisms have been taken up by later critics, for example, Paul Millar (2010), who in his introduction to Baxter's *Selected Poems,* suggests that Curnow's selection of Baxter's landscape poems was not representative of Baxter's output (xv). In his journal, Charles Brasch declared his love "for this lavish country with its great contrasts of wild mountains & foaming green trees [. . .] it goes to my head like wine, and it touches my memory & my heart" (CBH December 26, 1957). Yet he too was later critical of what he saw as Curnow's narrow view of New Zealand poetry outlined in Curnow's introduction to the 1961 *Penguin Book of New Zealand Verse*, complaining in his Journal about "Curnow preaching again; the gospel according to A. C." (CBH February 12, 1961).

Frame does not appear to have engaged in this debate, focusing more on the South Island poets she admired: the poets who were her contemporaries and became her friends, in particular James K. Baxter, Ruth Dallas, and Charles Brasch. In her letter to Baxter from Christchurch in 1947 she wrote about her belief that "poetry is in memory [. . .] the more I read of your work the more I feel you are remembering the real way" (King 2000, 94–95). Writing many years later to Bill Brown, Frame (2016) described the Baxters as "a gifted, sensitive family" (24), and sent Brown "some very fine translations" (251) by James K. Baxter of Rimbaud's "Seven Year Old Poet". In an earlier letter that year to Bill Brown, Frame described Ruth Dallas as "a gifted poet" (100).

Frame comments a number of times on her enjoyment of Brasch's poems. Frank Sargeson relates an incident in a letter to Brasch when Frame had returned to New Zealand that year and was visiting, but finding Sargeson was out, made herself at home and settled down to read his new books. Sargeson tells Brasch he returned to find "she had read all your poems. She was astonished (I think that is the right word)—she didn't say much, but it was some time before she came out of her bemusement" (CBH July 4, 1964). The poetry book in question was probably *Ambulando*, published in 1964, containing poems which recall the distress of a very painful homosexual love-affair, and the need for silence and concealment, as in these lines:

> For life? Your life and mine?
> This moment of waking dream is all the life
> I dare ask or imagine;
> These words: this silence: the heart instructed:
> And in your eyes life and death new-born.
> (Brasch 1980, 96)

These raw and agonised poems by the austere and reticent Brasch amazed Frame, and she would draw on them later for *Daughter Buffalo*.

Frame's empathy with the natural world of New Zealand and the way in which it was represented in landscape poetry is evident in her novels, and occasionally quoted or referenced directly, particularly that of the South Island poets. Frame's major declaration of her love for New Zealand poetry, however, occurs in *Towards Another Summer*, begun in 1963, in which the home-sick Grace Cleave takes up her host's copy of Curnow's *Book of New Zealand Verse*. She recalls a train journey through the town of Waianakarua, of the "plantation of gum trees crackling smooth grey flames of leaf, shaking blue dusty smoke as the wind touched them" (*TS*, 53); and Brasch's poem "Waianakarua", which tells of "Tall where trains draw up to rest, the gum-trees/Sift an off-sea wind" (Brasch 1980, 4; Curnow 1951, 128). Grace reads Brasch's "A View of Rangitoto"—Rangitoto is an iconic volcanic island, clearly visible from Auckland's shore—and cites the final two stanzas, lines which connect with a comment made by Mavis in *Living in the Maniototo* about her home in volcanic Taranaki, noted earlier, where she is "a guest, as all are who live here, of the Taranaki mountain" (*LM*, 133); and which belongs, like Rangitoto, to "A world of fire before the rocks and waters" (Brasch 1980, 17–18; Curnow 1951, 132). Reading these lines, Grace, ecstatic, "made a wild movement with her hand as if she were trying to lift the volcano from between the pages" (*TS*, 62). Grace watches her host's New Zealand father-in-law dozing and dreaming of home "of the Canterbury plains" and in a phrase from Curnow's (1951) poem, "Time" (139), one of the poems Grace returns to in Curnow's anthology—of "the Nor'wester 'nosing among the pines'" (*TS*, 44).

In his introduction to this anthology, Curnow (1951) stresses the importance of *place* in New Zealand writing, and arguing that "it is this vital discovery of self in country and country in self, which gives the best New Zealand verse its character" (21). Frame's feeling for the land and for Taranaki more closely resemble Brasch's feeling for New Zealand's mountains, which he expresses in his journal as "among them, visibly, audibly, the earth is still being made—in grandeur and terror, as yesterday" (CBH February 3, 1949). A full account of New Zealand landscape poetry is beyond the scope of this study, but the South Island poet Ruth Dallas (2000) also encapsulates a sense of being rooted in the landscape, "O far from the quiet room my spirit fills/The familiar valleys, is folded deep in the hills" (26). Although Frame travelled widely and made a number of long-distance journeys in later years, including a year spent mostly in the USA during 1970–71, she made New Zealand her permanent home when she returned from London in 1963 after seven years away. Writing in her autobiography some years later, she expresses a sense of being at one with her native landscape, its history and its future, so that "living in New Zealand would be for me like living in an age of mythmakers; [. . .] to know the unformed places and to help form them, to be a mapmaker for those who will follow" (*CA*, 415). This was a perception of landscape which Charles Brasch knew Frame shared with him, expressed in the poem which Brasch (1984) dedicated "to Janet":

> I am there, sleeping in the rocks,
> under the houses, below the promontories,
>
> I am the sea, I am the wind,
> Everything and nothing, with you. (204)

Walt Whitman, Frame's America and *Daughter Buffalo*

During her trips overseas, Frame spent a considerable amount of time in the USA, especially in the late 1960s and early 1970s, staying in writers' colonies or with American friends. In the USA, she reacquainted herself with the poetry of Walt Whitman, which she had read as a schoolgirl in *Mount Helicon*, and in her subsequent letters from New Zealand to American friends, makes frequent reference to it. Writing in 1885 about *Leaves of Grass*, Whitman declared his pride in being "An American bard at last! [. . .] We shall cease shamming and be what we really are" (www.loc.gov/exhibits/ treasures/ Whitman). In this aim we can see a parallel with Allen Curnow: Whitman, a century earlier in another new country, aiming for a specifically American poetry.

Whitman abandoned conventional rhyme schemes and verse-forms and aimed to express himself freely in the voice of the American vernacular. His best known or most anthologised poem is "O Captain! My Captain!" (*Mount Helicon* 1948, 203), an elegy for Whitman's hero, Abraham Lincoln, but in its conventional metre and rhyme scheme it is atypical of Whitman. Most of Whitman's poetry is characterized by its freedom from traditional verse-forms and its colloquial language; and his stated desire to create a purely American style of verse—indebted to the British poets of the past, but unshackled, creating its own style and in an American vernacular idiom.

Mention has already been made of the solace Frame found in Whitman's "The Lost Mate" (204) when her sister Myrtle died, and her letters to Bill Brown reveal her continuing delight in Whitman's poetry, as well as an appreciation of Emily Dickinson. From the MacDowell artists' colony in the USA, Frame (2016) wrote to Bill Brown in lines she had "recovered from the secret manuscripts of Emily Dickinson" and which read

> *B you are gone away*
> *even au revoir only*
> *was hard to say.*
> *We are lonely* (6; Frame's italics).

Frame was amused by the American habit of referring to people by their initials, as she does in this poem, referring to Bill brown as "B". In a more serious vein, she later wrote to Brown from Dunedin that "life continues very much a la Emily D with little of her courage and none of her talent" (196). In her correspondence with Bill Brown, Frame refers often to him and to his partner Paul Wonner as her "live-oaks" from Whitman's (2009) poem "I Saw in Louisiana a Live-Oak growing" (106). Whitman declared in the poem that the live-oak "makes me think of manly love", and for Frame it was an image of her friendship with these two American artists, both, like Whitman, homosexuals.

Frame (2016) also comments frequently on the sequence of poems that Whitman later added to *Leaves of Grass,* and which forms the elegy to Abraham Lincoln, especially "When Lilacs Last in the Dooryard Bloom'd", taking one of its lines to describe her daily life "in the large unconscious scenery of my land" (153; Whitman 2009, 259). In the USA, Frame listened to Paul Hindemith's *Requiem*, written in 1946 after the death of Franklyn D. Roosevelt, with a libretto drawing on Whitman's eloquent elegy for Abraham Lincoln. Bill Brown sent Frame a recording of it to listen to again at home in Dunedin, and in thanking him Frame (2016) wrote, now is the time for me to listen to it when my thoughts are so much in the U.S. [. . .]. Whitman's words are a large part of the beauty of The Requiem but I love the music too, the words are embedded there as if they were growing. (130)

Frame's reading of Whitman's poetry permeates *Daughter Buffalo* (1972), which is set largely in New York. Talbot Edelman, a young American medical student of "death studies" has an encounter with a stranger, who introduces himself unexpectedly: "I'm Turnlung", and who bears a physical resemblance to the common image of Walt Whitman, "an elderly man with a trim triangular beard and straggly grey hair" (*DB*, 414). Turnlung is not American, but has come to America "to take a closer look at death" (415). As he takes over the narrative from Edelman, Turnlung invokes T.S. Eliot's repetition of "an old man" (Eliot 2009, 21-23) in "Gerontion" when he declares: "I am an old man, a traveller down Instant Street" (420) and biblical lines from The Book of Job (422). His words gradually take on an increasingly Whitmanesque and prophetic tone in their simple diction, repetition and biblical cadence.

Figure 4: Walt Whitman in Washington, DC, circa 1863. Uncropped print made from glass negative. Photo by Mathew Brady. National Archives NARA.

In her novels, Frame uses—in among prose chapters—sections of free verse with diverse functions, reflecting imaginative processes; the layering of voices; and the subtle and sometimes unknowable workings of the human mind. Turnlung's words echo Whitman's "Song of Myself" when he says: "I am a bottle with a message in it. I will float back and/forth in the dark for many years" (426), lines which resonate with Whitman's message that

I am the poet of the Body and I am the poet of the Soul,
The pleasures of heaven are with me and the pains of hell
are with me. (Whitman 2009, 45)

There are specific references to Whitman's tropes: the lilac bushes, for example, which were laid on Abraham Lincoln's coffin—Lincoln died in May when the lilac was in flower. Turnlung and his former lover Selwyn had planted lilac bushes in memory of Turnlung's Aunt Kate, with their "heartshaped leaves which defy a writer to trespass on the territory of Walt Whitman and T.S. Eliot" (*DB*, 446). Frame reworks the story of the solace she gained from Whitman's poetry after her sister Myrtle died, as Turnlung's headmistress friend says, "I was able to use the incomparable facilities for grief and mourning given by Walt Whitman", quoting the opening lines of "The Lost Mate": "Once, Paumanok, when the lilac-scent was in the air and the fifth-month grass was growing" (454).

Frame's matter-of-fact portrayal of Turnlung's homosexuality as an ordinary aspect of his life—and Edelman's difficulties in acknowledging his—mark the rare inclusion of a positive portrayal of sexual desire in a Frame novel. Physical passion is usually either thwarted, as in Malfred Signal's rejection of Wilfred in *A State of Siege*, or reduced to farce as in the "love-a-dove" antics of Peggy Warren in *Intensive Care*. *Daughter Buffalo* was published in 1972, when anti-sodomy laws, inherited from the British, were still on the statute books in many American states. The process of repealing these laws began in some states from 1961 onwards, but they were only finally and completely overturned in 2003. The law in England and Wales was partly liberalized in 1967, in response to the Wolfenden Report published ten years earlier; but not in Scotland, Northern Ireland or the Channel Islands until 1982; and not in New Zealand until 1987.

Frame was aware of the tension the legal situation created in the lives of homosexual men—and this included a number of her closest friends—and it was reflected in their writing. She was living in London when the Wolfenden Report was published in 1957, and sent Sargeson a copy of it, as the wrapping around a little present of what he described as "some pansily-scented snuff" (Sargeson, 2012, 266) much to Sargeson's amusement. Sargeson had received a letter from the English novelist E.M. Forster, whose novel *Maurice* with its subject of homosexual love, was published posthumously. Forster had read Sargeson's novel *I Saw in My Dream*, and found it "extraordinarily haunting" (FSH December 29, 1949). Sargeson shared this letter with his friend E.P. (Peter) Dawson, one of the many people with whom he maintained a correspondence. She was an English writer who made her home in New Zealand between 1925 and 1962, when she returned to England. Commenting on his letter from E.M. Forster, Sargeson felt it necessary to ask her to "please never refer to it in print. I should feel such a worm—at least if any reference to the letter appeared in print until after the kind man was dead" (FSH December 29, 1949). We might assume that in this letter that Sargeson was protecting his own interests as well as showing respect for Forster's.

Frame's reading of Charles Brasch's (1984) *Ambulando* made clear to her the inner turmoil of the reserved, austere and fastidious Brasch, who reveals his feelings in "Break and Go", which begins:

> No one has clean hands,
> None a pure heart.
> We shall be part of one another to life's end
> Whether we would or not.
> But now break, go.
> Let silence fall like snow:
> Together we offend. (105)

Given the need for secrecy, Whitman (2009) is possibly as open as he could be in his expression of his own sexuality in *Leaves of Grass*, declaring

> Here to put your lips upon mine I permit you,
> With the comrade's long-dwelling kiss or the new husband's kiss.
> For I am the new husband and I am the comrade. (98)

Frame takes up Whitman's coded ambiguities of "manly love" and "comradeship", as Edelman oscillates between love and hate, retreat and abandonment, resentment and gratitude for Turnlung who, he says, "gave me permission to mourn and rejoice over my own life [...]. We made love to our own lives and deaths" (*DB*, 256).

In *Leaves of Grass*, Whitman's view of the unending cycle of life is expressed in his answer to the child's question '*What is the grass?*' (Whitman's italics). The grass is not only a symbol; it is the evidence of the unending cycle of life, since as Whitman replies to the child:

> The smallest sprout shows there is really no death
> And if ever there was it led forward life, and does not wait at the end to arrest it. (33–34)

Turnlung expresses this sense in a paradox of his own in the prose Epilogue to *Daughter Buffalo* as he ponders the final stages of his own life, "what matters is that I have what I gave; nothing is completely taken" (*DB*, 587). The reversion to prose in the Epilogue, the details of Charles Brasch's *Ambulando,* the New York Dead Letter Office and to Turnlung's retirement home in subtropical New Zealand with its "lovely beach" and "magnificent view" (587) mark the return from Turnlung's dream and memory world of Whitmanesque verse, to tangible prosaic reality.

Chapter Three: Frame's Use of Poetry in the Novels

Prose, Poetry and Poetic Prose

In an interview for the Australian National Library's sound recordings, in 1977, Frame (2011) talks about various aspects of her novel writing and her poetry. She says she's never written "a real poem, but I keep trying", and then reads a piece which she describes as "just an idea I wrote down, just developed it. I don't call it a poem, I don't call it anything. Well, I call it 'Hypotenuse'" (102). Frame used a revised version of this piece in *Living in the Maniototo* (1979), one of a number of insertions into the novels of poetry and significant sections of free verse or a prose-poetry hybrid.

The term "prose-poem" is most famously the coinage of Charles Baudelaire (2013), the 19th-century French poet, who wrote to his publisher, Arsène Houssaye, that he had dreamed of writing with "le miracle d'une prose poétique, musicale sans rythme et sans rime, assez souple et assez heurtée pour s'adapter aux mouvements lyriques de l'âme, aux ondulations de la rêverie, aux soubresauts de la conscience" [the miracle of poetic prose, musical without rhythm or rhyme, supple enough and jarring enough to adapt itself to the soul's lyrical movements, to the ebb and flow of dreams, to the sudden start of awareness] (4–5). Frame (2016) had read some of Baudelaire's work while she was at Yaddo, and continued to do so when she returned to Dunedin in 1970, both through library books and on tapes that Bill Brown sent her (210).

Baudelaire's well-known description of his "prose poétique" makes an interesting fit with Frame's cross-genre poetic style and her use of free verse within the prose novel facilitates the layering of multiple voices, combining suppleness and sudden shocking jolts as well as the lyricism of which Baudelaire writes. Baudelaire's hybrid style was revolutionary in its time, and Frame had read avidly the modernist novelists—James Joyce, Virginia Woolf, D.H. Lawrence, William Faulkner—who had also attempted to embody Baudelaire's ideals in their writing. Frame's cross-genre writing has been called "subversive", for example by Gina Mercer (1994). Frame does indeed counter and confound expectations, and her poetic sections serve a variety of purposes.

The verse sections of Frame's novels, very obscure in places, often serve as more than just an addition to or subversion of the narrative, and draw on the nature of poetry to delve more deeply than the conscious mind, to reveal, like dreams, the workings of the unconscious. In Frame's first novel, *Owls Do Cry* (1957), the "Songs from the Dead Room", the adult Daphne's cell in the mental hospital, are sections of poetic prose within a novel in which the prose itself is densely metaphorical. These songs are Daphne's thoughts and unspoken feelings, when she is unable to express herself to the people around her, and not given the opportunity to do so. They are italicized to mark them out from the main body of the writing, appearing at intervals like a Greek chorus, a voice for the voiceless, encompassing her joys and fears and presaging her fateful end.

Owls Do Cry, written in "a poetic, imagistic, allusive style" (Jones 1987, 175) draws on experiences of childhood and Frame's time in mental hospitals and weaves a variety of poetic voices from her prolific reading into a richly textured portrayal of inner life and the outside world. The child's ability to see beauty, significance and magic in the everyday, and the literalness of understanding which is confused by euphemism and cliché are exploited to point up corruption and spiritual hollowness in the adult world. Frame draws on her memory of lines from Wordsworth's "Ode on Intimations of Immortality", which she had learnt by heart at school, as the four Withers siblings—Daphne, Chicks, Francie and Toby Withers—enter the story "trailing clouds of glory" but find as they begin to mature that the "shades of the prison-house begin to close" around them all too quickly.

The novel is interspersed with Daphne's songs from "the dead room", in which she brings together her family in memory, imagination and poetic allusion. The novel opens with Daphne's first song, its densely figurative language resonant with imagery of childhood innocence, consciously recalling the first of Blake's *Songs of Innocence* in its description of daybreak and birdsong: "piping like the child in the poem, drop thy pipe, thy happy pipe". The rhapsodic and poetic cadences of Daphne's song retain in adulthood the imaginative language and vision of the child: "and I planted carrot seed that never came up, for the wind breathed a blow-away spell" (*OC*, 9). The syntax of Daphne's rapturous lines, "And the place grows bean flower, pea-green lush of grass [. . .] and the days above burst unheeded, explode their atoms of snow-black beanflower" (*OC*, 9), fuses Dylan Thomas's (1988) celebration of childhood, "Fern Hill", "Nothing I cared, in the lamb white days, that time would take me/Up to the swallow thronged loft by the shadow of my hand" (135) and Gerard Manley Hopkins's (1967) "Spring", his joy in springtime and childhood innocence, "When weeds, in wheels, shoot long and lovely and lush" (28).

The imagery of Frame's childhood poems was drawn from the fields and gardens around her, and from the view of the world as she lay in the grass, observing the skies above her. Like Blake and Hopkins, Frame had a sense of the paramount importance of the beauty and sanctity of the natural world, an essentially Romantic view of nature as both consoling and uplifting, where nature is invested with personality and in which human moods and moral impulses are reflected. A striking example is the end of the disastrous picnic outing in *Owls Do Cry*, as the picnic-party leaves the "long-faced cow, melancholy now, because no-one came to milk it, standing by the manuka fence, under the fir tree that heaved not in any wind or storm but out of its own sorrow" (*OC*, 146). Frame's own poetry is full of birds, trees, the seasons, and the elements of life:

> Every morning I congratulate
> The icicles on their severity.
> I think they have courage, backbone,
> Their hard hearts will never give way. (*ST*, 46)

Her anthropomorphic description of icicles draws on primordial imagery of the earth's elements, which Frame pursues with wit in "hard hearts". In 1958, Frame changed her name by deed poll to

Janet Clutha, after New Zealand's Clutha River, and the significance of this identification cannot be underestimated. It is central to her identity, and she saw the river as

> a being that persisted through all the pressures of rock, stone, earth and sun, living as an element of freedom but not isolated, linked to heaven and light by the slender rainbow that shimmered above its waters. I felt the river was an ally, that it would speak for me. (*CA*, 166)

Daphne's songs end with a refrain which sounds through the novel like a death knell: "Sings Daphne from the dead room" (*OC*, 9). Blake's "dark satanic mills" and his chimney-sweep are imaged in the Dickensian references to the woollen mills where people believe that "years ago small children had worked in mills, never seeing the sunlight for years" (*OC*, 27), and in a polyphonic texture of poetic allusion drawn from a timeless continuity of poets, echoes of Blake's chimney sweep, sold into servitude, merge with Eliot's "Little Gidding" to form Daphne's vision:

> *The singe on the sleeve is worse than fire*
> *The half-place than the knowing where,*
> *Like seas between to the unhappy sailor.*
> *Poor trafficking child, with no treasure.*
> (*OC*, 83; Frame's italics)

As Jeanne Delbaere remarks: "Like the *Four Quartets* Janet Frame's novels are full of echoes, silent shades glide through them, vaguely recognisable, beckoning to us for a while before making way for others" (Delbaere 1979, 707). The voices of poets speak through *Owls Do Cry*, as they do in Frame's subsequent novels, and to each successive reader.

The use of poetry to access underlying thoughts or feelings is addressed in a variety of ways by other contemporary poets. For example, in an interview for *The Paris Review*, Ted Hughes (1995) suggests that poetry is often "a revealing of something the writer doesn't want to say but desperately needs to communicate" (75) and in Frame's hands is a powerful tool in *Intensive Care* (1970) in the gradual revealing of Naomi's hidden distress. The poet and critic Ruth Padel (2004) notes the importance of the reader's response when she asserts that "the reader's unconscious as well as conscious mind is at work in reacting to the poem, just as the poet's conscious and unconscious thoughts work together to make it" (59). Verse sections give a greater insight into the mind of characters unable to communicate; create a parallel version of the prose story; provide a commentary akin to a Greek chorus; develop a multilayered, multivoiced structure; or serve as a kind of allegory, like the "Hypotenuse" in *Living in the Maniototo*.

In *Living in the Maniototo* (1979), the desire for freedom from authority and convention is a recurrent theme. Mavis, tired of obeying the "Thou Shalt Nots" of her creative writing class "decided to break the rules" (*LM*, 58). She elaborates the creative process with her "Hypotenuse" poem and begins by declaring:

> I am not Scalene, old warrior with the shortened foot hobbling by,
> nor isosceles prayer-pointing the sky,
> but part of the whole only, hypotenuse. (*LM* 68–69)

The artist is the hypotenuse, the linking agent, creating shape and wholeness. This is a poem without a metrical or rhyme scheme, relying on alliteration, lineation and a division into irregular stanzas to distinguish it from prose. The following chapter—Chapter 12—consists entirely of further lines from "I Am Hypotenuse", celebrating the artist and declaring the futility of trying to create a work of art by playing by the rules, like the man with the steam-cleaning business, trying to write a novel: "He unloaded all his stored-up drama/Which fell apart at birth, lacking the life-dealing want" (72).

Elsewhere, verse sections are used enigmatically, and as an alternative commentary on the narrative, and in later novels achieve a level of poetic density which begins to require a level of "decoding", to indicate a subtext to the surface level of meaning. In *The Edge of the Alphabet* (1962), the third chapter interrupts the narrative with a verse commentary on timelessness, introduced with a line from a common traditional ballad form, "So I walked one evening" (*EA*, 16) in an echo of W.H. Auden (2006), "As I walked out one evening" (84–85) and continuing with lines about "the monster in the mudflats", the primeval, pre-lingual monster who dies out "unwilling to change or camouflage". Auden's poem declares that "Time will have his fancy" and that "the glacier knocks in the cupboard", and Frame's lines follow a similar theme, asking "Will Time publish us too as grotesque, purposeless, /beyond the range of human language, between the pages of ice" (*EA*, 17). Auden's poem ends "And the deep river ran on", and Frame's narrator, returning to prose, asserts that "The dead return, they mingle, their smell is layered over the living and the present" (17).

In *The Edge of the Alphabet*, the protagonist, Toby Withers, Daphne's brother from *Owls Do Cry*, is likewise inarticulate, and although he has insights is for the most part portrayed as simple-minded. In verse the narrator articulates thoughts and ideas that Toby is unable to find words for or comprehend. Or the narrator, in this case Thora Pattern, paints a word-picture in verse of the post-war London in which Toby arrives, of winkle-picker shoes and West Indian immigrants, with an alternative to Toby's limited point of view in its commentary on the repetitions of life: "A man receiving treatment at King's College Hospital/For nails driven through his hands and feet" (118–19). Charles Brasch records his appreciation of Frame's insights in his journal, noting that in *The Edge of the Alphabet* "one feels [. . .] the exposure of the gulfs, abysses, that underlie all our lives, of the constant attempt to conceal reality from our gaze which nearly all our activity represents" (CBH February 42, 1963), a comment which applies increasingly to Frame's later novels, in particular *Intensive Care*.

Sylvia Plath and *Intensive Care*

In *Towards Another Summer*, which Frame began writing in February 1963, a few days after she had heard of Plath's death, Frame alludes in lines of verse to Plath's themes of violent death and family relationships, and to Plath's interest in bee-keeping:

> Dear mother, dear father dear husband dear child,
> there is no answer,
> this microphone like a beehive celled with honey
> is blocked forever with the sweetness of death. (*TS*, 49)

Plath's poetry makes itself even more pervasively felt in Parts One and Two of *Intensive Care* (1970). The novel is remarkable in its use of free verse and its relationship to Plath's poetry, especially her late poems, which were published individually in journals, magazines and newspapers between 1959 and 1962 when Plath was living in London, and published posthumously in *Ariel* in 1965.

Plath and Frame share an ability to focus on states of crisis derived from a personal experience of anxiety and despair, transformed by extraordinary linguistic skill and dazzling, often savage imagery and given universal significance. Carole Ferrier (1995) notes that Frame's treatment of psychological depths has "affinities to some of the poems of Sylvia Plath" (213–14) and that in *Intensive Care*, daughter Naomi's verse letters to her "First Dad", Tom Livingstone, suggest that he "takes on for his daughter the colossus-like qualities of Sylvia Plath's Daddy". Ferrier's intuition is surely correct here. The character and situation of Naomi strongly suggest a link with Plath's poetry and Plath's pre-occupation with the dysfunctional dynamics of family relationships.

Plath's final contribution to the BBC radio programme, "The Poet's Voice" was broadcast three months before she died, and was broadcast again, in her honour, a few days after her death. Frame, a regular listener to the BBC Third Programme which carried these broadcasts, wrote her listening and her grief into *Towards Another Summer*, as quoted in Chapter 2. In her introduction to her poem

"Daddy" on this programme, Plath (1989) said "here is a poem spoken by a girl with an Electra complex. Her father died while she thought he was God" (293). Plath's use of the term "Electra complex" may well have triggered a response in Frame, who had personal experience of the gender inequality of committals to mental hospitals. Grace Cleave, the protagonist in *Towards Another Summer*, remarks on the unquestioning acceptance of Freud's theories, commenting that "it's no use saying Freud, Freud. People do, you know. Like squeezing a stale sponge" (*TS*, 13).

Adherence to the Freudian theory of infantile sexuality remained largely unchallenged into the 1970s. Bruno Bettelheim (1976), the Freudian psychoanalyst and influential advocate of the importance of reading fairy tales for children, restated Freud's belief that "what his female patients recollected was not something that had happened, but what they wish would have happened [. . .] that the patients when little girls had been far from innocent" (320). This was a conclusion Freud (1985) came to in 1897, when he came to believe that his original view—that all of his patients had been subject to incest—had been in error since "in all cases, the *father*, not excluding my own, had to be accused of being perverse [...] whereas surely such widespread perversions against children are not very probable" (264). Freud then developed his theories of infantile sexuality and the Oedipus complex, which Carl Jung termed the Electra complex in girls. Freud (1924) concluded that in adult neuroses "it appeared that between the symptoms and the infantile impressions were interpolated the patient's phantasies (memory-romances), created mostly during the years of adolescence" (277).

Both Bettelheim and Freud have since been strongly criticised, for example by Alice Miller (1985), the Swiss German psychoanalyst, who was herself originally a Freudian, but whose extensive work with disturbed children led her to challenge Freud's theories. She relates Freud's 1896 report that "in all eighteen cases of hysterical illness treated by him [. . .] he discovered [. . .] repression of sexual abuse by an adult or by an older sibling who had in turn been abused by adults" (277). Miller's views "conflict sharply with Freud's theory of infantile sexuality. [. . .] Genuine sexual maturity", she asserts, "coincides with physical maturation in puberty" (122). Miller takes the view that Freud rejected his 1896 findings of abuse, swayed by what seemed to him to be apparent probabilities, his patriarchal bias, and by the powerful Judeo-Christian commandment to "honour thy father and thy mother". These pressures caused Freud to respond "by treating a subject that he wished to bury under the weight of taboo" (1997, 42). She takes the view that as remarkable as Freud's work is, there is now more information available than Freud had access to.

Miller's (1985) earlier book was originally published in German in 1981, and for the American edition she added a note that:

> when this book appeared in Germany in 1981, I was virtually alone in my thinking, for the sexual abuse of children was still a forbidden subject in Europe. I didn't know that the situation had already changed in the United States, that the topic was being discussed openly there and had become a matter of public concern. (309)

Among other commentators on this issue is Marina Warner (2014), who has described Bettelheim's Freudian views as "controversial and flawed" (113), criticizing him for overlooking changes in cultural attitudes over time and for his continuing patriarchal stance: "he enrages me as he has done many other lovers of fairy tales—especially feminists who take issue with the psychoanalytic premises about female nature, destiny, and sexual identity" (125). In 1970, when *Intensive Care* was published, the sexual abuse of children had not received the recognition it has in more recent years, and any suggestion of such abuse was more likely to be disbelieved, ignored, suppressed or ascribed to a fault or psychological state in the child, as in an Electra complex. Frame was aware of the way in which sex-role stereotypes often lay at the heart of how mental illness was seen, and how society treats girls and women, responding to the victim with blame or disbelief.

A recent study by Judith Holloway (2001) of pre-war inmates of Seacliff Mental Hospital near Dunedin revealed that "women who failed to keep their households clean [. . .] could be liable to incarceration" (153). Committals were often initiated by family, authorised by two general doctors and a magistrate. Evidence of Frame's awareness of these gender inequalities and iniquities in the treatment of mental health comes in her gift of a copy of *Women and Madness* (1972) by an American psychologist, Phyllis Chesler, to her friend Phillip Wilson, the New Zealand writer. Her sardonic inscription is "something romantic from Janet". The book's subtitle is *When is a Woman Mad and Who is it Who Decides*?

The experiences of abused children have long been overlooked through taboo, the fear of destroying a family, and the fear of losing parental love. Virginia Woolf (2002), writing in 1939 in her late fifties, describes her frightening and shame-inducing experience at the age of six, when her half-brother—a young adult—set her up on a table and began an increasingly intimate exploration of her body; and though she "stiffened and wriggled" he would not stop. She wondered "what is the word for so dumb and mixed a feeling? It must have been strong, since I still recall it" (82). Who could she possibly have told, who would not simply have dismissed or scolded her? Even at eighteen, Virginia could cause embarrassment amongst her family with a comment about Plato, reprimanded with a whispered "they're not used to young women saying any̱thing" (40). In later years she narrated her experience of abuse as a six-year-old in letters to friends, and recalls it in her "Sketch of the Past", which was not published until 1972.

Frame takes up this theme in *Intensive Care* (1970) in her treatment of Naomi and her sister Pearl in a way which is psychologically subtle, and initially ambiguous. Naomi's verse hints at the turbulence lying beneath the surface and combines Baudelaire's "ondulations de la rêverie" [the ebb and flow of dream] with his "soubresauts de la conscience" [sudden starts of awareness]. Frame shares Plath's disdain for cliché and platitude as well as her use of savage images of pain, violence, and anger, the "boot in the face" of the Daddy whose daughter feels he has betrayed her, as Pearl and Naomi are betrayed. Naomi's father, Tom Livingstone, is damaged by his experiences as an 18-year-old soldier from New Zealand in Europe during World War 1, and his subsequent life-long family relationships have been distorted by shell-shock and the impact of the horrors he witnessed during the combat. Tom spent time as a patient in a wartime convalescent home, a former English country mansion, Cullin Hall, and after the armistice he returns to a loveless marriage in New Zealand where he continues to cherish the memory of the young nurse, Cissy Everest, with whom he fell in love in England. The devastating effects of war leave him unable to engage in a loving and caring relationship with his wife and two daughters, Pearl and Naomi, and after his retirement Tom, now a widower, returns to England to look for Cissy.

The novel opens in free verse with dreams of the loved and protected child in which: "the child played a poem/protected by mild adjectives" (*IC*, 27). Frame moves swiftly to violent images of cruelty and copulation, where children are:

> tripped, trodden on, pulled apart
> limb by limb, bonfire
> in feast, explosion, and orgasm. (27)

No-one is named in this opening choric verse which forms the novel's first chapter. The reader is left with startling images, not knowing who the speaker is, or whether this is dream, fantasy or a reflection of reality. The brief second chapter, again in verse, takes A.A. Milne's "Happiness" and suggests a reason for Tom's "great big waterproof boots" in language which reflects the viciously angry battlefield destruction of life. The reader then meets Tom Livingstone, convalescing from his wartime injuries, in chapter three. Here the prose narrative begins, as Tom returns to England to look for his lost love, Cissy Everest, and the novel moves backwards and forwards in time between Tom's convalescence at Cullin Hall, his married life in New Zealand, and his return to London where he breaks his leg by slipping on the ice and then finds himself back at Cullin Hall, now a "Recovery Unit". Here, "all dreams lead back to the nightmare garden" (32). The loss of innocence, and the loss of Eden, are established.

Naomi introduces herself in terms reminiscent of the younger Plath, "student, typist, writer-of-verse", in images of internal bleeding with "I picked raspberries, haemorrhaging them into a tin bucket" (*IC*, 40). Blood, betrayal, pain and death combine with recollection of unacceptable truths. Plath's "Daddy" died when his daughter was a child, young enough to think of her fearsome father as God, ascribing to him in her anger an imagined Nazi past. Naomi re-lives her pain as she matures and gains an increasing understanding of her betrayal, "the pain of grief brought to birth by thinking" (87). The loss of innocence and of the paradise garden is brought about by the father who, she says in a biblical phrase, "gave us knowledge" (86).

The reader is kept in a fluctuating dream-filled sense of ambiguity as Tom fantasises about an alternative life and family with Cissy Everest, and the truth about the death of his wife Eleanor is clouded. Did he really push her into the slurry pool, or only imagine it in his desire to be rid of her? Or did Naomi poison her with the weed-killer? (*IC*, 146). Was Pearl adopted and subsequently sent away to boarding-school? (145). The narrators are unreliable and Pearl, Naomi and Tom all attempt to escape into a fantasy world. The reader is certainly led to believe Tom killed the ailing Cissy—not out of merciful compassion, but in a fit of anger that she had "failed" him (60). Tom's other daughter, Pearl, attempts to deceive herself in the language of an imagined fairy-godmother as she struggles unsuccessfully, in misery and anger, with the consequences of her suppressed feelings: the weight she cannot lose and her habit of trying to control everyone else's life (144). In a final unspoken comment on her relationship with her father, Pearl does not attend his funeral.

The relationship between Naomi and her father is frequently couched in language which describes an Electra complex. Naomi notes Tom's understanding—and not jealousy—of her bringing her boyfriend, Donald, to the Bonfire Night party, but insists that "I had to be loyal to you, dear First Dad" as Donald hangs himself (*IC*, 156).

Tom's sudden brush with truth, when Peggy Warren, the current woman in Tom's life, crudely wonders about his daughters, "surely you didn't love-a-dove them?", leaves Tom reduced to angrily embarrassed bluster (113).

Naomi is destroyed by the impossibility of telling the truth, illustrated at Christmas, when the meal is "followed by the love-sleep" (*IC*,183), and she uses her present of a John Bull printing set to print only formulaic phrases and conventional symbols. Like the six-year-old Virginia Woolf, Naomi does not have the words to express that which she in any case feels obliged to conceal, and Frame's poetry suggests the tension caused by the breaking of sexual taboo. Christmas for Naomi is "Pain and Santa" (236), and in Naomi's penultimate verse chapter the language of anguish and destruction runs through the lines of verse unmistakably, suggesting the cause of her illness was that "we never grew out of Christmas". The intensity and bitterness of the language, "pain", "break", "stain", "startle", "harm", "cut" and the crudity of expression create a picture of childhood betrayed and destroyed:

> Growing up we grew in
> Like unhealthy fingers and toenails;
> You cut us to the quick. (*IC*, 236)

Naomi sees the green crickets, "carolling with their arse as men and women are doing/on the lupined beach". She has to pretend "the sticky mess" is bird lime; performing "the favour, your favour" leads her eventually to "wake to grief of destruction" (236).

Frame ends the second part of *Intensive Care* with Naomi's final choric verse as she faces her imminent death in quieter mode, with a sense of resignation and detachment, self-consciously acknowledging the coming end, now that "all is a dream at Christmas time" (*IC*, 250) and "the barrier is broken with death". She recalls the deceptions of her childhood with their false hopes and promises: "Look, there's a honeybee/with a basket of poisonous fruit under its arm". She leaves unsaid the words she found unsayable, unable to solve "the crossword pain", looking

at the words between the lines between the words
between the pages
of the going going gone book. (*IC,* 250)

as she and her father "are recovered" (251) under the earth. The sense of finality in the last piece of choric verse, provides a fitting conclusion to what was originally envisaged as the end of a novel. Frame's lines are suggestive of Plath's final poem, "Edge", written a few days before she took her own life, with its imagery of a darkening world closing itself down:

as petals
of a rose close when the garden
Stiffens and odors bleed
From the sweet deep throats of the night flower.
(Plath 1987, 273)

These closing chapters have arguably received less attention than they merit by critics, perhaps through the greater interest in the dystopian future of Part III, and Frame's decision to join Parts I and II with Part III and make them fit somewhat loosely with the connecting device of the Livingstone tree.

It is clear from Dr Alice Miller's comments in 1984 about the taboo nature of child abuse that in *Intensive Care*, published in 1970, Frame was ahead of her time in her shrewd perception and in her honest delineation of dysfunctional family dynamics and the hidden cruelties which could be suffered by children in such families, especially girls and young women. She acquired this understanding from listening to stories she heard from fellow inmates and "from my observations in hospitals" (*CA,* 367) especially during her years in Seacliff Mental Hospital where she had become aware of the "Ophelia syndrome", the acceptance and internalization by young women of the opinions of powerful male authority figures.

Frame uses verse throughout her novels to experiment with narrative styles, but in Parts I and II of *Intensive Care* she makes a different use of poetry both to disguise and hint at the concealment of taboo subjects and to express the lifelong impact of sexual abuse on the individual. She invites the reader to probe beneath the surface, reading closely—decoding almost at times—to make connections, to transcend the barriers of taboo, and to acknowledge the secret fear and pain experienced by Naomi. In Frame's multi-layered texture of language, Naomi's verse chapters give voice to unspoken or unutterable thoughts and feelings as Frame alludes to the savagely honest poetry of Sylvia Plath.

Chapter Four: The Bible—Eden and Apocalypse

Biblical Poetics

The two major canonical texts in the English language and the most pervasive texts of western culture, the King James Bible—also known as the Authorised Version—and Shakespeare's plays, have left an indelible mark in the English language, their phrasing and stories firmly embedded in our modes of expression, thinking, ethics and cultural life. In addition, the King James Bible and Shakespeare's plays are among the most widely-translated of texts, are known throughout the world and have long had a global readership. Frame had an especially close familiarity with the Bible. Her mother, Lottie, was a devout Christadelphian, who believed in the Day of Resurrection and the Second Coming of Christ. Above all, Lottie believed in the paramount importance of biblical scripture, "knew many of the passages by heart" and "insisted we read from the Bible" (Alley and Williams 1992, 42). The Bible was entrenched in Frame's imagination, biblical poetic forms of expression make a major contribution to her novels, and its language is part of her habits of thought. The influence of religion diminished for Frame while she was still at school, "and was replaced, possibly, by the influence of words. I had an abiding memory of Bible-reading days, of the red-letter Bible which I used to pore over" (42). Her novels illustrate how the loss or absence of faith may leave people with the legacy of a love of the Bible's poetry, words and music, evident in her explorations of ethical and spiritual issues. She calls on the Bible's stories, poetry and ancient psalms and their links with mythology, and she exploits biblical poetic rhythms and syntax for their sense of timelessness.

Frame makes frequent reference to the poetry of the Psalms, the Beatitudes, the Song of Solomon, and Ecclesiastes, weaving echoes, themes and cadences through her prose and storytelling. She takes poetic biblical verses as inspiration, and uses biblical cadence and rhythm in her own prose and poetry. At certain times, she employs direct quotation, allusion, parody of biblical texts, biblical syntax and style interwoven with snatches of poetry and the voices of characters in a verbal orchestration of text and speech. At other times she follows a theme or a "load-bearing word", one of those words which Mavis, the novelist in *Living in the Maniototo*, believes "stop the sky from falling" (*LM*, 78), and which Frame examines from many angles.

In *Faces in the Water*, for example, the inmates of a mental hospital learn that "weeping is a crime" (*FW*, 9) and they are exhorted by the nurses "like Lear and Cordelia to pray and sing" (36) in an allusion to Psalm 137, the lament of the Hebrew captives, which begins:

> By the rivers of Babylon, there we sat down, yea, we wept,
> when we remembered Zion.
> We hanged our harps upon the willows in the midst thereof.
> For they that carried us away captive required of us a song;
> And they that wasted us required of us mirth, saying,
> Sing us one of the songs of Zion.
> How shall we sing the Lord's song
> In a strange land?

Here Frame weaves a direct reference to *King Lear* 5.3, where Lear and Cordelia are prisoners, "like birds in a cage" (*FW*, 9) and Lear urges Cordelia to "live, /and pray, and sing" (11–12) which in itself alludes to Psalm 137. Further allusions to the same psalm reverberate all through the novel, layering echoes of the lament, which has resounded in literature from biblical times, of distress in captivity, powerlessness and the humiliation of captives. Frame is here reworking the theme of a text which dates from nearly three thousand years ago, and is familiar through a number of musical settings: by Bach for example, and Verdi's *Nabucco*, as well as more recent popular versions, appropriations for book titles, and the psalm's use in Jewish and Christian ritual. The reader is thus invited to meditate on a shared history and a shared humanity, made all the more forceful by Frame's use of Holocaust imagery in both *Faces in the Water* and *Owls Do Cry*.

For the inmates do feel like prisoners in "a strange land". They are powerless, enclosed and subject to humiliation and punishment, expected nevertheless to smile and appear cheerful. Like a Hebrew captive in Babylon, Istina is exhausted by her treatment, saying "I could not absorb any more fearful possibilities; I was so tired; if it rained, the harp hanging on the willow tree would get wet, and still I did not care" (*FW*, 59), the abandoned harp a symbol from Psalm 137, of the feeling of desolation which inhibits song, art and music. As Istina sinks ever lower in the institution's hierarchy of wards and personal hopelessness, "wasted" in her incarceration, she "remembered the weeping willow, and the harp now destroyed by frost and damp" (82). When she returns from the depths of Lawn Lodge, the section of the hospital reserved for the most intractable inmates, to the relatively liberal regime of a convalescent ward she "stayed all day and every day near the willow tree circling it and trying to charm it with riddles" (107), the harp a constant symbol of Istina's inability to feel or express happiness.

Other inmates sing the songs required of them by the nurses, and dehumanised by the regime, incongruously launch into recent popular and romantic, optimistic tunes of the 1940s and 1950s. Hilary sings of her passion for Harry in the words of "My dreams are getting better all the time", and soon after she is severely punished for acting on the feelings behind the song. Their brief encounter, two days of freedom together in the secluded bush at the back of the hospital, resulted in a period of solitary confinement for Hilary (*FW*, 158). At the dance where the women are made up "like stage whores" (165), Istina dances with Eric to the tune of "Destiny" (167). Carol, who talks incessantly of marriage and her engagement ring, sings snatches of her favourite song, "Some enchanted evening, you may see a stranger" (140).

Frame makes a connection between the dehumanised and sometimes sadistic behaviour of the nurses in the mental hospital to that of the Babylonian captors who required "mirth". This affinity is stressed constantly on the wards, where the inmates "learned not to cry in company but to smile" (*FW*, 32) and with the "amusement" of the degrading lolly-scramble which fills Istina with disgust. The Hebrew origin of Istina's surname, "Mavet", meaning "death", the shaved heads and the Holocaust imagery of the ECT procedures link the biblical Hebrew captives with the hospital patients and with the Jewish and other inmates of 20th-century death camps, pointing up a timeless, endless cycle of inhumanity.

In other novels, Frame's invocation of the Bible points up the characteristic powerlessness and distress of characters who live on the edge of society, through poverty, mental capacity or fragility, and whose hopes for a better life are undermined by life's cruelties. A number of Frame's characters invoke lines from the Beatitudes, the affirmation of morality, humanity and compassion which begins:

> Blessed are the poor in spirit: for theirs is the kingdom of heaven
> Blessed are they that mourn: for they shall be comforted.
> Blessed are the meek: for they shall inherit the earth.
> (Matt. 5:3–5)

In *Owls Do Cry*, these verses are one of the biblical texts which inform the life of Amy Withers, Daphne's mother, but which promise more than they deliver. Daphne frequently recalls them in her hospital cell, referred to as her "dead room". Amy is one of life's peacemakers, poor and meek, but feels far from blessed at the end of Christmas, as she "cried herself to sleep for disappointment and loneliness" (*OC*, 95). At the girls' school, religious observance is shown to be little more than a formulaic and conformist routine, as the Beatitudes are followed rather too swiftly by banal announcements from the Headmistress, the music of the lines truncated by a teacher who is oblivious to their meaning and their poetry (24). Daphne later recalls these lines in one of her songs from the dead room where she merges her mother's Christadelphian belief that angels live among us and in the Second Coming of Christ with Christ's promise of salvation for the dispossessed:

for angels walk upon the earth among people, and the day Christ comes He too will walk unknown upon the earth. And blessed are the poor in spirit, for theirs is the kingdom of heaven. (49; Frame's italics)

In this extended song from the dead room, Daphne intersperses lines from the Beatitudes and further biblical references, "*Lay not up for yourselves treasure upon earth*" (Matt. 6:19; *OC*, 49; Frame's italics) with her grandmother's Dixieland song, "*Grandmother breaking her back on the hot Virginny sun/Grandmother what big eyes you have*" (*OC*, 49; Frame's italics). This song, "Take me Back to Old Virginny", from which Daphne inferred that her grandmother had been an African slave, is mixed with her mother's admonitions after her daughter Francie Withers's death by drowning, "*Francie, come in you naughty bird*", fairy stories—"Red Riding Hood" here—Christadelphian beliefs and repeated allusion to Ariel's piercing cries in *The Tempest*, "*Oh the wind is lodged forever in the telegraph wire for crying there*" (48; Frame's italics) until Prospero freed him. The lines form an orchestration of memories, scripture, song and poetry which seem to sum up the whole of Daphne's life so far, a life lived through literature.

The long years of Daphne's incarceration are expressed in biblical rhythms and psalm-like cadences: "And Daphne lived there alone for many years" (*OC*, 132). The use of biblical repetition, anaphora, here is suggestive of timelessness and the long reach of history: "nor do the people there move, nor can you walk there" (128). Daphne wants to look at the outside world "to see if God were saying 'Blessed are the meek and poor in spirit'" (130). Frame's repeated use of biblical syntax suggests a poetic, visionary prophet in the wilderness, both literal and metaphorical: "And Daphne lived there alone for many years, amid the assault and insinuation of sound in days unshining and night without darkness" (131).

Frame makes consistent use of particular load-bearing words from the Bible, of which "treasure" is a notable example in her challenge to materialism which recurs throughout her œuvre. The first part of *Owls Do Cry* is subtitled "Talk of Treasure" from St Matthew, "Lay not up for yourselves treasures upon earth" (Matt. 6:19), and Frame repeatedly interrogates the word "treasure" in its secular and material, spiritual and ethical senses. A picnic organised by the nurses—a rare trip into the world outside the hospital for some of the inmates—descends into dark farce as it comes to a confused and ill-tempered end, and the nurses grumble and ask Daphne what she thinks. This rare occurrence of the nurses beginning to treat an inmate humanely, by asking their opinion, serves to emphasise that the nurses tend to become as institutionalized and dehumanized as the inmates. Daphne keeps her thoughts to herself, but expresses them in a fusion of biblical echoes, thinking, "if I travel a hundred miles to find treasure, I will find treasure. If I travel a hundred miles to find nothing, even if I bring money with me, to lay it down in exchange, I will find nothing" (*OC*, 145–46). Matthew's exhortation to "Lay not up for yourselves treasures upon earth" (Matt. 6:19) is a key biblical image for Frame, and one which she pursues throughout her novels. Daphne's thoughts echo St Matthew again: "what shall a man give in exchange for his soul?" (Matt. 16:26), and are overlaid with those of St Paul: "And though I have the gift of prophecy and understand all mysteries, and all knowledge; and though I have all faith, so that I could remove mountains, and have not charity, I am nothing" (I Cor. 13:2). Alone, and in her silent thoughts, Daphne shows her understanding of St Matthew's concept of the "treasure" of the human heart.

Frame draws on allusions to the Bible by other writers, Shakespeare, T.S. Eliot, Walt Whitman, and W.H. Auden for example. The Bible is the supreme intertext in the English language, a pervasive linguistic presence. Poets and writers of all ages have assumed their readers' or audience's common understanding of allusion and reference, for example the dying Falstaff who "babbled of green fields" (*Henry V* 2.3.17; Ps. 23) and Keats's imagining, in his *Ode to a Nightingale*, of Ruth the Gleaner "in tears amid the alien corn" (Ruth). There are secular references such as "The Samaritans" as the name of a befriending charity, and idiomatic expressions which most people no longer recognise as biblical, such as "a fly in the ointment"

(Eccles 10:1) and "the skin of my teeth" (Job 19:20). Literary titles and music frequently draw on the Bible: Golding's *Lord of the Flies*, Yeats's *The Second Coming*, and Handel's *Messiah*, and advertising slogans plunder and adapt phrases from the scriptures. Frame's characters make frequent allusion to the Bible, both directly and through remembered lines of poetry.

Like Daphne, Naomi in *Intensive Care* (1970) is a patient in an unspecified hospital and expresses her deepest thoughts and feelings in verses which only she and the reader hear, and like Daphne she draws on familiar lines from the Bible as well as remembered snatches of song and poetry. Near the beginning of *Intensive Care*, Naomi writes from her hospital bed to her father, Tom Livingstone, addressing him as "Dear First Dad", Auden's phrase for Adam, the first man in "Bucolics: I Winds" (Auden 2006, 285). Although Tom does not visit his daughter during his time in England, Naomi's letter is addressed to him in the Recovery Unit at Cullin Hall in lines which invoke the Beatitudes, Isaiah, and a punning play on the word "recovery", and this reference recurs all through the novel. Part of Naomi's letter is set in italics as a poem:

> *Blessed is he whose sin is recovered.*
> *I do hope to recover the city by nightfall.*
> *The woods hope to recover their primeval*
> *silence, intervals and rests and music, the*
> *heart its belief and hope.*
> *The day will recover its night.*
> *The night its morning.*
> *The death its birth.*
> *The valley its lost mountain.*
> *The mountain its departed valley.*
> *Stop! Stop!'* (IC, 42; Frame's italics)

In these lines we hear the voices of Naomi and an echo of Psalm 32, "Blessed is he whose transgression is forgiven, whose sin is covered" (Ps. 32:1). Frame makes play with "covered" and various meanings of "recovered" and "recovery". Naomi alludes to the lines from Isaiah which begin "comfort ye my people" (Isa. 40:1) and there are echoes of Isaiah's promise of comfort and the restoration of Jerusalem, "the city", to which Frame makes repeated reference in this novel: "Every valley shall be exalted, and every mountain and hill shall be made low: and the crooked shall be made straight and the rough places plain" (Isa. 40:4). These biblical references are suggestive of comfort, a safe haven and of the expiation of sins and in addition they prefigure strands of the coming narrative. We hear the former violinist and Cullin Hall patient Miriam, "silence, intervals and rests and music" and in a final startling shift of register we hear the horrific protest of Cicely—former nurse and Tom's first love—being suffocated when Tom presses the bedspread against her face in an uncontrolled fit of anger and who could only think, being unable to speak the words: "Stop! Stop!"

There are varying layers of time in this polyphonic piece and a variety of voices and voiced thought; it is a collection of different discourses, expressing a variety of values and ironies. There is also an assumption of prior knowledge of biblical phrasing which not all readers would possess. However, readers may nevertheless appreciate the poetic rhythm of the lines and an awareness of the way in which the different voices from within and without the novel come together, in Bakhtin's (2011) phrase, in "co-existence and interaction" (28). This quality of Frame's prose was noted by, among others, the American critic Kenneth Burke who wrote an endorsement for *Intensive Care* for George Braziller's use. Burke begins: "What lovely writing this is, with its sorrow for all lostness!" and notes that "the pages are rich in their development by associative turns, the range of modulations by which she depicts her characters' attitudes and circumstances" (GBP April 30, 1970). Burke's comment suggests a greater complexity in Frame's technique from the more readily accessible polyphonic poetic prose of her first novel, *Owls Do Cry*.

In the final chapters of Part Two, *Intensive Care* returns from the narrative of Tom Livingstone and his grandson Colin in New Zealand to the Recovery Unit at Cullin Hall, England, with Tom Livingstone among his former fellow-patients. There is a reprise of the fusion of biblical cadence, with allusion to Isaiah and Miriam's music. None of them have "recovered the city by nightfall", and the biblical prophecy has delivered neither the promised solace, nor "that the crooked places will be made plain instead of being made acceptably, recognisably, crooked" (*IC*, 249). The only "recovery" is the grave, "six feet down and three across" (251). Tom Livingstone's brother Leonard comes to the same conclusion as he lies dying, thinking about his own death and the words of Psalm 24, "The earth is the Lord's and the fullness thereof, the world and they that dwell therein" (Ps. 24:1). Soon, he thought, the earth would "recover all", leaving no trace of him, because the earth was "its own recovery unit" (*IC*, 203).

Biblical prophecy is both invoked and undermined in *Daughter Buffalo* (1972), Edelman, "medical graduate, a student of death" (401) expresses his suspicion of the biblical comparison of different aspects of life with the seasons as expressed in Ecclesiastes, "that each held their sadness or joy" that:

> To every thing there is a season,
> And a time to every purpose under heaven:
> A time to be born, and a time to die. (Eccles. 3:1–2)

The novel is a meditation on the place of death in people's lives. Death is sanitised, automated and financed out of sight of the living. In this novel, references to Shakespeare, Walt Whitman and T.S. Eliot are interwoven with references to the Bible. Turnlung is an elderly writer, visiting the USA, about whom we gain uncertain hints and who becomes Edelman's lover. The epitaph to T.S. Eliot's Gerontion's from *Measure for Measure,* spoken by the Duke to Claudio, could also apply to Turnlung:

> Thou hast nor youth nor age
> But as it were an after-dinner's sleep
> Dreaming on both. (*Measure for Measure*, 3.1.32–34; Eliot 2009, 21)

The Duke's reflections on the value of life and death, and his words of comfort for Claudio were conceivably Frame's starting-point for this novel, and more specifically for the dream-like character of Turnlung. By the end of the novel, the reader is uncertain whether Turnlung dreamed Edelman and his time in New York, or if Turnlung was a figment of Edelman's imagination and dreaming, however real both characters seem during the narrative, and the multiple voices here invite the reader to read beyond the lines to the other texts.

Turnlung is the one character in Frame's novels who displays the traits of an Old Testament prophet. His language is couched in the cadences of the Bible, which he quotes and echoes. At his first meeting with Edelman, Turnlung complains of the violations of language, the euphemisms for death, each one a "password", with the psalmic retort: "He sendeth out his word and melteth them" (*DB*, 421). He quotes Job's cry of anguish: "*How long will you vex my soul and break me in pieces with words?*" (422; Job 19:2; Frame's italics). Echoes of Psalm 23, "a mountainous banquet set before me" (*DB*, 424) are blended with snatches of timeless nursery rhyme "round and round the mulberry tree on the cold and frosty morning of language" (424). Turnlung expresses himself in the style of an Old Testament prophet in his repeated declarations: "I write from a land where the Bible is written in the daily newspaper [. . .]. I write from a land where the obsession is the death of all [. . .]. I write from a land as haunted by death and guilt as the Ancient Mariner" (425). His assertions are in the style of biblical rhetoric characteristic of American oratory, from Abraham Lincoln to Martin Luther King and Barack Obama, layered with reference to "dangerous days" (425) in the poetry of Burns, Coleridge and Genesis, and the invocation of the authoritative text of the Bible invites the reader to concur with the suggestion that the biblical and secular poets of all ages understood the human condition.

In *The Adaptable Man* (1965) biblical scripture and the priestly vocation come together in the character of the Reverend Aisley Maude, the clergyman who has come to convalesce and recover from TB at the home of his brother Russell in Little Burgelstatham, Suffolk. Russell recognises that it is the beauty of the Bible's language that has drawn his brother Aisley to a life as a clergyman as much as faith or their clergyman father's example; and that he, Russell, lacks "the complex My Son, My Son, which if truth were known, is perhaps the reason behind Aisley's pursuit of religion" (*AM*, 208). Indeed, Aisley is experiencing something of a crisis as his church attempts to modernize, and Aisley suffers the repeated sensation that "God had moved". Aisley is a lover of poetry, from Anglo-Saxon elegies and epics to Stephen Spender, and had cringed at his late wife Katherine's unpoetic and inappropriate banalities in her attempt to "reclaim Aisley from his drab parsonic Anglo-Saxon dream", especially when Katherine led the local newspaper to report that they wanted to "transform the church from a medieval white elephant to a bang-on space-age tiger" (99).

The biblical theme in *The Adaptable Man* also refers to and incorporates contemporary debates about the recent translation of the Bible into modern English, the *New English Bible* (*NEB*), published in 1961. For Aisley, the poetry of the King James Bible is an intrinsic part of his life, and his ear, like Frame's, is keenly attuned to its music. The point is emphasised by the inability of Aisley's nephew Alwyn to respond to a John Donne sermon: Alwyn can hear only the archaic inflections with which one can "think a fancy trite thought and make it sound meaningful" (*AM*, 51). Aisley settles in his room with the copies of the Bibles left for him by his sister-in-law, Greta, and begins to read from the King James version St Paul's familiar letter to the Corinthians, "For now we see through a glass darkly, but then face to face" and as he reads on "Aisley could feel the peace and love steal over him" (56). Turning to the *NEB*, Aisley finds that "glass darkly" is rendered as "puzzling reflections in a mirror". For Aisley, moving between the two versions was to go "from Beauty to Abomination" (213). Aisley's sense of the discordance of this wording chimes with the view of T.S. Eliot, among other scholars and critics. In a letter of December 16, 1962 to the *Sunday Telegraph*, Eliot expressed the view that the *NEB* failed even to achieve a level of "dignified mediocrity", and had lost the essential "music of the spoken word". The controversy and debate surrounding the *NEB* was widely aired on radio and TV as well as in print media, and would doubtless have been familiar to Frame who was living in London at the time.

On its publication in 1961, the *NEB* dominated the front page of the *Times Literary Supplement* on March 24, with an article about translation issues, and a further article on "Language in the New Bible". From the beginning, most of the criticism was of the infelicities of wording and the failings of the literary panel, "dozing brothers of the craft" (Gifford 1962, 470). Aisley clearly agrees, and in an image which recalls Frame's repeated reference to St Matthew's words on material and spiritual treasure, Aisley expresses his view that modern scholars "had undertaken the task of convicts breaking stones, monotonously striking day after day until they destroyed a quarry of jewels which they still imagined to be stones" (*AM*, 57). For both Aisley and Frame the King James Bible is one of the poetic jewels of the language.

Ethics and Spirituality

When *Owls Do Cry* was reviewed for the first time, in *Landfall*, the reviewer Winston Rhodes made striking use of religious discourse to convey his reaction to the spiritual and ethical qualities of Frame's first novel, which "glows with the light of a poetic vision of life" (Rhodes 1957, 331). He comments that

> The emotional effect of *Owls Do Cry* is such that instead of confining myself to the language of criticism, I feel tempted to talk about life and human suffering, about the values of civilisation and the search for meaning, about the empty heart and the bewildered mind [. . .]. [Frame] is concerned

with the gradations of human sensitivity, with our kinship in suffering, with the pathetic variations of death in life, and with man's pain-swept pilgrimage in search of he knows not what. (327–28)

Successive critics have similarly employed religious and spiritual discourse to discuss Frame's work—"spiritual", "ethical", "visionary", "utopia", and "pilgrimage"—whilst noting Frame's lack of adherence to an orthodox religious doctrine. As Mark Williams (1990) remarks, "for Frame, the trick is to learn to live religiously, but without the gods" (54). Frame shares with William Blake not only a profound sense of the way in which human behaviour falls short of its potential in society's concern with material gain, but also Blake's sense of the possibilities of transformation. In some undated notes she made for potential but unspecified interviews in the 1980s, Frame (2011) asserts that "it's my belief that there's an indestructible goodness in all things, states, everything. Religious people would call it God" (120).

Frame's secular spirituality is a concept which causes devoutly religious critics such as T.S. Eliot and C.S. Lewis problems of semantics and philosophy. For orthodox Christians, "secular spirituality" is a contradiction in terms, and the incorporation of religious discourse within works of literature is also an issue for critics who hold fundamental adherence to the Bible as doctrine. T.S. Eliot (1986), writing about *Paradise Lost*, takes the view that: "it is a glimpse of a theology that I find in large part repellent, expressed through a mythology which would have been better left in the Book of *Genesis*, upon which Milton has not improved" (12). Writing about Blake, Eliot (1979) admonishes him for his lack of doctrinal orthodoxy:

> What his genius required, and what it sadly lacked, was a framework of accepted and traditional ideas which would have prevented him from indulging in a philosophy of his own, and concentrated his attention upon the problems of the poet. (157–58)

C.S. Lewis (2013) sternly asserted that "those who read the Bible as literature do not read the Bible" (310). A fixed viewpoint of this kind would preclude an appreciation of Frame's subversive treatment of doctrine and religious texts. Marc Delrez's (2000) humanist endeavours to find an appropriate form of words to convey Frame's concern with the "beyond", a spiritual, but not necessarily a biblical or a religious search for Enlightenment, led him to suggest that "her pursuit of totality is spiritual in essence" (76) and a few pages later that "her primary impulse is not political so much as existential, philosophical and possibly even religious" (79). In a further quest for words, Simone Drichel (Cronin & Drichel 2009), disagreeing with Delrez's use of "spiritual", opts for "ethical" (184), taking the term from the philosopher Emmanuel Levinas. This continuing semantic and philosophical search to define Frame's idea of a world beyond this one, beyond the corona, is in itself testament to Frame's outward-looking world view and her desire to "explore beyond the object, beyond its shadow to the ring of fire" (*SS*, 239), and her interest in Buddhism. Cindy Gabrielle (2015), in her account of Frame's interest in Buddhist thought, calls attention to the interest in Buddhism shown by a number of Frame's close friends (4). Gabrielle notes the discussions Frame had about meditation with James and Jacquie Baxter and Charles Brasch; as well as evidence of her reading in eastern and Buddhist philosophy from the books she borrowed or had in her own possession. Aspects of Buddhism, silence, meditation and stillness of mind, for example, are also common to non-conformist Christian sects, and Frame's interest in Buddhism is likely to be part of her broad interest in spirituality.

Lottie Frame's Christadelphian faith would have sown the seeds for Frame's radical rejection of orthodox dogma: Christadelphianism shares a number of features with other non-conformist sects which developed in Britain from the 17th century, notably a challenge to the authority of the established church, elected unpaid lay preachers and more democratic egalitarian governance, meeting houses instead of churches, and pacifism. Mark Williams (1990) perceptively asserts that Frame's "debt to the Christadelphians is registered chiefly in her religious sense of the commonplace" (32), and he rightly highlights the influence of Lottie's faith and bible-reading. Frame's belief in the "indestructible goodness in all things" is one which is shared by other dissenting sects, of which possibly the most familiar, both in Britain and the USA is the Religious Society of Friends ("Quakers"), whose watchwords are "silence" and "witness". Silent meditation is a central feature of Quaker meetings, and an awareness of this practice among British and British colonial societies may make an interest in Buddhism appear a less esoteric departure than it might for readers from other parts of Europe more accustomed to Huguenot or Lutheran Protestantism. Frame's friends included a number of people with an interest in Buddhism: Bill Brown and Paul Wonner in California; Ruth Dallas, Charles Brasch and Karl Stead in New Zealand. They would have encouraged her reading and added to her own knowledge of Buddhist thought and practice.

Frame felt strongly about a range of ethical issues, as evidenced by her surviving correspondence. In a draft letter she condemns the homophobia with which the New Zealand Labour MP Colin Moyle was treated. In 1977 the Prime Minister Robert Muldoon accused Moyle of being questioned by the police about homosexual activities, apparently in an attempt to gain political advantage, at a time when homosexual activities were still illegal in New Zealand. Frame (2011) wrote that

> A politician's sexual preference is surely irrelevant. What is always relevant is the reminder that humanity has a tragic history of using itself and its supposed obligations ('they were only being human.' 'They were doing their duty') as an excuse for inhumanity. (176)

There is further testimony in her letter to the *Otago Daily Times* over a proposal to build a very large 100-bed institution for handicapped children, urging a more humane approach to their welfare, in which Frame notes that

> Our country with its small population has an unequalled opportunity to practise being human instead of identifying itself always with its larger population of sheep and aspiring to Sheepity and Sheephood rather than to Humanity. (171)

Frame opposed the 1981 Springbok rugby tour, joining the protest march in Wanganui against the blatant racism of the New Zealand rugby sector, and writing to the local newspaper, the *Wanganui Chronicle* on August 3, 1981, mocking the overriding importance of sport, partly in verses of a 'song':

> My name is Footy Pool, of Rugby I'm the fount.
> I'm a faithful Rugby son.
> I have so many freedoms, far too many to count,
> Responsibilities I have none. (178–79)

Writing to Bill Brown about *Intensive Care*, Frame (2016) says "I put a lot of myself into it, I think, I don't mean me as a person, but me and how I feel about many issues" (126), and Frame's concern with racism, the treatment of anyone not conforming to social norms, and the inhumanity of people who unquestioningly follow orders make themselves felt in her novels.

In Part Three of *Intensive Care* (1970), set in a post-atomic future in the 21st century, Frame makes extensive use of biblical quotation, allusion and parody in the apocalyptic tale of "the time of the fires in Waipori City," and the horrendous issues it raises, of genocide and eugenics and the dismissal of anyone deviating from the "normal" (*IC*, 389). *Intensive Care* was first published in 1970, at a time of considerable anxiety about the possibility of nuclear war and the fear of a man-made apocalypse. The novel draws on prophetic Old Testament sources in its account of the inhumanity of people who through fear of losing their own lives comply with the requirements of an authoritarian regime and agree to carry out the dictates of the Human Delineation Act, designed to eliminate anyone deemed abnormal, a chilling reminder of the 20th-century Nazi destruction of

Jews, gypsies, homosexuals and people with a variety of physical and mental disabilities. One of the victims of the Human Delineation Act is Milly Galbraith. Milly is the "doll-normill" chronicler of the approach of "Deciding Day", when the decision will be made about who is, and who is not fit to live, by the authoritarian government, deaths carried out by the "Early Disposal Units" organised by the "Humane Department" (*IC*, 270). She is encouraged to read the Bible by the local clergyman, but she finds the print in her Bible is "too small for comfort" and that "many of the words don't have enough meaning" (289). Nevertheless, Milly, with her particular "in-telly-gents", becomes the voice of conscience in her post-Atomic community, drawing on her semi-understood readings of random pages of the Bible, feeling the importance of these texts and the power of the language, even though they are not fully accessible to her. Sandy, Milly's imaginary friend, introduces himself as "a Hero, the Reconstructed Man" (291) whom she expects eventually to marry. In their conversation, Milly responds to Sandy's familiar phrase from the Song of Solomon, "I should say the winter should be past", and refers to the rest of the verse, which reads:

> For lo, the winter is past, the rain is over and gone;
> The flowers appear on the earth; the time of the singing of birds is come, and the voice of the turtle is heard in our land.
> (Song of Sol. 2:11–12)

The reference to Solomon's love-song forms an incongruous prelude to Sandy's detailed quotation of the speech given by Prime Minister who is responsible for the implementation of the Human Delineation Act, which is couched in the specious language of a corrupt politician as he outlines his plans for "disposal, with other waste" of "broken bits of humanity" (*IC*, 293). The winter, the post-atomic nuclear winter for much of the world, is very much of the present; the lush and abundant natural beauty of Solomon's world destroyed by man's wanton quest for power through world-destroying warfare, a victory which has turned to ashes in the mouth.

As Milly continues her account, she includes lines from the random Bible pages she has found. Errors in her transcription suggest her lack of understanding, but in the extracts she quotes Frame makes her show how the biblical desolation parallels the fictional nuclear destruction of the 21st century. Isaiah's picture of the wondrous restoration of Jerusalem for the returned exiles, "and I will make the place of my feet glorious" (Isa 60:13), is followed immediately by the lamentation on the state of Zion, "how is the gold become dim" (Lam. 4:1; *IC*, 349). When Milly quotes the call for six executioners to slaughter the idolaters, and the man "with a writer's inkhorn" (Ezek. 9:2) to mark the foreheads of those to be spared, she reminds Sandy that the Bible "is all blud and fyre, desserlitt cities" (*IC*, 349). The Bible is used in this context as a holy text, in Bakhtin's words as "the authoritative and sanctified word of the Bible" (Bakhtin 2008, 69): Sandy and Milly's use of its stories and poetry underline their status as victims of a cruel and deliberate destruction. Sandy, filling his own inkhorn, responds to Milly's quotations in verse of biblical cadence and imagery,

> That is a God's intention
> a city of desolation
> the sun to crack open all life and draw forth
> the shimmering garments of growth. (*IC*, 350)

Sandy decries the death of compassion and the darkness of man's heart. In a punning mix of registers, using finally the language of international telecommunications, he declares:

> But the receiving dark
> Blinder than blind love took
> Wholly the mature care
> Of hand heart compassionate look.
> How can I read you Roger, if they have destroyed the
> book? (*IC*, 350–51)

In *The Rainbirds* (1968), Frame also uses biblical allusion to explore ethical issues surrounding people's treatment of those who are thought to fall outside the bounds of social convention, but in a quieter, smaller-scale domestic setting in Dunedin, New Zealand. She draws two biblical narratives, the Easter story and the story of Lazarus, to explore the inability of the people around Godfrey Rainbird to see beyond the trivial and the conventional. In her subversive use of the Lazarus story, Frame employs biblical imagery to explore the consequences of an ordinary death which leads to an apparent rebirth and a second life. She parodies biblical texts to illustrate the absurdity, hypocrisy and callousness of the community's response to Godfrey's recovery from an apparently fatal accident. Godfrey's wife Beatrice is at a loss. From the outset she is unsure about coping with the rituals and conventions of death and bereavement, which ought to have brought comfort. She does not know how to manage "the absurd and tragic inconvenience of his resurrection" (*RB*, 316) and seems unable to turn to her local community for help. The local Dunedin community's failure of compassion is highlighted by the insensitivity of the clergyman who refers to the "biblical happening in Dunedin" without offering any practical or pastoral help and wonders at Easter if Godfrey would "care to be welcomed again into the Church" (44).

Godfrey's increasing despair and the absurdity of his situation are marked by the strikingly odd developments in his reading of conventional words on the page. In Godfrey's interpretation, his dismissal letter informs him that it is "no longer soppible for me to plomey you", and the minister reads the "Drols Pryer" (408). Godfrey's speech only returns to normal towards the end of the novel when he begins to experience "his new abundance of warmth and life" (492). Frame's enigmatic version of the Lord's Prayer, forms a critical parody relying on the reader's knowledge of the biblical source, and as such it belongs to an ancient tradition of ridiculing sanctified texts. Bakhtin (2008) gives an example from 14th-century French, which reflects on the horrors of war:

> Pater noster, tu n'ies pas foulz
> Quar tu t'ies mis en grand repos
> Qui es montés haut in celis.(78)
> [Our father, you are not crushed
> For you have set yourself in comfort
> Who have ascended high into heaven.]

The French prayer interrupts and usurps the sacred Latin between "pater noster" and "in celis", and complains about God creating an easy life for himself in heaven—the French verb is reflexive—compared with the deprivations of earthly existence. Frame's choice of anagrams and neologisms, creating pejorative or negative new words, conveys a similar feeling of betrayal and disenchantment: "Our afther which rat in heaven; hollowed be thy mane [. . .] for veer and veer, mean" (*RB*, 411). The callous betrayal of Godfrey and society's unimaginative failure of compassion, its hollow meanness, is further emphasised by the Good Friday trip to the beach, from which Godfrey comes away "shivering, exposed to a winter loneliness" (361). The wintery darkness of this phrase echoes St Matthew's "there was darkness over all the land" (Matt. 27:45) as Christ dies on the cross.

Ministers of the established church do not fare well in Frame's novels: there is a considerable distance between the sense of human potential on the one hand, and on the other the platitudes and conventional piety with which the clergy preach, unable to give either effective ethical and spiritual leadership or offer succour to those most in need of their help. Milly Galbraith declines the Reverend Polly's invitation to pray, and her father's response to the departing clergyman is "Good riddance" (*IC*, 363). Benign, on the whole, but banal, ineffectual, and trapped by conventions and church hierarchies, they may find themselves with "a congregation of two women and a dog" (*AM*, 236). Or they may entertain, like Aisley, the somewhat Trollopeian criticism of clerical self-important pomposity that "God once had the power of weaving in and out of precedence, at times clumsily marshalling Himself behind the Bishop" (21). Aisley articulates his dilemma by referring to the "cynic" who identified the need for a different way of looking, "that what I needed was a new camera". Fearful of the immensity he glimpses, however, Aisley "longed once more to set up the obsolete camera before the moss-covered monument of my Christian faith" (5).

Aisley takes refuge in contemplation of an era of pre-church monasticism. He muses on the life of the 7th-century monk St. Cuthbert who was at one with the natural world and "had the faith to walk in the waves" (*AM*, 213), just as Aisley desires to be "close to the first fluid world, the sea" (78). The desire for simplicity does not, however, preclude a level of self-perception and an awareness of the behaviour of others, and Gabrielle's discussion of the influence of Buddhist teaching is surely well founded here. Aisley is mindful, aware, and attentive, though still disconcerted by his inability to find answers, or for his beloved Bible scriptures to supply them. Weary of pretence, of hiding his "candle under a bushel" (Matt. 5:15), he is disturbed by his perception that his nephew Alwyn "is all that everyone thinks he is not" (*AM*, 52). Eventually Aisley wonders if Alwyn "will confess to having murdered Botti Julio" and whether "he may even be the father of Greta's child" (213–14). Retreating from these anxieties to the imagined age of Cuthbert, Aisley wonders if he can take comfort from the promise that "the last shall be the first" (Matt. 20:16), and that his day will come.

Religious discourse is, of course, what one would expect of a clergyman, and in complete contrast to Aisley's charitable and introspective spirituality is Brother Colman in *Living in the Maniototo* (1979), an American evangelical pastor who cynically exploits the language of the Bible for his own material advantage. The narrator,

Mavis, is living in the house of her friend Brian in Baltimore, and Brother Colman preys on the soul of Mrs Tyndall, Brian's African-American cleaner, in jewelled malignity, "with diamonds glittering at the lapels" (*LM*, 87), the personification of false treasure. He has subverted the instruction to "go and sell that thou hast and give to the poor, and thou shalt have treasure in heaven: and come and follow me" (Matt. 19:21). Mrs Tyndall is the poor, donating her $5 a month, a widow's mite, to Brother Colman's "Diamond Account Book" (*LM*, 84), and seems to gain some warmth, some hope of a better life hereafter. However, in Frame's parody of St Matthew Brother Colman exhorts his congregation to "Give all you have to God [...] empty your purses at God's feet" (88); the rapacious self-styled evangelist has converted spiritual treasure into a money-making scam. Brother Colman's corrupt world is one "where thieves break through and steal" (Matt. 6:19), as Frame repeats St Matthew's view of material and spiritual treasure, which she had first investigated in *Owls Do Cry*, and to which she returns time and again in subsequent novels.

Biblical Narratives

Frame's use of the Bible to provide part of a narrative framework is most apparent in the two novels which are sometimes treated as companion pieces, *The Rainbirds* and *A State of Siege*. In Frame's version of the Lazarus story in *The Rainbirds*, it is Godfrey who supplies the cynical alternative narrative to the simple joy and gratitude of Martha and Mary, sisters of Lazarus, and the reader sees the parallel with Lazarus through Godfrey's consciousness. By contrast with the biblical sisters, Martha and Mary, Beatrice is more concerned for the cost of the unused coffin than with planning the kind of celebration prepared for Lazarus by his sisters when they learn of his miraculous resurrection. The banal financial embarrassment occurs to Godfrey too, who thinks about Lazarus having to "fork out for his expensive perfumed shroud and the funeral feast" (*RB*, 372). Godfrey muses further on alternative possible outcomes for Lazarus: that his wife might have another man, or that his recovery might excite jealousy among less fortunate neighbours, based on his own experience of people who step outside the accepted conventions. His sense of being "*baptised* in the joyousness of being alive" (Frame's italics), as in Lazarus's second chance of life, is a short-lived reverie (347), an apparent reversal of the biblical story. His "green pastures" and "still waters" (Ps. 23) "had become without warning a torrent that dropped suddenly into a small dark hole in the earth" (348).

Godfrey is conscious of other people's revulsion and fear, and that "Lazarus had been wrenched by death out of people's lives; he was not going to be accommodated so readily into the living" (*RB*, 372). He thinks about being buried alive, and "the fear of being pronounced dead and in another man's power haunted him" (442). Godfrey's story contains echoes of Balzac's subversion of the Lazarus story, *Le Colonel Chabert*, as Marc Delrez (2002, 185) briefly notes. The University of Otago Calendar for 1943-44 shows that Frame would have encountered Balzac's novels at the University of Otago, in classes she was able to attend as a student at Dunedin's Teacher Training College and Frame uses Balzac's subversive novel in a complex intertextual framework. *Le Colonel Chabert* nudges the reader towards a complementary view of the dilemma faced by Godfrey and Beatrice, and a layered used of the Bible narrative is interwoven with the grimly realistic 19th-century French novel.

Balzac's (2007) Chabert, one of Napoleon's chief officers, is left for dead after battle. Buried under other corpses in a common grave, he gruesomely struggles out and spends several years recovering. Returning to Paris, he can no longer find a place in society, and like Godfrey Rainbird is seen as an embarrassment and a threat wherever he goes. Referred to throughout as "le défunt" [the deceased], as that is his legal status, Chabert struggles unsuccessfully to regain his money, his previous living status, and his hostile, bigamously remarried, and terrified wife. He is ridiculed by street urchins who resemble those of Anderson's Bay, Dunedin in Frame's novel, and is supported by one lone voice of compassion, his lawyer Derville—more outspoken than the lone doubting voice in Godfrey's community, the father of one of the Anderson's Bay urchins, who knows Godfrey has "had a raw deal" and thought "there's some injustice here" (*RB*, 488) without stirring himself to do anything about it. The living would prefer Chabert and Godfrey to remain dead, and Chabert's (Balzac 2007) words could have been Godfrey's: "J'ai été enterré sous des morts, mais maintenant je suis enterré sous des vivants, sous des actes, sous des faits, sous la société tout entière, qui veut me faire rentrer sous terre!" (36). [I was buried beneath the dead, but now I am buried beneath the living, beneath the red tape, beneath the whole of society, which would send me back under the earth!]. Both men suffer lost illusions: Chabert returns to post-revolution France to find a Bourbon king back on the throne and Godfrey, an immigrant from England, finds New Zealand failing to live up to the promise of "all those posters of painted cows generously yielding their milk" (*RB*, 249). Godfrey and Chabert both experience an overwhelming sense of loss and despair, and are threatened by a society which tried to deny them Lazarus's second chance of life.

That *The Rainbirds* is not Frame's most successful novel appears to be a matter of common agreement. Critics have been less enthusiastic about this text, especially the earlier and initial reviewers, who appear to agree that the novel lacks creative power and find that the narrative requires "forbearance" (Panney 1993, 107), or "an effort" (Evans 1969, 193), or is "something of an anti-climax" (Dalziel 1980, 16). In these instances, Frame's use of the biblical narrative is viewed solely as a critique of New Zealand society of the time. More recently, Jan Cronin (Cronin & Drichel 2009), asserts that "what prevents the Lazarus model from being a viable context for the interpretation of Godfrey's experiences is context itself: the different settings of their stories" (54) and it may be that earlier critics also felt that the Lazarus story just did not work in the Dunedin context, or that the critics' focus was too much on the familiarity of the localised Dunedin setting and social satire. Frame's aim is much broader than this, and in her use of biblical narrative, reworking and subverting, like Balzac, the story of Lazarus, she points up the universality of Godfrey's sense of loss, and what Marc Delrez (2002) refers to as "the inner dimension of Godfrey's quest" (186).

Balzac's novel is a classic of 19th-century physical and psychological realism, rooted in the detail of the French legal, financial and social system of the time. Chabert's return from the grave may be gruesome, but it is located in French history. Frame's concern is with the inner reality of the minds of Godfrey and Beatrice and their struggle to make sense of, and come to terms with, the bizarre events of their quiet lives and Godfrey's desire to live again beyond the tight social codes and restrictive attitudes of his community. Both novels are much more complex than the biblical story of Lazarus. Beatrice has no comprehension of Godfrey's "inner dimension", as Delrez describes it. His repetitive occupation assembling plugs leaves his mind free to wander and wonder, and to notice small details, like flyspecks on windows, and differing perceptions of the speed of time passing. Her imagination, like her speech, goes no further than commonplace cliché: "People are only human aren't they? I mean they've their lives to live"; and using "the sun and the sky", as Godfrey perceives, "as a personal smoke-screen" (*RB*, 430).

Godfrey ruminates on death and the passage of time, and refers to an epoch before anno domini, to biblical times when life was apparently uncomplicated "if you had no desire to survive and no sense of smell" (*RB*, 373). He looks across at Dunedin, which to him resembles "a biblical city", Jerusalem (441). Later, in an allusion to the Book of Revelation, he expresses his desire to "lie here in my deckchair while the sun shines on the city of Jerusalem" (452). These deliberations take on a broader personal and spiritual significance for him, which he is unable to share with Beatrice: "I don't think you understand what I'm talking about. I'm talking about destruction, about the lie and the truth, the white lie, the grey lie, the yellow, green and technicolour lie, and the black lie" (430).

The dominant emotion for Beatrice, as for Chabert's wife, now a "Comtesse", is fear. Balzac's (2007) graphic delineation of Parisian poverty, the legal position of women as possessions, and Chabert's implied threat, clearly convey what the future holds for the Comtesse if Chabert proves his identity: "Je vous ai prise au Palais-Royal" (86): [I picked you up at the Palais-Royal] a return to the streets and to prostitution. Beatrice's fears are more mundane and far less defined—but her descent, the loss of the children, her increasing reliance on alcohol, and her suicide, are final. She can see no other future than the grave. She lacks even Godfrey's faint apprehension of a new Jerusalem, and none of the simple pleasure of just being alive, which Lazarus and his sisters felt, and which Godfrey woke to, sensing a "new abundance of warmth and life" (*RB*, 492) on the morning of Beatrice's death, as "he stood complete once more upright on the earth his space secured" (493).

Of all Frame's novels, the use of biblical narrative structures is most apparent in *A State of Siege* (1966), the story of Malfred, an unmarried art teacher from South Island, who retires to an island in the warmer climate of the North Island, to make a new life for herself as a painter. The novel opens with a simple minor sentence: "A South Pacific paradise" (*SS*, 31), which the narrative subverts, and it ends with an apocalypse. In the course of the novel, references to Genesis and to the Book of Revelation, key texts for the narratives of life and death, would perhaps appear to offer the reader the hope of a definite pathway through the narrative, as the protagonist, Malfred, makes her early daily adjustments in her new life which are linked to the Genesis account of the stages by which God created the earth. The trail, however, leads to ambiguity and mystery, as Malfred—in her experience of this new start in life—confronts the unknown and the unknowable.

Karemoana is a sunny island of subtropical fruit and year-round flowers, a favoured retirement destination and holiday venue, which seems to offer Malfred, free finally of her filial duties of care for an aged invalid mother, the chance to retire early, lead her own independent life, and find "a New View" (*SS*, 48) as a painter. Malfred's journey north is a "pilgrimage" (34). The island's link with the Garden of Eden, in spite of Malfred's protestations of "I don't expect a paradise" (40) continue in her journey towards Karemoana, in her anticipation of her arrival. In the language of the narrative, this is most explicitly "on the afternoon of the fifth day" (78) as Malfred prepares to paint the sea, in an echo of God's fifth day creation of the sea and its creatures in Genesis (Gen. 1:20–23).

Malfred's time on Karemoana is from the outset beset with ominous signs of menace, whether real or imaginary, playing on her underlying loneliness and isolation, as the biblical imagery of the paradise garden is interwoven with threatening elements of the distinctly secular film noir, one of the dominant film genres of the 1940s and 1950s in films such as *The Big Sleep*, *The Third Man*, *Notorious*, and *Casablanca*. On her arrival, Malfred is immediately struck by the remoteness of the bach, the odd stares of the other people in the taxi, the broken panes in the call box, and the problems with the telephone line: all the stock-in-trade of the film noir.

The film noir tone of the novel, ominous and doom-laden, develops in conjunction with biblical allusions: Malfred rings the agent from the call box and hears a voice "like a prophet's voice to her ear" (*SS*, 60). Her insecurity, anxiety and despair increase as the narrative moves towards its apocalyptic conclusion. The mood of the film noir develops with her feelings about her lost love and stifled sexuality, love being "the most treacherous invader" (71). Her paranoia increases as she listens to the unexplained knocking in the darkness of the long night, as "the enormity of what lay outside began to touch Malfred with a cold brand that slid in a snail-track of sweat across her forehead" (82). She is overtaken by repressed fears, distorted memories and unresolved ambiguous desires of her abortive affair with Wilfred, the would-be lover whose sexual advances she rejects and who died in World War 1 and the tension escalates as she makes her desperate mock phone calls.

The film noir element of the narrative was not lost on Vincent Ward and Timothy White, whose highly acclaimed film of the novel won a number of awards in 1978, much to Frame's delight. The film won both the Chicago Film Festival's "Best short film" prize, and the "Special Jury Prize" at the Miami Film Festival. In an interview with Vincent Ward in the *New Zealand Listener* on September 29, 1979, Frame is reported as saying she thought the film was "a beautiful poem" (23). Ward appears to have had an appreciation of Malfred's attempts to find a "New View" (*SS*, 48). In a discussion about film-making for *Art in New Zealand* 30, in the autumn of 1984, Ward suggested that:

> the more beautiful the surface of a picture, the more it operates like a windowpane and separates you from the content [. . .]. You have to break the lovely surface of things; smash your fist through the panel of glass and pull the people out from behind it. (38)

Further layers of literary allusion in the novel, interwoven with those to film noir and Genesis, increase the sense of impending doom. Malfred recalls Macbeth's dark night, with the knocking that appalled him and his musings on sleep, and Wilfred reappears in Malfred's imagination in his soldier's uniform, with a bloody face like that of Banquo. Frame links the knocking in *Macbeth* with the Book of Revelation: "Behold, I stand at the door and knock" (Rev. 3:20), and a doom-laden echo of Macbeth, facing his fears. The knocking is insistent, and Malfred's response to it relates to both the "prowler" and to Wilfred: "however hard he knocked at the door, and however long he stayed, she would never let him in" (*SS*, 139). The stone is biblical too, a further reference to Revelation: "To him that overcometh [. . .] I will give him a white stone, and in the stone a new name written, which no man knoweth saving he that receiveth it" (Rev. 2:17).

As Malfred clutches the stone hurled through the window, she tries to read the print on the newspaper surrounding it. The handwritten words "Help! Help!" are clear enough, but the newsprint, which seems as if it should be meaningful, is composed like "Jabberwocky" in words which have recognisably English morphology, endings and English word elements, repetition and a sense of shape. It is tantalising in its suggestion of unfulfilled desire, "sorrowbride"; fire, "fuming of perburning"; threat, "wolpe"; and death, "done to fleath" (*SS*, 244), a technique of neologising and jumbling lexical elements suggestive of both confusion and inner truth which

Frame exploits to delineate Godfrey's distressed state of mind in *The Rainbirds*.

The ambiguity of Frame's version of her biblical source—Malfred's stone does not deliver redemption and enlightenment—is highlighted by Jan Cronin (2011). However, in deviating from the original source, Frame invites readers to ponder and explore ambiguous possibilities of interpretation rather than solve a puzzle with one single answer or interpretation; and to make connections of their own, as Frame's literary allusions and references weave in and out of each other, specifically or as just faint echoes, explicitly or ironically. Gina Mercer (1994), in contrast to Cronin, interprets the novel as a feminist study, casting Malfred as an Eve figure, who "desires knowledge of the most disturbing, even deadly kind" (115), an interpretation which might be considered too narrowly feminist in its focus on Frame's use of Genesis.

Other interpretations argue that *A State of Siege* is a post-death account of existence. In her study of Frame's interest in Buddhism, for example, Cindy Gabrielle (2015) argues that "the *Tibetan Book of the Dead* forms the backdrop" (55) to the novel, and that Malfred has already died, Karemoana being a version of Hades or Limbo. This is an interpretation which still references Christianity, though framed by Roman Catholic doctrine rather than biblical text. Similarly, Marc Delrez (1992) in an article published in *The Ring of Fire*, intuits a link with William Golding's *Pincher Martin*, published in 1956, and finds the similarities "truly remarkable" (127–28): Martin's story is a seaman's tale of apparent island survival after shipwreck, the reader only learning at the end of the novel that Martin drowned at the time the ship sank, and was therefore presumably in limbo or purgatory. Although at a literal level, the stone Malfred is still clutching when she is discovered contradicts this idea, Delrez maintains in *Manifold Utopia* that Malfred is metaphorically dead at the beginning of her journey, and that through the imagery of decay and decrepitude on the island, "the idea of her death is never allowed to slip from the reader's mind" (139).

The remarkably wide range of critical writing about *A State of Siege* highlights the novel's ambiguities and the extent to which readers bring their own experience, reading and perceptions to bear in their interpretation of it. These multiple possibilities are surely entirely deliberate, evidenced by the interlacing of the ambiguities of film noir with the apparent certainties of the biblical texts of Genesis and Revelation in Malfred's doomed search for a paradise garden, creating a level of ambiguity on which Charles Brasch (Frame 2010) remarks in his comment on the novel as "above all a poem–much-veined richly-coloured stone that one wants to turn over and over in one's hand–a crystal that seems to contain all worlds" (19).

The Bible is the one inescapable text common to all readers in English, both indirectly by virtue of its legacy within the language itself, and by the ways in which writers over centuries have responded to its language and rhythms. Frame exploits the particular place of the Bible in the English language, with its lexis, syntax and narratives so firmly embedded in both everyday expression and in spiritual and ethical discourse, as part of the woven texture of the language. She calls on the Bible's stories, poetry and ancient psalms with their links to mythology, especially creation myths, exploits biblical poetic rhythms and syntax for their sense of timelessness, and draws on its ethical exhortations to humanity and compassion. In doing so, Frame invites the reader's complicity in interpreting these borrowings from the Bible in exploring the novels' layers of allusion, ambiguity and significance.

Chapter Five: Engaging with Shakespeare

Upon the Heath

As an aspirant author, the schoolgirl Janet Frame knew that she had to engage with Shakespeare as "it would be impossible to think of being a writer if I didn't like reading Shakespeare" (*CA*, 115). At Waitaki Girls' High School, the vivid reading by Miss Farnie of the witches' opening speech from *Macbeth* captured Frame's imagination, and she was cast to play Lady Macbeth in a school production of the sleep-walking scene, though the project was overtaken by the pressure of exams and did not materialize (115). Her thoughts were for "the wild Scottish moors and battles and battlements and the hauntings [...] and in the language used to describe the weather, the sky, the dark, to match the nightmare within the characters" (114). As she matured, read more and gained confidence, she developed an acute awareness of the magical power of words to create a world on a bare stage, as well as a blank page.

  Frame shared her love of Shakespeare with Frank Sargeson, and had the opportunity to discuss their favourite plays with him while she was living in the army hut in his Takapuna garden. Sargeson (2012) reveals in a letter to Winston Rhodes that he had once been cast as Ariel, soon after he went to live in Auckland in 1925, although this proposed production of *The Tempest* was abandoned (382). Michael King (1995, 178) refers to Sargeson's habit of reading in bed in the morning—often Milton or Shakespeare. In 1940, Sargeson (2012) wrote to his literary friend Peter (E.P.) Dawson, referring to the imaginative letters he received from her, telling her that "I prefer the *poetic* (if I may use the term) people who make you expand to the *scientific* people who try to tie you down. The difference to my mind is the difference between Shakespeare and Bernard Shaw" (29). Having tended to dismiss Shakespeare in his youth, Sargeson (1964) describes in his Shakespeare centenary essay for *Landfall*, "Shakespeare and the Kiwi" the attachment to Shakespeare he developed as an adult, becoming "drunk with the understanding that the totality of splendour which attached to the world of Shakespeare's imagination was inseparably rooted in *words*", and accepting the "positive invitation to enter the landscape of the poet's imagination" (51; Sargeson's italics), a view which Frame's autobiography suggests she had developed as a child at school.

The early settlers valued their Bibles and volumes of Shakespeare's plays and brought them to New Zealand, a testimony to their sense of the importance of literacy and the power of the written word, and this was the culture in which Frame grew up. Mark Houlahan (2000b) refers to the arrival of settlers with "double-columned Bibles and Shakespeares", brought from Britain as "twin talismans of sacred and secular English authority" (113). Frank Sargeson makes the same point in "Shakespeare and the Kiwi" when he writes of "powers attaching to his [Shakespeare's] name which were as mysterious as they were undefined" (1964, 49). These comments bring to mind the ways in which Frame describes her attachment to her copy of Shakespeare when she was a patient in the mental hospital, "hiding it under straw mattresses, having it seized and scheming for its return" (*CA*, 239), and just by turning the pages had "absorbed the spirit of *The Tempest*". Istina Mavet, the hospital inmate in *Faces in the Water* (1961) clings on to her copy, too. Both Frame and the fictional Istina use their Shakespeare editions as talismans for protection and support in the harsh world of the hospital. For Istina "it seemed as if the book understood how things were and agreed to be company for me and to breathe, even without my opening it, an overwhelming dignity of richness" (*FW*, 98). In his article for the *Shakespeare Survey*, Mark Houlahan (2000a) asserts that "Shakespeare pervades Frame's fictions more elusively" than is the case in the work of other New Zealand writers. He notes Frame's "freewheeling implosions" (180) and her idiosyncratic and original intertextual use of her knowledge of Shakespeare, "a Shakespeare deeply recalled, a Shakespeare of isolated fragments of words which float into Frame's worlds to radiate their textual power" (178).

Frame's love-affair with Shakespeare's plays and poetry developed further at the University of Otago, where she attended lectures as a Teacher Training College student, with her life-long friend Sheila Natusch. She listened in awe to Professor Ramsay

> analysing each word of Shakespeare, transmitting to us his own sense of wonder at Shakespeare's language and its meaning. Like the sea from Oamaru, Shakespeare and his language travelled with me to Dunedin and were treasured for sharing my new life and the life of 'the girl that was gone'. (*CA*, 157)

Professor Herbert Ramsay was appointed Professor of English Language and Literature at the University of Otago in January 1921, when he was 34, and led the University's English department until his retirement in 1950 (Morrell 1969, 174). A Scotsman, he had taken First Class Honours in Classics at St Andrew's, Scotland, and had been Associate Professor at the University of Western Australia, Perth, before coming to Dunedin. Professor Ramsay's influence on Frame endured, and Natusch (2004) records that his "magnificent lectures on Shakespeare [...] all delivered in a rich Scots burr, stayed in our minds for good" (29).

Professor Ramsay remained in the thoughts and correspondence of Frame and Natusch for many years afterwards and in 1966, Frame wrote to Sheila agreeing with her that it was "exciting that Shakespeare and Prof may be published together at last" (Natusch 2004, 27). Although Frame's letter does not mention the nature of this proposed publication, Sheila Natusch makes it clear that Professor Ramsay had difficulty getting his work published, as it failed to "cut much ice with these [sic] who decide these things, the makers-or-breakers" (29). Ramsay's fellow lecturer, Dr Gregor Cameron, also had work turned down by the University of Otago Press. Frame wrote to Sheila suggesting Dr Cameron try the University of California Press, at Berkeley, after she had met Kenneth Burke, the American academic, at the Writers' Colony at Yaddo. Burke, she said in a letter in1980, "reminded me of our great professors and lecturers at Otago—full of daring imaginative thought, engrossed in literary studies" (26). In Morrell's 1969 historical account of the university, Ramsay is described as a man of "often unorthodox views" (174).

The two friends, Frame and Natusch, visited Professor Ramsay in his retirement, Frame marking one such occasion with a poem, "A Visit to the Retired English Professor", celebrating the love of language they shared and their joy in just listening to him talk:

> Clone,
> plene in his rale after so calid a time had milled its fee,
> durant, he burndered, cleamed in the day's coltering zone.
> Then we sat under the plum tree
> on the wet grass-covered stone
> while he talked of Hamlet. (*PM*, 31)

The plays Frame draws on most in her novels are *The Tempest*, *King Lear* and *Macbeth*.

Macbeth's witches visit several of Frame's protagonists and make their presence felt early in the Suffolk village of Little Burgelstatham in *The Adaptable Man* (1965), where "the Heath is a lonely place. It's damp and cold; witches get rheumatism" (*AM*, 3). This is the primeval heath which links Little Burgelstatham's wild and magical pagan past with its apparently sleepy present, where the "train stops briefly, and will soon not stop at all", words reminiscent of Edward Thomas's "Adlestrop". Beneath the apparently Arcadian pastoral scene is the "burgel, [. . .] a burial place of the heathen" (12), after which the village is named, and reference to the witches on Macbeth's Heath alerts the reader at the outset to the hidden irrational feelings which lurk behind the everyday human facade. The journalist Unity Foreman, ostensibly one of the village residents, but in reality sitting in her London office, decides to disregard her early copy for her "Letter from the Countryside" column,

> Surely nothing is drowned, face-downwards,
> Turning in violence from the Olde English dream?
> [...]
> Is there a place for the dying toad, like a lump of wound
>   lava? spurt of blood,
> the adder, grinning rat, deadly nightshade? (45)

In referencing Macbeth's witches, however, these lines are in fact closer to the undercurrents of death and violence of village life than the imaginary Arcadian idyll she writes from "The Charming Village of Little Burgelstatham".

Frame uses the dreams, hallucinations and witchcraft of *Macbeth* to create an atmosphere of malice and evil. In *Towards Another Summer* (2007), the protagonist Grace Cleave is herself a novelist, and encourages the journalist wanting to visit and interview her: "Do, do". Her words echo the witches' chant from *Macbeth,* and cause her to envisage herself as "the old frustrated witch dancing round the cauldron" (*TS*, 28), her own words bringing to mind the incantation:

> And like a rat without a tail,
> In a sieve I'll thither sail
> I'll do, I'll do and I'll do. (*Macbeth* 1.3.8–10)

Frame's intertextual musing is in keeping with her assertion that "nothing was simple, known, safe, believed, identified. Boundaries were not possible, where nothing finished, shapes encircled, and there was no beginning" (*TS*, 13). The witches come in a dream to Toby Withers, one of the four sibling children in *Owls Do Cry* (1957), disturbing him in the words of their incantation which his sister Daphne had taught him, "on the heath with Hecate, in thunder and lightning". In his dream, they reveal themselves as his three sisters, Francie, Chicks and Daphne, rehearsing all his fears and insecurities before reverting to "bony women shrieking Aii-aii-aii", as his dream fades (*OC*, 79–83).

In *A State of Siege* (1966), Frame draws on *Macbeth* again as the lonely, retired art teacher, Malfred, spends a long sleepless night in her isolated Karemoana bach. Frame takes issue with Macbeth's view of "sleep that knits up the ravelled sleeve of care" (*Macbeth* 2.2.37) as "neither hopeful nor exact" (*SS*, 179). She continues by asking if it "would not be more comforting for the many who are not Shakespeare if sleep were to destroy rather than knit up all the ravellings?" The Shakespearean links between dreams, sleep and comfort are pursued as Malfred's anxiety gradually increases, and initially, "she had not time to let her fear make way for fantasy, though she remembered the knocking on the gate in *Macbeth*" (84). Frame brings together key motifs from both *Macbeth* and the Bible as the fearful knocking in *Macbeth* on the night of Duncan's murder is interwoven powerfully with the images of the knocking at Malfred's bach and the stone from the Book of Revelation. Malfred's rejected lover, Wilfred, appears as an image of Banquo's bloody ghost, as Malfred's fear and the tension increase, exacerbated by her lack of meaningful contact with her external surroundings on Karemoana. When finally the stone crashes through the window the wild Shakespearean storm enters Malfred's house, and all the comforts and safety of home are shattered.

Images from *Macbeth* alluding to unbearable distress, life crises, murder and annihilation appear elsewhere in Frame's novels. In *Daughter Buffalo* (1972), Lennox's account of the tempestuous night of Duncan's murder also makes its presence felt to Edelman, dreaming of his father's visit to his grandfather at his old people's home. The two ageing men, engaged in mutually incomprehensible monologues, warn of "dire combustion and confused events new hatched to the woeful time" (*Macbeth* 2.3.56; *DB*, 417). In *Intensive Care* (1970), Frame uses an elliptical reference to Macduff's horror at the murder of his wife and children, "all my pretty ones at one fell swoop," (*Macbeth* 4.3.216–19) to convey the devastating sense of loss of part of themselves felt by the maimed and disabled inmates of Cullin Hall, the English war-time convalescent home for injured servicemen and women (*IC*, 38).

The tempestuous storms in *Macbeth* and *King Lear* are associated with the barren heath and the absence of shelter, a timeless, isolated terrain. The epigraph for *Living in the Maniototo* (1979) is attributed to the *Encyclopaedia of New Zealand*, which describes the Maniototo as "unforgettable landscapes composed of severe lines" deriving its name from the Māori, "mania, a plain; toto, bloody" for a novel which explores the significance of place as well as of Shakespeare. The decision of Maniototo resident Peter Wallstead, a man of imagination and erudition, a novelist and history teacher, to spend all his life in the Maniototo, suggests that this particular wild heath does not lack spiritual wealth. In *Living in the Maniototo* the heath becomes a metaphor for the artist's imagination, in contrast with the urban wastelands of Blenheim (Frame's name for Auckland in this novel) and Baltimore, an American city of cages and howling wolves.

In Frame's imagination, the Shakespearean heath of *Macbeth* and *King Lear* connects with Thomas Hardy's Egdon Heath, the Brontës' wild Yorkshire moors, and the titular terrain of the Maniototo. The heath is a wilderness where people are either at one with the forces of nature, or at their mercy. Frame alludes repeatedly in her novels to the wild places of *Macbeth*, *King Lear* and *The Tempest*. In *The Carpathians* (1988) the American Mattina Brecon, musing on the devastation wrought by the Gravity Star in Kowhai Street where she has made her temporary home in New Zealand, ponders on "the rediscovery of the old truth that human beings everywhere had not travelled very far from the heath in *Macbeth*" (*CP*, 152), recognising the elemental nature of human beings in spite of the trappings of modern civilization. The heath in *King Lear* is the ultimate expression of desolation, grotesque cruelty, and helpless suffering. It is the setting for a consideration of humanity and what it is to be a human being, above the level of the dumb beast. The heath and Lear's distress are recalled in the experiences of two inmates of mental hospitals, Daphne in *Owls Do Cry* (1957), and Istina Mavet in *Faces in the Water* (1961). Daphne's experiences of the enforced electrotherapy operating procedures in the mental hospital call to mind the blinded Gloucester as the nurses order the women to take their teeth out "as a precaution against choking, your eyes out, like Gloucester, to save you sight of the cliff and the greater gods who keep their 'dreadful pother' above your head" (*OC*, 41). The inmates of Lawn Lodge, the ward for the most intractable patients, recall for Istina the figure of Lear, wandering on the heath and the "Poor naked wretches wheresoe'er you are/That bide the pelting of this pitiless storm" (*FW*, 98; *Lear* 3.4. 28–29). These allusions to Shakespeare allow Frame to convey the crass cruelty and inhumanity of the treatment that the inmates suffer, without appearing to exaggerate it. Like Daphne, Istina thinks of "the confusion of people, like Gloucester, being led near the cliffs" (*FW*, 98).

Memories of Lear and the wild heath are lodged in the minds of several of Frame's other characters, for example Godfrey Rainbird, the latter-day Lazarus in *The Rainbirds* (1968) and Edward Strang, Vera's imagined husband in *Scented Gardens for the Blind* (1963). Edward Strang is unsettled by his daughter Erlene's lack of speech, and sees it as a threat to both sanity and survival, since spoken language for Edward is an essential part of being fully human, and sane. Edward recalls Lear on the stormy heath, addressed by a semi-coherent Mad Tom, who appears bereft of all the trappings which separate man from animal. He quotes the words Lear addresses to Tom, "thou art the thing itself; unaccommodated man is no more but such a poor, bare, forked animal as thou art" (*SG*, 106. *Lear* 3.4.108–10), linking Erlene's speechless predicament to that of mad Tom.

A vaguer memory of *King Lear* comes also to Godfrey Rainbird. His inability to find answers to his family's questions and their lack of empathy with him prompt a pained remembrance of Cordelia's compassionate response to a confused and tormented Lear, "No cause. No cause" (*Lear* 4.7.75). The words are "from some play he'd seen" lodged somewhere in his mind, title and playwright's name forgotten. In his distress and bewildering sense of loss and abandonment, the half-remembered play re-emerges from deep in Godfrey's memory as he identifies himself with "an old man on a heath and thunder and lightning" (*RB*, 436).

Wild Waters

Although Frame quotes, echoes or alludes to lines from several of Shakespeare's plays, it is *The Tempest* which appears to have stirred her imagination more than any other. The play's ambivalence, uncertainties and challenge to preconceptions of reality and the human condition pervade the whole of Frame's œuvre, and its deployment of theatrical magic features strongly in her later novels. Diane Caney (1993, 152–71) writes interestingly about the inspiration of *The Tempest*, drawing chiefly on Frame's life-writing, with some reference to the early novels, *Owls Do Cry* and *Faces in the Water*. She focuses on the imagery of stormy seas, magic and otherness, and on the themes of exile and return, drawing on colonial issues and the control exerted over Caliban, an obvious connection for Frame, born into a colonial culture. The focus in this section, however, is on the storm, Prospero's magic, and the magic of language.

Frame writes of learning Ariel's song, "Where the bee sucks", at school, and of studying *The Tempest* with Professor Ramsay at the University of Otago. By the time she found herself in a mental hospital, Frame "had absorbed the spirit of *The Tempest*. Even Prospero in his book-lined cell had suffered shipwreck and selfwreck; his island was unreachable except through storm" (*CA*, 239). The identification with Prospero is intensely personal, as Caney illustrates. Both Frame and Prospero are exiles from their own lands. Prospero, the word-magician, is saved by his books, just as Frame, whether confined to a hospital or living in Europe and America, is saved through writing hers. Words for Frame (1965) had always been "instruments of magic" (40), just as they are for Prospero.

When Jane Campion's film, *An Angel at My Table* (1990), based on Frame's autobiography, won the special prize at the Venice Film Festival in 1990, the Italian academic Claudio Gorlier asked Frame in a written interview in *La Stampa* on September 29, 1990 about her relationship with Prospero:

> Magia è una parola chiave per la sua opera. Uno dei suoi romanzi, «Gridano le civette», trae il titolo da un verso della «Tempesta» shakespeariana. Sente una certa parentela con

Prospero, protagonista della «Tempesta», e la sua arte magica? (*Tuttolibri*, 1)
[Magic is a keyword in your work. One of your novels, *Owls Do Cry*, takes its title from a line in *The Tempest* by Shakespeare. Do you feel a certain kinship with Prospero, the protagonist of *The Tempest*, and his magic art?]

Frame (2011) plays down the personal connection, however, and is reluctant to stress the closeness of the kinship, "because if I was I would be Madame Prospero"; and stresses what is for her the important point that "*The Tempest* is about an artist finishing his art, somehow with overall magic help" (148). The influence of *The Tempest* is diverse and runs deep.

Ariel's song in *The Tempest*, "Where the bee sucks, there suck I" supplied the title for *Owls Do Cry*, an image of seeking refuge from life's cruelties. Ariel's phrase, "tricks of desperation" (*The Tempest* 1.2.209), is his response to Prospero's question about the shipwrecked travellers and their irrational state of mind: what "would not infect his reason?" (1.2.208). It forms the title of the first part of Volume Two of the *Complete Autobiography*, and this same exchange with Prospero provides its epigraph. Frame's novels are suffused with the imagery of infected reason, storms, islands, the sea and magic, and the stormy seas become an image of inner turmoil. Ariel, trapped and howling in a tree until Prospero "made gape the pine" and freed him, suffered "torment/To lay upon the damned" (*The Tempest* 1.2.292). His piercing cries find an echo in Daphne's "songs from the dead room" of the mental hospital, where telegraph poles replace Ariel's tree and "the wind is lodged forever in the telegraph wire for crying there on a grey day" (*OC*, 48). The same image occurs in the description of the storm on Karemoana, as "the wind screamed in the telephone and electric wires", and here the wild storm abates only to leave Malfred with a terrifying silence rather than a release from her turmoil (*SS*, 74).

Toby Withers, Daphne's brother in *Owls Do Cry*, resurfaces in *The Edge of the Alphabet* (1962), becoming a protagonist and taking a more central role in the later novel. His desire to return to his homeland leads him to embark on the sea-voyage to Britain, and in a confused pre-seizure state while waiting for his ship to set sail, he addresses his rescuer from the turbulent sea as, "You witch-octopus whom I loved, who in the dark distressful ocean manoeuvred for me" (*EA*, 292). The imagery of the tempestuous sea forms a link between *The Edge of the Alphabet* and *Owls Do Cry*. For Daphne, in *Owls Do Cry*, "the sea will creep into the sleep of people and flow round and round in their head, eating out caverns where it echoes and surges till the people become eroded" (*OC*, 19). At night in Daphne's dormitory were "the rigid, afraid and wandering people, knowing the mountain outside and the wild storms there, huddling into their bedclothes" (137). Toby dreams of his sisters, Francie and Daphne, "in a storm they could not see or understand" (30). In *Faces in the Water*, the natural dangers of the sea, central to *The Tempest*, form Istina's "festering dreams" where

> a great gap opened in the ice floe between myself and the other people whom I watched, with their world, drifting away through a violet-coloured sea where hammerhead sharks in tropical ease swam side by side with the seals and the polar bears. I was alone on the ice. (*FW*, 4)

Istina is as powerless and isolated as the victims of the shipwreck in *The Tempest* and at the mercy of forces she cannot control. Standing up to get dressed, she is "buffeted by the waves in the mid-ocean of the room" (58), and at the point where she faces the possibility of a leucotomy and feeling "no longer human" Istina knows she would have to find shelter in "a safe nest between two rocks on an exposed coast mauled by the sea" (190), a haven, like Prospero's, to shelter her from the stormy elements of her life.

Shakespearean Dreams

In her 1964 article for the *Times Literary Supplement*, "Memory and a Pocketful of Words", Frame (2011) wrote that she aimed in her writing "to make the shape best suited to the time, the place, and the dream" (35), and she alludes frequently to Shakespearean dreams and dream-like states, magical happenings and the irrational unconscious feelings and desires that dreams express. She wrote of the supreme power of Shakespeare, such that "even at night when most of the city of tragedy is quiet one can hear the inner explosions of Shakespeare's unattended works as new layers of meaning are cast spontaneously from their context" (30–31). In a further piece, "Beginnings", written for *Landfall* in 1965, Frame (2011) recognizes a personal imperative to devote her "time wholly to making designs from my dreams" (46) and described her mother "who wrote poems as remedies" as "a dreamer" (40). Like Shakespeare, she uses dream as a creative device. The common experience of unsettling or terrifying nightmare creates a serious response in Shakespeare's plays and Frame uses this awareness of the importance of dreams in exploring an alternative reality.

References to Shakespearean dreams are frequently suggestive of a romantic possibility, and alternative life. Francie, Daphne Withers's sister in *Owls Do Cry*, had studied *A Midsummer Night's Dream* as she was preparing to leave school, and knew "that a man called Shakespeare, in a wood near Athens, contrived a moonlit dream" (*OC*, 20). But Francie, who dreamed of singing in opera, and had "sent away for the free book on becoming an opera singer" (28), finds those dreams come to an end when her father announces that she will go to work at the dreaded, deadening local woollen mill. Grace Cleave's homesick musings find expression in "I know a place", not where "the wild thyme grows" (*MSND* 2.1.249) but where "the matagouri, the manuka, the cabbage tree grow" (*TS*, 59), substituting native New Zealand flora. Frame alludes briefly to other plays of Shakespeare to conjure up both imaginative landscapes of the mind and a sense of awe. Toby day-dreams as he pores over the atlas: "How simple to travel, and on a night like this, a spring night with the air outside so thick with hawthorn and plum and powdered catkin that it had to be elbowed and brushed aside before it could be breathed" (*OC*, 77) and his thoughts echo Lorenzo's wonder at the beauties of the natural world: "In such a night as this,/When the sweet wind did gently kiss the trees" (*Merchant of Venice* 5.1.1-2). Alwyn, in *The Adaptable Man*, contemptuous of both his uncle's religious faith and his father's old-fashioned dentistry, muses on the futility of people's hopes and dreams, perhaps echoing those of *A Midsummer Night's Dream*, as Francie does in *Owls Do Cry*, but chiefly referring to the dreams of *The Tempest* (4.1.156–57):

> a pitiful hope [. . .] that the new world was near, that this was the new time, that man could at last, feeding upon his burden of dreams, become his dreams, prove the truth of "we are such stuff as dreams are made on"; dreams would blossom from dreams. (*AM*, 157)

The dreams of Frame's protagonists often turn to nightmare, rather than delivering a "new world", and are linked to a collapse of the rational mind and to madness, like Lady Macbeth's sleepwalking. Shakespeare's readers and audiences have always been indebted to his insights into the human psyche and his dramatic use of dreams to convey the disturbance of troubled minds. A widely-held view of Shakespeare's omniscience is expressed by Charles Dickens (2011), passing Bethlehem Hospital (Bedlam) on a night walk through London in 1860. Linking dreams and sanity, he wonders:

> are not the sane and the insane equal at night as the sane lie dreaming? [. . .] I wonder that the great master who knew everything, when he called Sleep the death of each day's life, did not call Dreams the insanity of each day's sanity. (235)

In *Faces in the Water*, Istina, confined to a modern-day mental hospital, and feeling herself as if on the edge of King Lear's cliffs, cannot escape her nightmares. She tells the reader "I dream and cannot wake and I am cast over the cliff and hang there by two fingers that are danced and trampled on by the Giant Unreality" (*FW*, 7).

Dreams are a link with memory, often suppressed memory, and the inability of Frame's characters to escape from the past. In *Owls Do Cry*, Chicks, like her brother Toby, is distressed by her dreams. Obsessed with improving her social status, she dreams of herself at a circus with a panther, but "I could not remember my act" (*OC*, 103). She is even more unnerved by her dream of the desert in which "the sand was grains of gold" (115), where she calls out for her parents and Francie, Toby and Daphne, but "nobody came" (117). Chicks deceives herself. She suppresses any imaginative or questioning thoughts within herself and in her dreams is confronted with the fears she cannot face in her waking life. When Amy dies, Chicks is embarrassed by the prospect of her more sophisticated acquaintances sneering at her. In her italicized reverie, however, she remembers her mother who, "*knew her bigness and sweetness and could not move for spilling some of it*" (*OC*, 118; Frame's italics.). She stops herself abruptly, feeling "I am half Daphne in writing this, it is not my usual way, as if a spell had come over me" (*OC*, 119). Daphne had also seen that there was a spell on her sister Francie, and felt that Francie had got hold "of the wrong magic" (*OC*, 32).

Dream is also a nightmare for Grace Cleave in *Towards Another Summer* (2007), a modern nightmare of Prospero's storm in which "her ship explodes, is burned; flash in the sky, stain in the sea; nothing human recovered". As Grace emerges from her dream she asks "oh God why have I been deceived? Which world do I inhabit? Down, dream, down!" (*TS*, 66). She has no Miranda to plead for:

> A brave vessel
> Who had, no doubt, some noble creature in her,
> Dashed all to pieces. (*The Tempest* 1.2.6–8)

Dream as memory, intuition, and nightmare come together most vividly in *Intensive Care*, in Naomi's letters to her father, Tom Livingstone. Her letters act as a chorus, commenting on the action and the various strands of the narrative. She appears to absorb other people's dreams, and dreams of Tom's suffocation of Cissy Everest and parts of Tom's later life. As with Prospero's magic, we can never be entirely certain where reality ends and imaginative fantasy begins. Truth is elusive. There is a thread of violence and abuse which runs through the entire novel; the reader is uncertain whose testimony, or whose memory conveys the truth, and "all dreams lead back to the nightmare garden" (*IC*, 32). Naomi's letters suggest her father was sexually predatory. Tom's other daughter Pearl suppresses nightmares of her own. Loving and caring relationships appear to be beyond reach in the Livingstone family, but in the ambiguities created by this dream-like novel it is not possible to be sure if Tom has sexually abused both daughters, or alternatively abused only one of them and neglected the other.

The ambiguities of Frame's novels find their most striking form in *Living in the Maniototo*, with its "magical technology" (*LM*, 39) and the technical wizardry of Frame's writing. Magic intrudes on reality, as though Prospero were hiding in the shadows. The death of Tommy, the Baltimore artisan jeweller, early in the novel is a sudden shocking "plague of unreality" as he dissolves in "blue fury" detergent "and all that remained of Tommy were two faded footprints on the floor" (70). Baffled, Mavis and her friend Brian agreed to say nothing of the incident, trying to understand how "worlds that we know only in sleep and dream and mythology" (39) intrude into what they understand as reality.

While Mavis is living as a guest at the house loaned to her by Irving and Trinity Garrett while they are away travelling, so that she can get on with writing her novel, she finds herself having to accommodate further guests who introduce themselves as friends of the travelling Garretts. Mavis is diverted from her novel by the need to write the story of her guests, narrated to one of her alter egos, Alice Thumb. She then hears that the Garretts have died abroad, leaving the house to her in their will. At the end of the novel, Mavis is stunned, as is the reader, by the brutally sudden revelation of her own self-delusion regarding the imaginary guests and imaginary inheritance from the supposedly dead Garretts when they unexpectedly return home: "—how snugly I had nested myself within it!" (*LM*, 236). Like Prospero's actors, Mavis's guests "were all spirits, and/are melted into air, into thin air" (*Tempest* 4.1. 149–50). Even worse is the shocking news that her dear friend Brian really has died and that she had missed the telegram from his sister, a piece of "real" information lost while Mavis/Alice was consumed by her fantasy. Mavis had declared earlier that she had "decided to break the rules [. . .] because nothing in art is forbidden" (*LM*, 68). When the Garretts return, however, she desperately tries "seizing facts" (239), but to no avail, as reality and the world of the imagination painfully collide.

In her final novel, *The Carpathians* (1988), Shakespeare is once more the inspiration for Frame as she makes use of elements of the inexplicable which some critics refer to as "magical realism", notably Isabella Zoppi (1999), who extends the term to Frame's use of "dual realities" (151) in the novel. Though elements of magical realism are as old as story-telling itself, the term has come to be associated most with the Latin American writing of, among others, Alejo Carpentier, Jorge Luis Borges and Gabriel García Márquez for the inclusion of unreal elements within an otherwise naturalistic fiction, and with Franz Kafka, whose work Frame had discovered in the Oamaru Public Library in 1953 (*CA*, 225). Frame was essentially interested in legend, mythology and folklore, and it is this interest that she shares with Márquez. The first English translation of his novel *One Hundred Years of Solitude* was widely and favourably reviewed in the USA while she was living there in 1970. Frame spent the first three months of 1970 and the whole of 1971 in the USA, spending October and November of that year at the writers' colony, Yaddo (King 2000, 359–66). It is difficult to imagine that García Márquez's novel could have escaped her attention, but it does not appear to have been the kind of writing Frame was drawn to. There is no mention of it in her published correspondence or her autobiography. It would seem that "magical realism" was not a genre or term Frame identified with, and that Shakespeare remained her primary literary model.

Although Frame undoubtedly drew inspiration from a wide variety of sources, she segues suggestively from one to another, without adhering to any genre in particular. The major inspiration in *The Carpathians* for the Kowhai Street letter-storm is not "magical realism" but *The Tempest*, in which Prospero conjures up a storm to shipwreck his treacherous brother. Frame took a lifetime interest in Prospero from her time as a student, through the years of her incarceration and beyond. *The Carpathians* abounds with the imagery of *The Tempest*. The wailing, shrieking, sobbing Kowai Street residents with their torn clothes look and sound like victims of a natural catastrophe, and "from each house came a succession of horrifying human cries as if from someone trapped within the walls" (*CP*, 181). It is the sound of *The Tempest's* shipwrecked passengers, cursed by the boatswain: "A plague upon this howling! They are louder than the weather or our office" (*Tempest* 1.1.34–35). As the storm abates, Mattina sees "the halo of morning light on the farthest peaks of the mountains, as if beyond the peaks there were another world with another morning and promise of a day that bore no relation to Kowhai Street" (*CP*, 184–85). In this, she appears to have an intimation akin to Miranda's "brave new world" (*Tempest* 5.1.183), sharing the same sense of wondering uncertain awe.

The Tempest is an is an act of imaginative collusion between the writer-magician and the audience, just as *The Carpathians* is between the writer and the reader, and the reader is deceived as to the "truth" and to the identity of the narrator, John Henry Brecon [J.H. B]. J.H. B. warns us at the outset that this is his "second novel" (*CP*, 25), but our imaginative involvement with Mattina's journey of exploration causes us to forget these words, until we emerge from the dream and are disabused by the revelation that John Henry Brecon's parents, Mattina and Jake, died when he was seven years old. We have been deceived, but we are agents in our own deception, just as Prospero reminds his audience of their collaboration in the magic they have just witnessed: "Gentle breath of yours my sails/Must fill, or else my project fails" (*Tempest* Epilogue 11–12). Frame's spell, like Prospero's, is broken; and we return to our own worlds.

Chapter Six: Tending the Myths

Folklore

Frame's concept of myth is a broad one and she has a powerful perception of the significance of dream, myth and folklore and the interconnection of these primeval elements of culture. She makes repeated reference to myths and poetry from both modern and ancient oral cultures, embracing poetry and song from oral tradition, for example Anglo-Saxon poetry, the Psalms, traditional ballads, and nursery rhymes; the biblical myth of Genesis, classical and Māori mythology; and the myths that more recent cultures, such as the USA, Australia and New Zealand, have created for themselves. In her final novel, *The Carpathians* (1988) Frame draws on her developing interest in folklore, oral culture as well as Māori mythology, language and culture.

Frame had taken particular pleasure in folk tales since her early childhood, and in her 1975 article for New Zealand's *Education* journal, she writes of her delight in Grimms' tales, and of how much they taught her and satisfied her needs as a child:

> I found the book so satisfying. I think now, in the convention of its story-telling, the journeys, meetings, the matter-of-fact descriptions of marvels [. . .]. Any act was possible. Anything could happen. Nothing was forbidden. (Frame 2011, 56)

The English use of the term "fairy tale" for these folk tales is misleading. Fairy tales, with their magical elements, rarely feature fairies as such, and are certainly not as innocent as the term "fairy tale" might suggest; still less a triviality to be dismissed. The stories retold by the Brothers Grimm are *Märchen* [Tales], *Hausmärchen* [Household Tales] or *Kindermärchen* [Children's Tales]. Perrault's stories are simply *Contes* [Tales]. They are directly told folk tales of the vicissitudes of life, often of childhood, of cruelty and survival, related in a simple style accessible to very young children; and the terms "fairy tale" and "folk tale" are synonymous and interchangeable in this context.

Frame's attachment to these tales, especially Grimms' *Tales*, and her sense of their value are shared by a number of earlier scholars and writers. One of these is Louis MacNeice (2011), who would have been a familiar name to Frame through his work for BBC radio and his poetry, while she was living in England between 1957 and 1964. MacNeice attended an English boarding-school as a child, a long way from his home and family in Northern Ireland, and tells how "fairy stories have always meant much to me as a person, even when I was at public school where to admit this meant losing face" (7). Similarly, Charlotte Brontë's (2008) character, Jane Eyre, was enchanted by the stories her nursemaid Bessie told her on winter evenings "from old fairy tales and older ballads" (9).

The importance of fairy tales for children was confirmed by the eminent Austrian-American psychoanalyst Dr Bruno Bettelheim's hugely influential Freudian study of fairy tales, discussed in Chapter 3. It was published in the USA and the UK in 1976, shortly after Frame's 1975 article for the New Zealand *Education* journal. Bettelheim's work had appeared in the *New Yorker* in December 1975, was republished in the UK by Peregrine books in 1978 and reprinted as a Penguin book in 1991, so gaining a wide readership, in particular among people working with children.

Frame's only book for children, *Mona Minim and the Smell of the Sun* (1969) makes clear in its opening her feeling for the timelessness of fairy tale: "Once upon a time, not long ago, almost now" (*MM*, 7). She uses the traditional opening, but adds her own update, bringing the time-honoured beginning up to the present. The story tells the tale of a House Ant [sic], Mona Minim, who longs to see and smell the outside world and gain her independence, but falls through a crack in the stairs and is rescued and adopted by a kindly Garden Ant, before finally setting off on her return journey home: a lost-and-found theme common to fairy tales. As with Grimms' tales, Frame's story is a direct if lyrical tale for children—with a darker heart to it, a tale of loss, suffering and death—which younger and older children and adults can enjoy at their own level of understanding.

In her review for the *New Zealand Listener*, on September 25, 1992, Marion McLeod expressed her doubts about the suitability of *Mona Minim* as a children's tale "for the innocent child reader" as the "story is quite ominous in its overtones, and I suspect a sensitive young reader might well be upset by the dark paradox at the heart of the tale" (52–53). There seem to have been no such doubts in the minds of book reviewers for the *New York Times* on November 9, 1969 when the story was chosen as one of the ten best children's books in the 9–12 category, as a "wise and gently ironic fantasy", which Frame dedicated to the young son of her American friends, the Marquands, and to her niece, Pamela Gordon. Marc Delrez (2009) agrees with McLeod, however, asserting that "one can understand why her [Frame's] predilection for confronting themes and mediations was thought to make her tale unsuitable for its implied public", and he makes a brief mention of Bettelheim's views on the value of fairy tales to children, "if one is to believe Bettelheim". Delrez argues that the fairy tale is for Frame "a kind of facade for her more personal existential explorations, which are ushered in as it were through the back door of the text" (28–29), identifying links with her adult fiction.

These comments by McLeod and Delrez make it clear that they identify the "dark paradox" of the fairy tale, but they appear to miss the point that Frame and Bettelheim have identified, namely that the dark heart of all fairy tales, the elements of cruelty, suffering, loss and death, overcome by tenacity, courage and love, is an essential element of these tales. It provides a way for children to understand, and try to overcome, the vicissitudes of their own lives. Like the *New York Times* reviewer, Frame values the wisdom of these stories. Bettelheim (1976) held a view of fairy tales that "more can be learnt from them about the inner problems of human beings, and of their right solutions to their predicaments in any society than from any other source within a child's comprehension" (5), a point of view with which Frame demonstrably agrees. It is a view also expressed by the Swiss-German psychoanalyst Dr Alice Miller (1985), whose work was also discussed in Chapter 3. She made therapeutic use of fairy tales in her work with disturbed children, and asserts that fairy tales are "where the whole truth about human cruelty, as only a child can experience it, finds expression"(234).

Scholars and writers have been enchanted by these traditional tales, some through being asked initially to translate them. The American Professor of German, Jack Zipes, and the British Czech scholar, A.H. Wratislaw, began, like the Brothers Grimm, as translators of German and Eastern European tales. The novelist Angela Carter's translation of Perrault's tales from French inspired her feminist revisiting of the genre in *The Bloody Chamber*, as well as in the stories she wrote for children. The Russian Vladimir Propp (2013) attempted to analyse and codify the various types of Russian tales and their narrative elements in 1928, and his work was translated into English in 1958. Propp uses a series of symbols where, for example, a simple tale about a kidnapping and rescue may be expressed as

$$\beta^3 \eth^1 A^1 B^1 C\uparrow H^1\text{-}I^1 K\downarrow w^o \,(128),$$

and tabulated as in Table 2 below:

The Tsar's Three Daughters

β^3	Three daughters go walking
$\eth^1$	They stay too long in the garden
A^1	A dragon kidnaps them
B^1	A call for help
$C\uparrow$	Three heroes search
$H^1\text{-}I^1K$	Three battles with the dragon
K	Girls' rescue
$\downarrow$	Girls' return
w^o	Reward

Table 2: Propp's Analysis of a Folk Tale

Propp's study is specifically concerned with narrative structures and variants on narrative pattern. His analysis illustrates the patched and mended nature of fairy tales, the way in which story-tellers in oral and mostly illiterate cultures told and retold traditional stories adapted to suit their own circumstances. Similarly, Lorna Sage

(2001) notes that "fairy tales, in their multiple reflections on each other, and their individual and internal layerings of interpretations" have "no core, or point of origin, or ur-story 'underneath', just a continuous interweaving of texts" (235).

Most current commentators are more concerned with the content of the stories themselves, with their variety of interpretation, and their cultural and emotional significance. In his account of the Grimms' collection, Jack Zipes (1988) details the Brothers' concern "to preserve, contain and present to the German public what they felt were profound truths about the origins of both German culture and European civilisation" (12). Zipes describes the way the Brothers Grimm refined the stories: they were retold to appeal to a German bourgeois audience, eliminating erotic and sexual elements, and stressing the values of order, thrift and industry, so that the tales were tailored to the German social, religious and cultural contexts. Later writers have similarly interpreted fairy tales to suit their own conditions: the square-jawed clean-living hero of Disney's *Snow White*, for example, takes a more prominent role than in the traditional tale, and James Thurber's (1983) conclusion to his moral fable of a thoroughly modern American Red Riding Hood: "for even in a nightcap a wolf does not look any more like your grandmother than the metro-Goldwyn lion looks like Calvin Coolidge. So the little girl took an automatic out of her basket and shot the wolf dead" (3).

The apparently indestructible traditional fairy tale frees writers from the confines of empirical knowledge, taking the reader into the realm and imagery of dream and myth, and Frame exploits this literary genre to explore beyond perceived reality. Freud, in common with his compatriots, was well versed in the tales retold by the Brothers Grimm, while in the 20th-century psychoanalysts Bettelheim and Miller reaffirmed their value for children. Marina Warner (2014) notes "that fairy tales are cast in the language of the psyche, with the forest and palaces, snow, glass, and apples symbolizing deeper, concealed truths, has become widely accepted" (113–14). Frame makes extensive use of this primordial imagery of trees, snow and ice, and of mirror-reflections and dreams in her novels and poetry to explore the darker corners of the human soul. She blends fairy tale with other features of oral literature and song, to point up the sense of personal trial and exclusion from the mainstream of society, the "inner problems of human beings" in Bettelheim's phrase, and often weaves lines from disparate songs, poems and stories into a patchwork of her own, in keeping with the spirit of fairy tale retelling.

Fairy Tales

In *The Uses of Enchantment*, Bruno Bettelheim is emphatic about the importance of the darker elements of fairy tales, that they should not be shorn of their cruelty and pain, and that "an element of threat is crucial to the fairy tale" (1976, 144). *Mona Minim* shows that Frame thought so, too, in Mona's encounter with death and mortality. The traditional fairy tale served a "siren function" as Warner (2014) puts it, "saying the unsayable and tolling a warning in the night" (80). There is an abundant repertoire of tales of poverty, starvation, violence, child abandonment, imprisonment, rape, incest and wicked or hapless parents and step-parents. Children and young adults are tested and undergo trials of fortitude and tenacity before the final happy ending. On her way home, Mona Minim, Frame's intrepid House Ant, is not spared the distressing side of life, which comes as an encounter with the dying Queen Antonia in her spoiled wedding dress, trying to shed and eat her lacy wings so that she can lay her eggs and found a new colony while her husband also dies. She pleads with the horrified Mona to help her tear off her wings, and dies while Mona "looked up into the sky and saw there was no sky, only darkness and night" (*MM*, 93). Mona is a resourceful and robust, young ant, however, and soon returns to planning her route home.

Frame repeatedly expresses experience in terms of fairy tale, as well as legend and ancient poetry or ballads. During her time living in Sargeson's Takapuna hut in the mid-1950s, Frame (2011) used the language and protagonists of the fairy tale in an account of the generous and kindly but complex and confused male attitudes of her host and his circle of literary friends, in a form which is ostensibly less confrontational and more tactful than a direct statement of feelings may have been. The piece is an effective metaphor for the kind of exclusion from the mainstream which Frame experienced. "I am banished in a hut" she writes, "a scullion" receiving her food from a prince at the palace, who in turn is visited by other princes. She is not "our class of royalty" so the princes "humour her, certainly; but not speak much to her" [*sic*]. She dreams of leaving to "live my scullion's life, without the emptiness and loneliness of a grand palace" with "people who are scullions like myself" (221–22).

In Frame's first novel, *Owls Do Cry* (1957), written in Sargeson's hut, the book of Grimms' fairy tales with its curly writing is treasure itself. Daphne, one of the four siblings in *Owls Do Cry*, would quote from one of the stories which had captured her imagination when she was lost for an answer to what was said to her, "Rapunsel, Rapunsel, let down your hair; quoting from the prince who climbed the gold silk rope to the top of the tower" (*OC*, 11). In his rage, Daphne's father resembles Rumpelstiltskin. On the night of the dance in the mental hospital, the adult Daphne recalls *Cinderella*, but she finds there is no glass slipper and escapes wistfully into a reverie in which the unsympathetic and often cruel nurses, Flora Norris and Sister Dulling, are the Ugly Sisters. Nor is there a rescuing Prince, since "at ten o'clock sharp the people were stripped of their finery and thrust back into the ashes" (148).

Daphne's powerlessness and inarticulacy in the mainstream world and her dismissal by others as insane serve to hide her humanity, which manifests itself in her moral clarity, imaginative perception and compassion. Her innermost, inarticulate feelings are revealed when Frame links her with the imprisoned daughters of fairy tale and the words of past poets, though there is no happy ending for Daphne. Frame links Rapunsel in Daphne's songs from the dead room with the ancient Greek legend of Theseus unwinding silk thread in the labyrinth in his quest for the minotaur, and Blake's "Happy Piper", erasing the boundaries between Daphne's words, the author's voice, different poets and texts, weaving them in and out of each other.

> And we walk like Theseus or an ashman
> in the labyrinth, with our memories unwound on threads of silk or fire
> [...]
> Rapunsel, Rapunsel, let down your hair.
> Drop thy pipe, thy happy pipe. (OC, 32; Frame's italics)

Fairy tales are also part of the literary fabric of *Faces in the Water* (1961). Istina, who is by this time approaching the end of her committal to the mental hospital, likens herself to one of the little birds in *Hansel and Gretel*, picking up the crumbs which were not intended for her, as she listens to the conversation of two doctors (*FW*, 207). One of these doctors, a "tubby loud-voiced intelligent intuitive prince in the forbidden castle" (214), shows her unexpected kindness, rescuing her from the chaplain who had dismissed her. She describes another inmate, immobile on the grass with his roller, as one of those people who are "under a spell and stuck to whatever they touched" (220). Istina is more articulate than Daphne, but her humanity is just as effectively hidden beneath the concealment of hospital clothing and the hospital's punitive régime. The doctor rescues Istina from her prison by treating her like a human being, deliberately including her in everyday tasks, and as such is "an intuitive prince".

Greta Maude, the dentist's wife in *The Adaptable Man* (1965), finds refuge from the tribulations of her life in her hut in the garden with Maplestone's Chart of plant pests and diseases, living "her social life among vegetables" (*AM*,92) in the Suffolk village of Burgelstatham. Greta thinks in terms of Grimms' tales. She thinks of fairy tale rescuers, "Searchers", who take forlorn travellers "to the Great House for feasting and fires. For thousands of years these same

Searchers have been moving in and out of fables, myths, histories, stories" (126). Greta had given up all hope of acquiring the status of a metropolitan professional dentist's wife, lacking the patience, she felt, of the princess who ate and slept with the Frog Prince, in the hope that "one day he would bring fulfilment of all her desires" (92). Instead she expects to suffer the "pains and penalties of misbehaviour" (127) of fairy tale, and believes that her incestuously conceived child "will be a little prince with wrinkled skin" (94) as a punishment for her sin.

Anglo Saxon Poetry and *The Adaptable Man*

In *The Adaptable Man*, Frame links the traditional world of fairy tale and the genre's location with other elements of ancient oral culture in the Reverend Aisley Maude's feeling for Anglo-Saxon poetry, with which Frame had imaginatively identified at the University of Otago in the 1940s, and which is here rooted firmly in Suffolk and Northumbria. Frame was inspired by her university lectures in Anglo-Saxon, being imaginatively transported to the time and place where the Anglo-Saxon poems had been composed. In the copy of *The Adaptable Man* which Frame gave her former lecturer, Gregor Cameron, she apologizes for the uncorrected lines of the Anglo-Saxon poems "with the (human) request that once again the printer, not the author, may bear responsibility for the errors in quotation".

The Adaptable Man is set in the ancient county of Suffolk, part of the former Danelaw, the land settled by the Danes after the 9th-century battles between the Saxons and the heathen Danish invaders—the fictional village of Burgelstatham named after its heathen burial place. Suffolk remained a very rural county, barely touched by the Industrial Revolution apart from the railway, with an agricultural landscape largely unchanged for many centuries. Here "the place-names are more memories than names" (*AM*, 11), and during her time living in Suffolk, Frame found villages populated by people rooted in the apparent immutability of the place.

The Rev. Aisley Maude quotes from the Old English elegiac poems, "The Seafarer" and "The Wanderer", interweaving lines from each poem. "The Seafarer" relates the feats of endurance of a mariner alone at sea, and "The Wanderer" tells of the trials of a man exiled from his homeland, facing a hostile world alone, and Aisley, feeling at odds with the modern world, identifies with both. These elegies date from the 7th century, the time of St Cuthbert—a monk, sometime Bishop of Lindisfarne and finally a hermit—who lived in the early stages of the Golden Age of Northumbria, a period of cultural flowering of art that produced, among other artefacts, gloriously illuminated gospel-books between the mid-7th century to the mid-8th century in north-eastern England. Aisley relates to St Cuthbert and the legends that grew up around him, and in his mind he has

> returned to the Anglo-Saxon world of East Anglia, of Northumbria [. . .] he is St. Cuthbert himself, saying his prayers in the sea [. . .] while the two seals come out of the deep water to warm him *mid heora flyce* [with their pelts]. (*AM*, 77)

Frame uses the imagery of their yearning, tribulations and endurance to create a link between the fairy-tale imagery of Greta's feelings and Aisley's Anglo-Saxon poetry, as Greta sees her brother-in-law "living in a fairytale" (*AM*, 270). Greta identifies herself with characters of folklore, but the Rev. Maude identifies with the distant historic figure of St Cuthbert around whom myths have developed. Fairy tales and Anglo-Saxon laments are both from a distant past and anonymous; and both tap into primeval emotions, universal and unchanging human needs, the unending cycles of life, and the struggle to survive in a harsh world.

The Ballad Tradition and *Intensive Care*

Figure 5: BBC Third Programme, March 22, 1958. Courtesy of the Radio Times

Frame also uses snatches of traditional ballads, which were featured frequently in both popular radio broadcasting as well as the more erudite radio programmes on the BBC's Third Programme, during the Folk Revival of the 1950s and 1960s, when Frame was living in England. These ballads were re-worked and much travelled like the fairy tales; and like the fairy tale told their story with a sparse directness. Ballads, like fairy tales, often exist in a number of versions and variants throughout northern Europe and beyond: migrants took their oral culture with them, especially to America, as Francis James Child (1904) notes in his mid-19th-century numbered collection of ballads and their variants. Recordings of Child ballads and others were heard frequently on the radio, as in the illustration from the *Radio Times*. Alwyn in *The Adaptable Man*, sings snatches of one of them, the Appalachian ballad, "Tom Dooley". It is a story of a jealous killing, in the ballad tradition, suggestive of Alwyn's guilt in murdering Botti Julio, the Italian labourer.

Figure 6: BBC Third Programme, January 9, 1958. Courtesy of the Radio Times

In *Intensive Care*, Frame exploits this violent thread of ancient culture, the narrative structure and imagery of the traditional ballad in the story of Tom Livingstone's grandson Colin and the woman with whom Colin has an affair, Lorna. Frame cites lines from two ballads, "Lord Livingston" and "Lord Thomas and Fair Annet" (often "Clerk Tamas"), which both tell of thwarted love, jealousy, revenge and death. Although some ballads differ little from fairy tales, the traditional ballad rarely has a fairy-tale happy ending. Ballads for the most part relate stories of lost and unrequited love, revenge, violent death and bloodshed, as suggested by the illustration from the *Radio Times*.

Frame's use of traditional ballad poetry strikes an ominous note in her story of the Livingstone family in *Intensive Care*, and the lines which Frame takes from different ballads do not augur well for Colin and Lorna:

> *I dreamed a dream concerning thee,*
> *O read ill dreams to guid*
> *Your bower was full of milkwhite swans,*
> *Your bride's bed full o' bluid'* (*IC*, 207)

Frame begins Colin's story with a four line verse from "Clerk Tamas" who hunts down a woman he desires—"fair Annie"—in the woods, followed by a verse from "Lord Livingston" in which the Lord dreams of his beloved whose bed is "full o' bluid". Colin dreams of his colleague, Lorna, whose image haunts him. In spite of his marriage to May, his three children, and his respectable social standing, Colin embarks on an affair with Lorna which leads to their dismissal from work for adultery, and a decision to live together in Australia.

As in many of the ballads, a mother sounds a discordant note—Lorna's mother in this case—and sets in train events leading to a final catastrophe. Colin feels betrayed, and finds he can begin to understand his grandfather Tom's obsessions with Cissy Everest, and later with Peggy Warren, casting himself in the role of the traditional victim: "the settler robbed of his land by lovelight, he was the drowning sailor without a sea to drown in, the underprivileged beyond the castle gates" (212).

Colin arrives back in New Zealand from Australia in a state of frantic inarticulacy, and Frame quotes the stabbing and suicide with which "Lord Tamas and Fair Annet" ends. Colin cannot accept the end of his affair with Lorna, and like Lord Tamas again—who originally hunted Annie like a deer in one version of this ballad—Colin goes in pursuit of her. He finds the house on a day when the family is out, and his phone calls fail to persuade her to return to him. He hallucinates a meeting with Lorna in which they talk about the death of Colin's wife May and their children, and the new life which Colin and Lorna will enjoy together, until Colin emerges from his dream. In another version of the ballad Lord Thomas's life ends when he stabs himself after killing his unloved "nut-brown bride" while trying to save his true love, Annie, and Frame makes use of all these threads.

After some years of obsessively but fruitlessly pacing Lorna's street, Colin buys a hunting rifle, and the story ends as sparingly as any ballad, as he returns to Lorna's house, shoots her mother, her father and then Lorna, embracing her before turning his rifle on himself in a tale of betrayed, thwarted and unrequited love, violently avenged:

> *Now stay for me dear Ennet he said*
> *Now stay my dear he cryd*
> *Then strake the dagger into his heart,*
> *And fell deid by her side.* (*IC*, 219)

The use of these ballad references gives the story its awful inevitability; creates a link with ancient stories; provides Frame with a protagonist's surname, Livingstone, and part of her plot. She also draws partly on the story of her cousin Bill, who in February 1962 had shot his lover in Christchurch before turning his rifle on himself. Frame wrote a poem of her own about "Big Bill" whose early life had seemed full of promise:

> What happened between then and now, Big Bill,
> To bring madness, murder, suicide your way,
> Riding with us in triple nightmare to your funeral
> At St. Kilda on this cold dark winter's day? (*PM*, 5)

The elements of ballad form in the poem suggest the connection Frame made between family tragedy and the ballad tradition, the ballads articulating emotions which the characters cannot express, a mixture of obsession, despair and revenge.

Myth and Survival

In her early novella, *Towards Another Summer* (2007), written in 1963 and published posthumously, Frame makes a clear statement of the importance of myth when her protagonist, Grace Cleave, asserts that "it was an old tradition; we must tend the myths, she thought; only in that way shall we survive" (*TS*, 98). Frame emphasizes this point again, 20 years later, in the opening of her autobiography, linking mythology with familial and cultural memory in her suggestive interplay of Māori and Christian myth:

> From the first place of liquid darkness, within the second place of air and light, I set down the following record with its mixture of fact and truths and memories of truths and its direction toward the Third Place, where the starting point is myth. (*CA*, 7)

Frame is fascinated by both the workings of the human memory, and by the relationship of memory with mythology, and memory and art. The role of the writer is to preserve the continuity of that memory, walking like Theseus, using Ariadne's thread to find his way out of the Minotaur's labyrinth, with "our memories unwound on threads of silk or fire" (*OC*, 52). Even Colin Monk, the mathematician and "not a literary man" (*IC*, 389), narrating Part Three of *Intensive Care* (1970) and aiming to make a factual account of the workings of the Human Delineation Act which will obliterate memory, asserts that "I write to seize a place for myself and my memory in the folklore that will take root" (255). Monk has qualms about the morality of what he is required to carry out, in part because of the erasure of memory. "Time", he says "is glacier-long fire deep sun-high" (387) and asks himself, "do a few weeks of lost memory matter?"

The answer to Monk's question comes from Frame herself, confiding in her friend Sheila Natusch, to whom she lamented the effects of the ECT treatment, which robbed her memory of things she wanted to remember. Memory was an abiding concern for Frame. In a letter to the poet James K. Baxter to convey her admiration for his writing, Frame included the comment that "poetry is in memory", and adds that "you can annihilate time if you have enough power in you" (King 2000, 95). Memory can be traumatic, as the narrator of *The Edge of the Alphabet* (1962) remarks in relation to the discomfort of Zoe Bryce, a lonely failed school-teacher sailing from New Zealand to England, who is not so much disturbed by sea-sickness as ambushed by "thoughts, sadness, regrets [. . .]. For memory is so often a single explosion, like a firework in the face. One is blinded. One scrabbles about with damp matches trying to ignite an empty blackened little column of cardboard" (90).

Frame's sense of the "mixture of facts and truth and memories of truth" from the opening of her autobiography is apparent in her 1963 novella *Towards Another Summer*. Hilary Mantel notes in her review of the novella for the *The Guardian* on July 12, 2008 that this is where "her great work of memory began to take shape", referring to themes that Frame would later develop in her autobiography. Mantel also notes the connection with myth in her comments on Frame's use of language: "Intensely personal, her writing is always spiralling in on itself, towards the condition of myth, and yet it nails the moment, pins down experiences so fleeting that others would never grasp them".

Characters in Frame's novels struggle with the partly formed notion of what lies, in Malfred Signal's expression, beyond "the object, beyond its shadow to the ring of fire, the corona at its circumference" (*SS*, 239). As Frame discusses her ideas with Elizabeth Alley (Alley and Williams 1992), the New Zealand literary critic and broadcaster, she endeavours to explain her interest in "what is beyond the real, the invisible beyond the real". She comments on our fear of using our imagination, asserting that "the proper use of imagination is a form of courage, daring to explore beyond the horizons" (54).

In *The Edge of the Alphabet*, Toby dreams of writing about his "Lost Tribe", a dream undermined by magpies singing, in nursery rhyme fashion, "'A Wimbledon a Wombledon a fourteen miles'" (*EA*, 4). Asked where this tribe is to be found, he replies "behind a mountain approached through a secret pass" (216). Toby cannot match his insights with his limited powers of language, but the novel's other protagonist, Zoe, expresses a sense of another world when she meets a smiling man who introduces himself as Lawrence, in a bar in Soho, London, which she visits with her friend Peter. Lawrence invites them to come with him to the Serpentine, the lake in Hyde Park, and Zoe says to herself, linking dream and myth with the world of folklore:

> Of course I have met you in dreams and myths [. . .]. You appear at crossroads, at the entrance to mazes, on the outskirts of cities, at the edge of the alphabet. It is you who give warnings to the lost children and the eldest son to seek out his fortune. (266)

In her letter to Baxter, quoted earlier, Frame also comments on fruitless memory as well as Baxter's "true way of remembering". She writes that:

> You can walk a hundred years in time picking and pressing and saving the daffodils and buttercups and daisies that you find there till you have a mind full, and then you can sit down to fondle your treasure. [. . .] But what a dead smell your flowers have and the daisies will have fallen to pieces, petal by petal. (King 2000, 94–95)

In *Scented Gardens for the Blind* (1963), such a collector is Edward Strang, an obsessive amateur genealogist, who "was concerned that the human race should continue, that the generations should follow each other like the flowers which open at morning". His is "an ordinary family, in the chain gang of the human race", but Edward preferred to live and to exert power, "by remote control" (*SG*, 60–61). Edward's ancestors form an orderly list, with as much life to them as his collection of toy soldiers, or the disintegrating daisies of Frame's image.

Edward's lack of awareness contrasts with the envious yearning of Malfred Signal, the retired art teacher in *A State of Siege* (1966), who bitterly resents the gift of imagination her pupil, Lettice Bradley, reveals in her painting of Maui, the hero from Māori mythology. The girl seemed to have "been able to absorb, as a mindless sponge absorbs food from the sea, the myths and legends of her own country" (*SS*, 136). Frame displays a developing interest in Māori myth and culture in her later novels, and in her penultimate novel she takes for her title the Māori name of a real place, the Maniototo, a wild upland plateau of moorland on the South Island.

Frame's increasing interest in Māori culture comes both through her reading and through friendships, for example with the Māori writer, Jacquie Sturm, and her husband, James K. Baxter, the poet whose work Frame had so admired in her letter of 1947, and who developed a strong interest in Māori culture. Baxter held the Burns Fellowship at the University of Otago in 1966, the year after Frame. Frame had applied for a second year of the Fellowship, and when Baxter was selected she was invited to be "a guest of the university" in 1966, with an office and a cash grant to complete the work she was engaged in, so that their time there overlapped (Jones 2008). Baxter's book of essays from that time, *The Man on the Horse* (1967), is "dedicated to Janet Clutha", a clear indication of the close connection he felt with Frame, using the Māori river name which Frame adopted as her surname.

Baxter established a commune at a Māori settlement at Hiruharama (Jerusalem) in 1968 and took the Māori form of his name, Hemi. In *The Man on the Horse* he expresses a view of ancestry and timelessness which chimes with both a Māori view of the world and with Frame's, writing that he is "concerned perhaps chiefly with the search for the tree of Jesse, the sense of ancestral continuity, which the modern way of life tends to cut down and destroy" (1967, 9). Like Frame, he is concerned with the memory of the past, and the roots which lead down to it. At his death in 1972, he received the rare honour for a Pakeha of a tangi, a full Māori funeral held at Hiruharama.

Patricia Grace's *Waiariki* was the first commercially published collection of stories by a Māori woman writer, and Frame chaired the PEN jury which awarded Grace's *Waiariki* the PEN/Hubert Church Best First Book Award for Fiction in 1975. Frame recommended Grace's book for the award for because of its "loving comprehension of ownership". In her recommendation, Frame writes of *Waiariki*, that: "Patricia Grace has given us a complete clear picture of living people. *Waiariki* insists and moves, not only in its content and language but with the rhythmic quality that is an undercurrent of the writing, like a tide flowing" (Grace, personal communication). Frame's emphasis on rhythm and the image of flowing water is characteristic of her commentary on the writing of others and her sense of the organic nature of story-telling—she used the same image about West Indian writers she read in London—and Frame here affirms the value she places on indigenous forms of language.

Grace expressed her admiration for Frame as a "heroine" and "role-model" (Grace, personal communication). She made a contribution to Frame's 70th birthday book, *The Inward Sun* (Alley 1984), appropriately a version of a Māori creation myth, "Sun's Marbles" (99–104). Grace suggests that Frame's interest in Māori was more likely influenced by people she had met and knew, Jacquie Sturm, for instance, the Māori writer who became one of Frame's life-long friends. A reading of *Waiariki*, however, suggests that Grace had underestimated Frame's reaction to these stories—key works in the Māori Renaissance of the 1970s—and that Frame experienced a real sense of affinity with her writing. In the final *Waiariki* story, "Parade", Old Hohepa tells the young narrator that "it is your job, this. To show others who we are" (1986, 88). Frame appears to have assimilated his message, as just a brief look at these stories clearly shows.

Grace's (1986) stories tell of a variety of Māori people, their values, their consciousness, their traditional way of life, and their relationships with Pakeha New Zealanders, using both formal and colloquial styles of Māori English. The second story, "Toki", contains English modified by Māori syntax and cadence, for example, in this expression of feeling: "And she came to my side once more, the girl, and is there still though old lady now, she" (10). In their blend of distinctive Māori inflected English syntax with the English short-story form, these stories celebrate and affirm Māori cultural identity, *Maoritanga*; and family, *whanau*; its mythological context; and the Māori relationship with the land, the sea and the mountains, in life and in death. In *Living in the Maniototo* (1981), Mavis, born in a land of earthquakes, has a respectful sense of herself as "a guest, as all are who live there, of the Taranaki mountain" (*LM*, 133), a feeling in keeping with the Māori concept of *kaitiakitanga*, guardianship of the land. This respect for the natural world is also seen in the choice of title for Mavis's novel "The Green Fuse", from a poem by Dylan Thomas (1988), "The force that through the green fuse" (13), in which nature is seen as both creator and destroyer, just as the Taranaki volcano is both a creator and destroyer. In "And So I Go", this sense of oneness with the physical world is expressed by the dying Granny Roka as she prays: "Guardian hill you do not clutch my hand, you do not weep. You know that I must go and give me blessing. You guard with love this quiet place rocking at the edge of the sea" (Grace 1986, 47).

Pakeha attitudes are called into question. In "A Way of Talking", Rose, back at home from school, is angered by the Pakeha dressmaker Jane's demeaning reference to Māori labourers, and takes issue with her, speaking to her in standard English. Her sister is embarrassed by Rose's assertiveness, "Rose, the stink thing, she was talking all Pakehafied" (3). Rose is as stern a critic of the abuse of language as Mavis in *Living in the Maniototo*, who protests: "I have to cry out here that language is all we have for the delicacy and truth of telling, that words are the sole heroes and heroines of fiction" (*LM*, 92). In the final *Waiariki* story, "Parade", another Māori returns to her community, distressed by the patronising Pakeha reaction to Māori traditions. The story closes, however, with a confident reaffirmation of the value of Māori culture and language, as "I took in a big breath, filling my lungs with sea and air and land and people. And with past and present and future, and felt a new strength course through me" (1986, 89). The people sing their canoe chant in confident harmony, in Māori, with no translation given. The lack of translation encourages the reader who does not speak Māori to try to grapple with the meaning and cultural context of the words, and highlights the sense of the importance of indigenous language which Grace shares with Frame who argues against the translation of Māori words in New Zealand texts.

Frame's interaction with Māori writing and culture is harder to pin down than her inspiration from American and European texts, as it involves a spiritual identification and shared values around the guardianship of the land and social justice as much as a regard for indigenous forms of language, rather than the allusion, direct quotation and pastiche of the earlier novels. Frame was attracted by Māori myths and cultural practices, and had an interest in Māori language and its revival, which we see particularly in Frame's final novel, *The Carpathians*. Frame and Grace both express a sense of the importance of language and a spiritual sense of timelessness. Grace expresses her way of thinking in an interview with Antonella Sarti (1998), when she says "I think that we are our ancestors. We are here now because of our ancestors. [. . .] Past and future are part of the present" (49). Although Frame makes mention of the Māori in her earliest stories and poems, "The Lagoon", for example, it is clear that Grace's stories made a strong and lasting impression on Frame, and their impact can be detected in Frame's later novels. There is a sense of recognition and affinity, culminating in an increasingly direct affirmation of Māori values of kinship, community and antimaterialism in *Living in the Maniototo* (1979) and in her final novel, *The Carpathians* (1988). Frame's intertextuality is underpinned by her imaginative cross-cultural connections of mythologies from different traditions, from northern Europe, classical Greece, biblical scriptures and Māori mythology, and encapsulated in the opening words of her autobiography, quoted earlier, "where the starting point is myth" (*CA*, 7).

In *Living in the Maniototo*, in which New Zealand suburban streets are often named after British lords, country seats and battles, Mavis, from a Pakeha background, nevertheless comments on the use of more appropriate Māori place-names, which like "Burgelstham" in *The Adaptable Man*, stress the importance of belonging and of a linguistic union with the land: "Wanganui, Waikato, Tuatapere, Taranaki ... more powerful because they were welded to the place by the first unifying act of poetry and not stuck on like a grocery label" (*AM*, 96). In *Living in the Maniototo*, the Maniototo becomes a metaphor for the artist's imagination, an almost mythological place where Peter Wallstead, historian, teacher and writer lived in contentment. As Janet Wilson (1998) remarks,

> In establishing the Maniototo as the true home of the creative artist Frame makes a deserted unknown plain symbolise the elusive cultural treasure which is conspicuously lacking in the novel's spiritual wastelands: the metropolitan centres of Blenheim, Berkeley and Baltimore. (632)

In her final novel, *The Carpathians,* Frame's exploration of memory, myth, poetic imagination and language reaches its apotheosis, as she draws together their labyrinthine connecting threads in the story of the legend of the Memory Flower in Puamahara.

Memory, Language and *The Carpathians*

The Carpathians is narrated by novelist John Henry Brecon, son of the novel's protagonist, Mattina Brecon. He creates a story which merges details from his mother's notebooks and father's published writings with his own creative imagination to make permanent the memory of the parents he hardly knew, Mattina and Jake Brecon, embodied in language. John Henry is one of the "Housekeepers of Ancient Springtime" (*CP*, 278) who aims with "the use of words to continue the memory through centuries" as Frame further develops the theme of memory and its survival or its obliteration. Frame links her translation of Rilke's phrase, *printemps antique*, "ancient springtime", with the orchards around the fictional New Zealand town of Puamahara, a town named after the fictional legend of the Memory Flower and where its memorial is located. The town's name is a compound of the Māori words *pua*, a flower and *mahara*, memory.

The Puamahara Māori myth of the memory flower is Frame's invention, and reflects Frame's increasing interest in Māori culture and language, as well as her love of fairy tale and folklore and her sense of their importance. The Memory Flower myth tells the story of a young woman, "chosen by the gods as a collector of the memory of her land", who "journeys to a region between the mountains and the sea to search for the memory" (29). Her quest, in true folk tale tradition, is a journey of choices and judgements, and also mimics the Genesis myth of Eve tasting the fruit of the tree of knowledge so that "the woman of Maharawhenua tasted the yesterday within the tomorrow" (*CP*, 29). Like Mona Minim in Frame's fairy tale for children, she eventually had "no human function but that of a story-teller" (29) until she vanishes and is replaced by a tree from which the Memory Flower blossoms.

It is this legend of the memory flower which attracts Mattina Brecon, a wealthy Jamesian American who visits New Zealand and rents a house in Kowhai Street, Puamahara. The tourist board has promoted the legend because of its commercial value to tourism. Renée Shannon, a Kowhai Street resident planning to move to Auckland, is dismissive of it, telling Mattina that the Māori legends "don't often break into our *real* life" (*CP*, 163; Frame's italics). Renée has, however, a dawning awareness that "we're only now beginning to look closely at the place we're living in" (163). She senses the economic value of Māori legend as a tourist attraction and thus its commodification, in keeping with her materialistic view of the world. Frame's fictional legend embodies tenets of Māori culture—the essential link between past, present and future, and the importance of ancestral memory. This memory is an integral part of traditional Māori identity, illustrated in Patricia Grace's (2001) novel *Dogside Story* when she describes the building of a new *wharenui,* a meeting house, whose structural parts are named after the bones of the human skeleton, designed to keep the old stories safe:

> The reason for the piece of tahuhu, or ancestral backbone, being kept from the old house to be put into the new one is because the wharenui is the repository of talk, and rafters are its storage space. [. . .] It was a way of transferring the old stories into the new house for safe-keeping. (141)

The older residents of Puamahara, settlers of European origin, are generally lost and lonely figures—deserted like Connie Grant—by younger members of their families. Another such person is the "penultimate Madge", one of the last generation with links to the Scottish settlers, unnerved by her great-niece learning Māori at school, who finds that modern forms of language separate her from her grandchildren. "I speak the language of another age" (*CP*, 56) she wails, conscious that her memories and knowledge will die with her. Similar feelings are nursed by Hercus Millow, the retired sergeant-major, who enjoyed rereading the letters and children's poems of the 19th-century Scottish writer Robert Louis Stevenson, and a book of poems written in "Scottish" by his own ancestor, his great-grandfather. Now, as he merely dips into these books after his stroke, he feels as he reads "a sense of loss that a world still treasured had retreated from him" (106–07).

Millow's small collection of sea-faring novels and stories of war-time disaster, heroism and survival are allied to the Pakeha myth of the heroic New Zealand settler and are part of his armoury of defence, just as his memories of New Zealand supported him while he was a prisoner-of-war in a German camp. He understood that especially in times of stress the mind creates its own myths, that as an earthquake or volcano alters the world we inhabit, "memories are formed that as the years pass have the capacity to spread under seismic impact of their own stress, causing other memories to disappear and new details of the time, new scapes, to reappear in the present" (*CP*, 103).

Most of the Kowhai Street residents are Pakeha, except Mattina's Māori neighbour, Hene Hanuere, from whom Mattina learns about the near loss of the Māori language. Hene tells Mattina about Māori who have been "brought up Pakeha" (*CP*, 49), whose language and culture have been overwhelmed by the English-speaking majority. Hene explains that "it's been lonely without our language" (49) and that she's returning to it and making plans to renew contact with her Māori community. She is voicing a widespread concern among Māori, identified by Tracey McIntosh (Lui 2005) in her article on Māori identity, when she argues that "a significant number of Maori struggle to identify their tribal links and are ignorant of their wakapapa [*genealogy*] [. . .]. It is painful for Māori to confront this reality" (45). This theme of the deprivation of language and the reclaiming of it is a prominent one in Patricia Grace's fiction, as it is in *The Carpathians*, and in Frame's non-fiction. Hene's second name, Hanuere, means "January", and like "Mattina" suggests a new beginning. In contrast with the people in Kowhai Street, are the urban Māori:

> who here are mostly poor in the material possessions that the country values highly, who live in the streets of the orphaned cars, who are often out of work, staying at home to repair or rebuild their cars and to cultivate their flower and vegetable gardens. (*CP*, 34)

The images in the novel of cultivation, productive gardening, and recreation, contrast with the fixation of most urban Pakeha New Zealanders with technology, commerce and material possessions; for them gardening is a leisure pursuit, often a matter of mowing the lawn rather than an essential part of domestic economy as it would have been for most rural New Zealanders, Māori and Pakeha. Frame links the Māori with Rilke's "ancient springtime", their traditional legends with the biblical myth and poetry of the timeless "flower of the field" (37), which blooms, fades and blooms again, the biblical "lilies of the field", finer in their jewelled colours even than "Solomon in all his glory" (Matt. 5:28).

On her visit to Hene's *marae*, the Māori settlement, Mattina learns of her Māori neighbours' plans to relearn their language in their *kohanga reo*, language nests, rescue disaffected youngsters—both Māori and Pakeha—from substance abuse and crime and reconnect with their lands and crafts. Mattina meets Rua, a village matriarch, who talks about flax weaving, and her deeply-rooted knowledge of the craft: "I know flax and flax knows me" (*CP*, 131). These women, in their quiet, compassionate and even-handed tones, who nonetheless acknowledge iniquity and deprivation, resemble voices in Grace's short stories. As Hene points out, "both us and the Pakehas are at the long end of a poking stick" (128), sharing the critical but positive attitudes of a number of Grace's strong female characters.

Mattina sees that language is society's most precious asset and that words preserve the memory of the past. The Kowhai Street residents who negate this truth through their focus on materialistic acquisition and use of clichéd language are destroyed by the midnight storm of "shapes of the old punctuation and language–apostrophes, notes of music, letters of the alphabets of all languages" (*CP*, 183). The magical and incomprehensible devastation of Kowhai Street robs most of its inhabitants of the trappings of their lives and their "world of imposture" (84). As Janet Wilson asserts, Mattina is "spared the devastation wreaked by the gravity star because she understands the importance of artists in society and their value in recovering the meaning of the past through memory and language" (1993, 123). The devastation is wrought apparently by the Gravity Star, which brought "its overwhelming unacceptable fund of new knowledge from millions of light-years and centuries of springtime" (*CP*, 180).

It is Mattina's awareness of the importance of language which appears to save her from the fate of Kowhai Street's other residents, who are all destroyed in the storm, evidenced from the scab she is left with after the night of the storm, which she picks at. The scab crumbles onto the table and reveals itself to be "a pile of minute letters of the alphabet" from a variety of languages (185). She wonders if she has been saved by her retreat into memory and by her understanding of the inextricable link between memory and language. The key to her survival lies in the fate of her neighbours, "now unintelligible creatures with all the spoken and written language of the world fallen around them" (186), destroyed through their belief only in empirical knowledge. In the words of Dinny Wheatstone, the "graduate imposter", they surround themselves with "imitations of truth" (84). In her conversation with Hercus Millow, Mattina feels a sense of anger at the seductive power of stale expressions, commonplace phrasing and clichés, "the magnetic power that held words together so that few dared separate them or examine them, but used them, again and again" (69).

The phenomenon of the letter-storm in the novel has been referred to as magical realism by, among others, Isabella Maria Zoppi (1998), extending the term from its South American origins, to the literature of other cultures in which myth and ancestors are part of modern life, and in which surreal or anti-realist events occur without question or explanation. The relevance of the term "magical realism" to Māori culture is discussed by Witi Ihimaera (1992) in an interview with Paul Sharrad where he asserts that:

> We are talking about a culture that has embraced Christianity, but a tangi will always farewell its dead to a place called Hawaiki. [...] These magic realist elements are part of our history, and I cannot say they are folktales because I believe it too. (104)

Ihimaera, however, is arguably referring to a fusion of Māori mythology with present day realities rather than the "magic realism" of the Latin American novelistic tradition, where anti-realist events are accepted without comment.

The most notable exponent of magical realism, the Colombian novelist Gabriel García Márquez, published the first English translation of *One Hundred Years of Solitude* in early 1970, as noted in Chapter 5, while Frame was staying in California with Bill Brown, and the novel was enthusiastically reviewed on March 8, 1970 in the *New York Times* by Robert Kiely, then Professor of English at Harvard. Kiely sums up his view of the novel as "a South American Genesis", with Marquez writing in "the language of a poet who knows the earth and does not fear it as the enemy of the dreamer", a comment which could apply equally well to Frame. Frame, however, makes no mention of the South American novelists, and tended to avoid labels. She very much resisted the term "surreal" in her discussions with Elizabeth Alley (Alley and Williams 1992), preferring to suggest that her way of looking "becomes like staring at an x-ray of the real and visible" (54), a way of knowing which lies within the realms of scientific possibility. Frame used this comparison again in her autobiography, when she describes the process of writing about one's own life, which is "usually thought of as looking back" but which "can just as well be a looking *across* or *through*, with the passing of time giving an x-ray quality to the eye" (*CA*,191; Frame's italics). In *The Carpathians* most of the inhabitants of Kowhai Street suffer a single apocalyptic event. J.H. B.'s preliminary note to the novel quotes from a Press Association Report on the phenomenon of the Gravity Star "a galaxy that appears to be both relatively close and seven billion light years away" (*CP*, 25). This note suggests a natural explanation beyond human vision or understanding, rather than something surreal, and that Frame is like "an artist finishing his art" as she tells Claude Gorlier (1990) about Prospero in *The Tempest*, "somehow with overall magic help" (*Tuttolibri*, 1).

Frame's fusion of the real and the unreal, the empirical and the imagined is entirely her own. She makes connections between literatures and human experience over time, space and culture, creating an interconnected web, and these apparently magical elements in Frame's novel owe as much to Shakespeare, and to European folklore, Māori mythology, classical and biblical mythology as they do to the 20th-century novels with which the term "magical realism" is most closely associated. The Gravity Star is an extraordinary phenomenon, but the unexplained effects of the Gravity Star storm are not accepted without comment. People are disturbed by the cataclysmic event: Albion Cook has an embarrassed concern with property sales and wishes to gloss over it; and Connie Grant assumes a mass murder. But the Gravity Star does appear to have a scientific explanation, at least in part, which is only just beginning to be understood. In Kowhai Street, it could be said that "the time is out of joint" (*Hamlet* 1.5.189). The early reference to the phenomenon of the Gravity Star is a reminder of Hamlet's view that "There are more things in heaven and earth, Horatio, /Than are dreamt of in your philosophy" (*Hamlet* 1.5.166–67). Frame uses her intertexts to suggest imaginative parallels and similarities between the apparently quite dissimilar and "what is beyond the real, the invisible beyond the real" (Alley and Williams 1992, 54). To argue for the exclusive or labelling use of any particular form of literary terminology risks overlooking the breadth of Frame's scope, and limits the exploration which is central to her fiction.

When Mattina's husband Jake makes his visit to Puamahara after Mattina's death, he meets Connie Grant, the discarded grandmother, who makes him tea and urges him to be careful—in the manner of a character from Grimms' tales or classical mythology—and "had the manner of one of the old women, who, with the old men of myth and legend, wait by the side of the road, by the river bank, the edge of the forest, to warn, advise and assist" (*CP*, 275). In her discussion of *The Carpathians* with Elizabeth Alley (Alley and Williams 1992), Frame comments on her linking of older forms of literature and present-day New Zealand writing in explaining why she created an American protagonist, namely that "the technique of the stranger's point of view is an old tried technique going way back to fairy tales", adding "especially in our literature, which is full of journeys" (50). Mattina is conscious of New Zealand's earthquakes and volcanoes, "the almost sympathetic activity of the land itself", and their capacity for "fostering myths and legends old and new and inspiring superstition and hysteria" (*CP*, 152). As Mattina prepares to fly back to New York and rejoin her husband Jake, she knew she would "like the witches and story-tellers of old tales, pour her memories, like a potion, in Jake's ear" (222).

As Jake prepares to honour Mattina's dying wishes and visit Puamahara for himself, he ponders her repeated insistence on the importance of memory,

> not as a comfortable parcel of episodes to carry in one's mind, and taste now and then, but as a naked link, a point, diamond-size, seed-size, coded in a code of the world of the human race; a passionately retained deliberate focus on all creatures and their worlds to ensure their survival. (*CP*, 244)

In order for memories to survive, there needs to be a retelling of the old story, and as Lawrence Jones (1989) remarks, "*The Carpathians* celebrates art as the child of memory and language" (128). Mattina believes that "language reinforces memory, rebuilds its weakened foundations" (*CP*, 174), and exhorts Jake to find his way like Theseus and in his turn to pass on the story of Puamahara: "When all threads are broken, either though carelessness or ignorance of use, your remembering will renew the thread" (237).

In Puamahara, Jake muses on change and perception, and on the exultation of the first of Rilke's *Sonnets to Orpheus*, where "the trees, as in Rilke's poem, have their roots in the sky" (276).

> Da stieg ein Baum. O reine Überststeigung
> O Orpheus singt!
> A tree rose from the earth. O pure transcendence –
> Orpheus sings. (Rilke 1946, 34–35)

In Puamahara's orchard, in spite of the ravages of man-made pollutants which threaten to destroy the natural treasures of the environment,

> the blossoms had survived one more year. The acres of rows of glorious white and pink were no more nor less than a plan of time and space recorded by memory, the Housekeeper of Ancient Springtime, and reinforced by human memory using words, spoken and written language. (*CP*, 277–78)

These words, referring to Rilke's French poem, "Vergers" [Orchards], encapsulate Frame's belief in the power of language above all things, a belief she manifests in her character Jake, whose life "from its beginning had been accompanied by the works of Chaucer, Shakespeare, Spenser, Milton" (*CP*, 238) as well as great modern writers and for whom "words were his only valued property" (276).

Frame references literature from contemporary poets and novelists back to a time of predominantly oral culture and discusses her use of language, as Bakhtin does, drawing on a musical analogy. She explains to Elizabeth Alley (Alley and Williams 1992) that "the words are the instrument; I mean you are playing a musical instrument" (52). Music was vitally important to Frame and she told Charles Brasch that one of the joys of the writers' colony at Yaddo was the music she listened to there. Her friendship with Bill Brown began when she listened to his playing of Schubert and Beethoven. Frame notes that musical language, like written literature, is constantly being reworked and reinvented. The dying Mattina repeatedly asks to hear the Beatles' song, "Hey Jude", "the reconstituted Bach, the fresh youngsters from Liverpool allying themselves to the grand old cathedral master" (*CP*, 241), suggesting a parallel between the re-imaginings and re-workings of both music and literature, over hundreds of years.

In *The Carpathians*, Frame draws particularly on folklore and folk tale, from which she takes metaphor, elements of plot and characterisation, merging these with references to Rilke, Shakespeare and 20th-century poets and novelists. Frame uses the word "whirlpool" several times in her conversation with Elizabeth Alley (Alley and Williams 1992), to describe what she was striving for, the imaginative exploration of "the beyond"—and beyond folklore—saying that she was "in a whirlpool" while she was writing *The Carpathians* and that she wanted her readers to feel "within this whirlpool", too, sliding downwards in confusion, as Mattina does (48–49). Mattina recalls Dante's journey into hell as she contemplates "the invisible gap in the fabric of space and time", wondering if the Antipodes had been the entry to Hell or its exit (*CP*, 135).

From her first novel, *Owls Do Cry*, Janet Frame has drawn on the voices of writers—and chiefly the poets—who inspired her. With increasing complexity over the course of her subsequent novels she has shown her readers, in the words of Dr Cawley's tribute, "the evanescent nature of the arbitrary boundaries between knowledge and imagination, and art and science" (Alley 1994, 11). She has availed herself of a variety of literary traditions, old and new, from New Zealand, Europe and America, drawing on the multiplicity of her own reading for inspiration.

In all her novels, Frame writes as one of a communion, a community, a world-wide family of writers, with whom she creates a conversation. She takes from a life-time's reading the gifts of anonymous poets and story-tellers; of canonical writers of the past; and from present-day authors and poets. In a life devoted to the written word she shows that all this material transcends cultural and temporal borders. In her constant exploration of what lies beyond immediate perception, Frame's reworking and layering of narratives connects and celebrates the riches of the most ancient of oral and written narratives and poetry to the work of modern writers from across the world.

Afterword

My discovery of Janet Frame's brilliant novels began accidentally, on a trip to New Zealand and what started out as holiday reading became a dissertation and then a thesis. Academic explorations began with post-graduate and doctoral studies at the Open University, in the UK, and I thank my OU supervisors, Peter Lawson, Delia da Sousa Correa, Edmund King and Janet Wilson for their incisive feedback and their encouraging support. I owe an especially huge debt of gratitude to Janet, both for her endlessly generous and challenging support in my doctoral studies and for her editorial support during the preparation of this book, to Chris Ringrose for his tireless technical help and advice, and Valerie Lange at Ibidem. I am indebted also to a number of people who gave me information, answered queries in person and by email and pointed me in various directions. I have received a wealth of information from Dieter Riemenscheider, Monika Sobotta, Jeanne Delbaere, Paloma Fresno-Calleja, Andreia Sarabando, Masami Nakao, Tim Curnow, Patricia Grace, the late Sheila Natusch, Ann Cawley and from Kevin Ireland, who has come to the rescue a number of times. I have had wonderful support from the archivists at Princeton University, the Waikato District Archives and Public Library in Oamaru, and most especially from the terrific team of archivists at the Hocken Collections in Dunedin, who have been endlessly helpful and patient on line and in person during my research. Grateful thanks also to the Janet Frame Literary Trust for its timely posthumous publications and helpful information, to members of the University of Otago English Department, Jocelyn Harris, Lawrence Jones, and Greg Waite, Heather Murray and Alan Roddick, and Patrick Evans of the University of Canterbury, Christchurch, who gave me generously of their time during my research in Dunedin. Fondest thanks also to my dear friends Cynthia Greensill for her wonderful hospitality in Dunedin and her local knowledge, and to Mary Ensor for her endlessly enthusiastic and practical support. And thanks finally, but not least, to Sarah and Bryan who have spurred me on.

Index

A
Adcock, Fleur 111
Alley, Elizabeth 81, 199, 211–12, 214
Alvarez, Al 76–77
Anderson, Jean 38, 39
Arnold, Matthew 87–90, 108, 110
Atwood, Margaret 78
Auden, W.H. 20, 66, 98, 126, 142
Austen, Jane 60, 64

B
Baisnée, Valérie 95–96
Baker, Louisa 47, 48
Bakhtin, Mikhail 19–24, 85, 144, 156, 214
Ballantyne, Dorothy 11, 12, 40, 84
Balzac, Honoré de 18, 22, 66, 159–61
Barratt Browning, Elizabeth 108
Barthes, Roland 21
Baudelaire, Charles 62, 121, 130
Baxter, Jacqueline, see Sturm, J.C.
Baxter, James K. 67, 79, 83, 85, 111–12, 150, 199–201
Bazin, Claire 35
Bello, Eleonora 44
Benocci, Francesca 44
Bernardi, Daniele 43, 44
Bertram, James 98–99
Bettelheim, Dr Bruno 128–29, 186–87, 190
Bible, King James 19, 46, 50, 59, 66, 69, 81, 90–91, 117, 137–66, 153–66, 172, 185, 206, 209, 211
Bible, New English 147–48
Blake, William 18, 19, 24, 50–51, 56, 59, 66, 85–86, 89–90, 94, 122–23, 149, 192
Book of New Zealand Verse, A 47, 51, 67, 95, 111–14
Bragan, Ken 12
Brasch, Charles 28–30, 41, 51, 60, 69, 71, 74, 84–85, 94, 98, 100, 111–15, 119–20, 126, 150–51, 166, 214
Braun, Alice 35
Braziller, George 18, 30–31, 35, 36, 44, 45, 69, 71–72, 144
Brontë Sisters, The 17, 60, 64–65, 107, 173, 186
Brooke, Rupert 57, 64
Brouillette, Sarah 27
Brown, Theophilis (Bill) 16, 73, 75, 79, 85, 98–100, 104, 112, 116, 121, 124, 151–52, 214
Burke, Kenneth 144, 169

C
Campion, Jane 33, 35, 38, 44, 45, 175
Cameron, Gregor 169, 193
Camus, Albert 18, 69, 73–74
Caney, Diane 175
Carter, Angela 188
Casanova, Pascale 14
Cawley, Dr Robert 215
Chekhov, Anton 18
Chesler, Phyllis 130
Clare, John 110
Coleridge, Samuel Taylor 19, 65–66, 106, 110, 146
Conrad, Joseph 13, 78
Contes et Légendes 60, 62
Cronin, Jan 152, 160, 165
Curnow, Allen 51, 67, 85, 95, 111–14
Curnow, Tim 35

D
Dallas, Ruth 85, 111–12, 114, 151
Dalziel, Margaret 160
Damrosch, David 13, 16
Dante Alighieri 16
Daudet, Alphonse 64, 66
Davin, Dan 72

Dawson, E.P. (Peter) 69, 119, 167
Delbaere, Jeanne 17, 18, 33, 40, 85, 124
Delrez, Marc 83, 104, 150, 159–60, 165, 187
Dickens, Charles 22, 23, 59, 179
Dickinson, Emily 116
Donne, John 25, 147
Dostoevsky, Fyodor 21, 22, 64, 67,
Drichel, Simone 150
Drinkwater, John 50, 51, 60, 85–87
Duff, Alan 64
Dupont, Victor 18, 40

E
Eliot, George 60, 64
Eliot, T.S. 18–20, 64, 66, 85, 98, 117–18, 124, 142, 145–46, 148–49
Evans, Patrick 56, 67, 160

F
Faulkner, William 19, 68, 81, 121
Fenwick, William 48
Ferrier, Carole 127
Fielding, Henry 20–22
Forrester, Viviane 33
Forster, E.M. 119
Frame, Janet
   Adaptable Man, The 24, 65, 74–75, 107, 147–48, 157, 170–71, 179, 192–95, 205
   Autobiography 12, 14, 18, 36, 41, 44–45, 52, 54–55, 57, 60–61, 64, 66–69, 75, 78, 81–83, 86, 90, 103, 106, 114, 124, 134, 167–69, 175–76, 182, 198, 205
   "Beginnings" 83
   Carpathians, The 13, 32, 33, 36–39, 42, 79, 98, 104–05, 173, 182–83, 185, 204–15
   Daughter Buffalo 32, 71, 102–03, 113, 115, 117–18, 120, 145–46, 172
   Edge of the Alphabet, The 30, 71, 72, 102, 126, 176, 199–202

Faces in the Water 30, 31–32, 36, 68, 86–87,100–01, 138–140, 168,173–175, 177–179, 192
Goose Bath, The 43
Gorse Is Not People 38
Intensive Care 34, 71, 75–76, 78, 96, 118, 125–34, 143–145, 152–55, 157, 172, 180–81, 195–98
In the Memorial Room 20, 37, 70, 96, 104
The Lagoon and other Stories 11, 28–30, 35, 37, 38, 40–41, 84, 204
Living in the Maniototo 32–33, 71, 91–94, 101–02, 114, 121, 125, 138, 157–58, 173, 181–82, 203–05
"Memory, and a Pocketful of Words" 80, 178
Mona Minim and the Smell of the Sun 186–87, 190, 206
   Owls Do Cry 11, 12, 23, 24, 27–36, 38–40, 42–43, 63, 72, 90, 106, 122–24, 126, 138, 140–44, 148, 158, 171, 173–80, 190–92, 198, 215
Parleranno le tempeste: Poesie scelte 43
Pocket Mirror, The 32, 43, 82, 170, 197
Rainbirds, The 38, 155–56, 158–62, 165, 174
Scented Gardens for the Blind 31, 32, 83, 87–90, 109–10, 174, 200–01
State of Siege, A 73–74,107–10, 118, 158, 168, 162–66, 172, 176, 199–201
Storms Will Tell 43, 96, 123
Towards Another Summer 32, 37–38, 41, 77, 94–95, 99, 113, 127–28, 171, 178, 180, 198–99
You Are Now Entering the Human Heart 32

Frame, Lottie 19, 45–46, 48, 54, 83, 90–91, 103, 113, 137, 150–51
Fresno-Calleja, Paloma 40
Freud, Sigmund 128–29, 186, 189

G
Gabrielle, Cindy 150, 157, 165
Glover, Dennis 28
Goethe, Johann Wolfgang von 13, 15, 22, 25
Golden Book of Modern English Poetry, The 58, 64
Golden Treasury, The 59, 89
Gordimer, Nadine 78
Gordon, Pamela 187
Gorlier, Claudio 42–43, 175–76
Grace, Patricia 79, 202–04, 207
Grimm Brothers, The 40, 61–63, 67, 185–86, 190, 189–90, 192
Guignery, Vanessa 35

H
Hardy, Thomas 64, 78, 173
Holloway, Judith 130
Holroyd, Michael 44
Hopkins, Gerard Manley 24, 56, 64, 85, 123
Houlahan, Mark 168
Hughes, Ted 77, 124
Hugo, Victor 62, 64, 66, 75
Humphreys, Christmas 69

I
Ihimaera, Witi 210
Ils ont chanté: An Anthology of French Verse for Schools 61–62
Ireland, Kevin 68–69, 99, 111

J
Jacobsen, Dan 78
James, Clive 16–17
Jones, Lawrence 122, 213
Jordis, Christine 34
Joyce, James 70, 121

K
Kafka, Franz 15, 18, 68–69, 82–83, 95, 182
Keats, John 60, 63, 88, 107–08, 142
Kennedy, J.F. 25
Kiely, Robert 211
King, Michael 28, 32, 66, 69, 71, 79, 105
Kowhai Gold 51, 112
Kristeva, Julia 21
Kundera, Milan 15

L
Laboulaye, Edouard 62
Lawn, Jennifer 24
Lawrence, D.H. 64, 121
Leeming, Owen 46, 83–84
Leishman, J.B. 16, 75, 92, 97, 100–01
Lessing, Doris 78
Lewis, C.S. 149–50
Longfellow, H.W. 46, 60, 86, 113
Lueken, Verena 41–42

M
McIntosh, Tracey 208
MacIntyre, C.F. 100–01
McLeod, Marion 79, 187
MacNeice, Louis 66, 186
Malchow, Ruth 40
Mallarmé, Stéphane 73, 82
Manhire, Bill 96
Mansfield, Katherine 42–43, 50, 51, 64
Mantel, Hilary 199
Mare, Walter de la 50, 60, 85, 87
Márquez, Gabriel García 182, 211
Maupassant, Guy de 18, 73
Mercer, Gina 122, 165
Millar, Paul 112
Miller, Dr Alice 128–29, 134, 187, 189
Money, John 28, 67, 73, 99, 102
Mount Helicon: A School Anthology of Verse 61, 64, 86–87, 94, 106, 111, 115

N

Naipaul, V.S. 13
Nakao, Masami 17, 37
Natusch, Sheila 65, 67, 84, 169–70, 189, 199

P

Padel, Ruth 125
Panney, Judith Dell 160
Paterson, Don 16
Paton, Alan 78
Perrault, Charles 62, 185, 188
Plath, Sylvia 76–78, 85, 127–35
Plomer, William 11, 29
Poe, E.A. 61, 86–88, 111
Propp, Vladimir 188
Proust, Marcel 22, 69, 70

R

Radio Times 10, 75–78
Ramsay, Professor Herbert 65, 169–70, 175
Rhodes, Winston H. 12, 40, 79, 148, 167
Ribault, Nadine 38
Riemenschneider, Dieter 42
Rilke, Rainer Maria 15, 16,18, 67–68, 73, 75, 82–83, 85, 90, 97–105, 108, 206, 210, 213–14
Rossini, Rosanna Masioli 38
Rushdie, Salman 13, 31

S

Sage, Lorna 189
Sarabando, Andreia 39
Sargeson, Frank 11, 20, 28–30, 66–69, 72, 79, 84, 99, 105, 110, 111, 113, 119, 167–168, 190–91
Sarraute, Nathalie 18, 31, 69–72
Sarti, Antonella 204
Schreiner, Olive 78
Scott, Keith 22, 46–47
Seafarer, The 65, 194
Selvon, Samuel 80

Shakespeare, William 19, 22, 25, 50, 59, 64–65, 67, 69, 71, 86, 114, 137, 142, 145, 167–83, 214
 Hamlet 212
 King Lear 25, 65–66, 68, 78–79, 138, 170, 173–74
 Macbeth 65–66, 164, 167, 170–173, 179
 Measure for Measure 65–66, 145–46
 Merchant of Venice, The 60, 179
 Midsummer Night's Dream, A 60, 178–79
 Tempest, The 33, 34, 43, 65–66, 68, 141, 167–68, 170, 175–77, 179–83, 211
Shelley, P.B. 88–89, 106, 108
Siegel, Aaron 38
Smith, Stevie 110
Soper, Eileen 48
Spivak, Gayatri Chakravorty 17
Stead, C.K. 151
Steiner, George 15
Sturm, J.C. 79, 150, 201–02
Sullivan, Anita 38

T

Thomas, Dylan 22, 24, 56, 66, 85, 90–93, 95, 123, 203
Thompson, Francis 50, 64
Thurber, James 189
Tolstoy, Leo 69
Tom Sawyer 46
Torwaiwa, Naoko 37

U

Uncle Tom's Cabin 46

V

Valéry, Paul 62, 75, 99
Vaughan, Henry 103
Verse by New Zealand Children 47, 54
Vieilledent, Catherine 35

W

Walberer, Ulrich 33, 43, 39–40
Wanderer, The 25, 65, 194
Ward, Vincent 163–64
Warner, Marina 63, 129, 189, 190
Warwick Research Collective 13, 14
White, Timothy 163
Whitman, Walt 49, 61, 86, 111, 115–20, 142, 145
Whittier, J.G. 46, 86, 111
Wilde, Oscar 46
Williams, Mark 91, 149–150
Wilson, Janet 41, 205, 209
Wilson, Philip 130
Woolf, Virginia 17, 33, 66, 70, 121, 130, 133
Wordsworth, William 19, 50, 86, 89, 106, 122
Wratislaw, A.H. 62, 188
Wright, Albion 28, 29, 36

Y

Yeats, W.B. 19, 20, 50, 56–58, 64, 66, 85, 90–91, 93–94, 98, 143

Z

Zipes, Jack 188–189
Zoppi, Isabella Maria 182, 210

Selected Bibliography

Alley, Elizabeth. 1994. *The Inward Sun*. Wellington: Daphne Brasell Associates.
—, and Mark Williams, eds. 1992. *In the Same Room: Conversations with New Zealand Writers*. Auckland: Auckland University Press.
Anderson, Jean and Nadine Ribault. 2011. "Why Two Heads are Sometimes Better than One: Collaborative Translation of Janet Frame's *The Lagoon and Other Stories*." *Commonwealth Essays and Studies* 33 (2) (Spring): 21–32.
Auden, W.H. 2006. *Collected Shorter Poems*. London: Folio Society.
Baisnée, Valérie. 2009. "A Home in Language: The (Meta)Physical World of Janet Frame's Poetry", 89–106. In Cronin and Drichel, *Frameworks*.
—. 2014. *"Through the long corridor of distance": Space and Self in Contemporary New Zealand Women's Autobiographies*. Amsterdam-New York: Rodopi.
Bakhtin, Mikhail. 2008. *The Dialogic Imagination: Four Essays*. Edited by Michael Holquist and translated by Caryl Emerson and Michael Holquist. Austin, TX: University of Texas Press.
—. 2011. *Problems of Dostoevsky's Poetics*. Edited and translated by Caryl Emerson. Minneapolis, MN: University of Minnesota Press.
Ballantyne, Dorothy. 1952. Radio 4YA Review of *The Lagoon and Other Stories*.
de Balzac, Honoré. 2007. *Le Colonel Chabert*. Paris: Hachette Livre.
Barthes, Roland. 1977. "From Work to Text." In *Image – Music – Text*, translated by Stephen Heath, 155–64. London: Fontana.
Baxter, James K. 1952. *Recent Trends in New Zealand Poetry*. Christchurch: Caxton Press.
—. 1967. *The Man on the Horse*. Dunedin: Otago University Press.
—. 1976. *Aspects of Poetry in New Zealand*. Christchurch: Caxton Press.
—. 2010. *Selected Poems*, edited by Paul Millar. Manchester: Carcanet Press.

Bazin, Claire. 2011. *Janet Frame*. "Writers and Their Work" series. Tavistock: Northcote House and the British Council.
Bettelheim, Bruno. 1976. *The Uses of Enchantment: The Meaning and Importance of Fairy Tales*. London: Thames & Hudson.
Blake, William. 2004. *The Complete Poems*. Edited by Alicia Ostriker. London: Penguin Books.
Bragan, Ken. 1993. "Survival after the Cold Touch of Death: The Resurrection Theme in the Writing of Janet Frame." *Journal of New Zealand Literature* 11: 132–43.
Brasch, Charles. 1980. *Indirections: A Memoir 1909–1947*. Wellington: Oxford University Press.
—. 1984. *Collected Poems*. Edited by Alan Roddick. Auckland: Oxford University Press.
Braziller, George. 2015. *Encounters: My Life in Publishing*. New York: George Braziller Inc.
Brontë, Charlotte. 2008. *Jane Eyre*. Oxford: Oxford University Press.
Brouillette, Sarah. 2011. *Postcolonial Writers in the Global Literary Marketplace*. London: Palgrave Macmillan.
Caldwell, Thomas, ed. 1922. *The Golden Book of Modern English Poetry: 1870–1920*. London: Dent & Co.
Campion, Jane, dir. 1990. *An Angel at My Table*. Australia: Sharmill Films.
Camus, Albert. 1957. "La Femme adultère" [The Adulterous Woman]. In *L'Exile et le Royaume* [Exile and the Kingdom], 9–43. Paris: Gallimard.
—. 2004. *L'Étranger* [The Outsider]. London: Routledge.
Caney, Diane. 1993. "Janet Frame and *The Tempest*". *Journal of New Zealand Literature* 11: 152–71.
Casanova, Pascale. 2004. *The World Republic of Letters*. Cambridge, MA: Harvard University Press.
—. 2017. "Literature as a World." In D'haen et al, *World Literature*: 275–88.
Chesler, Phyllis. 1972. *Women and Madness: When is a Woman Mad and Who is it Who Decides?* New York: Doubleday & Co.

Child, Francis James. 1904. *English and Scottish Popular Ballads*. Boston & New York: Houghton Mifflin & Company.

Cronin, Jan and Simone Drichel, eds. 2009. *Frameworks: Contemporary Criticism on Janet Frame*. Amsterdam – New York: Rodopi.

Cronin, Jan. 2011. *The Frame Function: An Inside-Outside Guide to the Novels of Janet Frame*. Auckland: Auckland University Press.

Curnow, Allen, ed. 1951. *A Book of New Zealand Verse*. Christchurch: Caxton Press.

Dallas, Ruth. 2000. *Collected Poems*. Dunedin: University of Otago Press.

Dalziel, Margaret. 1980. *Janet Frame*. Wellington: Oxford University Press.

Damrosch, David. 2003. *What is World Literature?* Princeton NJ & Oxford: Princeton University Press.

Delbaere, Jeanne. 1975. "Daphne's Metamorphosis in Janet Frame's Early Novels." *Ariel* 6 (2): 23–37.

—. 1979. "The Divided Worlds of Emily Brontë, Virginia Woolf and Janet Frame." *English Studies* 60(6): 699–711.

—, ed. 2001. *The Ring of Fire: Essays on Janet Frame*. Sydney: Dangaroo Press.

Delrez, Marc. 2000. "Forbidding Bodies: Avatars of the Physical Work of Janet Frame." *World Literature Written in English* 38 (2): 70–79.

—. 2002. *Manifold Utopia: The Novels of Janet Frame*. Amsterdam-New York: Rodopi.

—. 2009. "The Legacy of Invention: Determinism and Metafiction in Janet Frame's *Mona Minim and the Smell of the Sun*." *Journal of Postcolonial Writing* 45(1): 28–29.

—. 2012. "Rilke in Frame." Unpublished conference paper, University of Liège.

D'haen, Theo, César Domínguez and Mads Rosendahl Thomas, eds. 2017. *World Literature: A Reader*. Abingdon: Routledge.

Dickens, Charles. 2011. "Night Walks." In *Dickens' London*, 230–39. London: Folio Society.

Donne, John. 1967. *John Donne: Selected Prose*. Edited by Helen Gardner and Timothy Healy. Oxford: Oxford University Press.
Duff, Alan. 1999. *Out of the Mist and Steam: A Memoir*. Auckland: Tandem Press.
Eliot, T.S. 1959. *Four Quartets*. London: Faber & Faber.
—. 1979. *The Sacred Wood*. London: Faber & Faber.
—. 1986. "A Note on the Verse of John Milton." In *Milton: Paradise Lost: A Collection of Critical Essays*, edited by Louis L. Martz, 12–18. London: Prentice Hall.
Evans, Patrick. 1977. *Janet Frame*. Boston, MA: Twayne.
—. 1993. "The Case of the Disappearing Author." *Journal of New Zealand Literature* 11: 11–20.
—. 2010a. "Reaching for Rilke's Angel: Janet Frame's Translations." *Journal of Post-colonial Cultures and Societies* 1 (1): 22–23.
—. 2010b. "'The Uncreating Word': Janet Frame and 'Mystical Naming.'" *Journal of New Zealand Literature* 28: 61–85.
—. 2011. "'They Kill on Wednesdays': Janet Frame, Modernity and the Holocaust." *Journal of Commonwealth Literature* 46: 83–101.
Ferrier, Carole, ed. 1995. *The Janet Frame Reader*. London: The Women's Press.
Fielding, Henry. 2004. *Tom Jones*. London: Random House.
Frame, Janet. 1965. *The Adaptable Man*. New York: George Braziller.
—. 1981. *Living in the Maniototo*. London: The Women's Press.
—. 1982. *Scented Gardens for the Blind*. London: The Women's Press.
—. 1986. *La chambre close* [*The Closed Room: Owls Do Cry*]. Translated by Catherine Vieilledent. Aix-en-Provence: Alinéa.
—. 1992. *The Pocket Mirror: Poems*. London: The Women's Press.
—. 1995. *The Edge of the Alphabet*. New York: George Braziller.
—. 1999. *The Complete Autobiography*. London: The Women's Press.
—. 2005. *The Carpathians*. Auckland: Random House.
—. 2005. *The Edge of the Alphabet*. Auckland: Random House.
—. 2006. *A State of Siege*. Auckland: Random House.
—. 2006. *The Rainbirds*. Auckland: Random House.
—. 2007. *Mona Minim and the Smell of the Sun*. Auckland: Random House.

—. 2007. *Towards Another Summer*. Auckland: Random House.
—. 2008. *Intensive Care*. Auckland: Random House.
—. 2008. *Daughter Buffalo*. Auckland: Random House.
—. 2008. *Storms Will Tell*. Edited by Bill Manhire. Tarset: Bloodaxe Books.
—. 2010. *Dear Charles, Dear Janet: Frame and Brasch in Conversation*. Edited by Denis Harold and Pamela Gordon. Auckland: Holloway Press.
—. 2011. *Janet Frame: In Her Own Words*. Edited by Harold Dennis and Pamela Gordon. Auckland: Penguin Books NZ.
—. 2012. *Gorse Is Not People*. Auckland: Penguin Books NZ.
—. 2013. *In the Memorial Room*. Melbourne: Text Publishing.
—. 2016. *Jay to Bee: Janet Frame's Letters to William Theophilus Brown*. Edited by Harold Dennis and Pamela Gordon. Berkeley, CA: Counterpoint.
—. 2017. *Parleranno le tempeste: Poesie scelte* [Storms Will Tell: Selected Poems]. Translated by Francesca Benocci and Eleonora Bello. Mendrisio: Gabriele Capelli Editore.
Fresno-Calleja, Paloma. 2015. "Reading (in) the Antipodes: New Zealand and Pacific Literatures in Translation." *Journal of New Zealand Studies* 21: 53–68.
Fresno-Calleja, Paloma and Janet Wilson. 2014. *Un pais de cuento: veinte relatos de Nueva Zelanda* [A Country of Tales: Twenty Stories from New Zealand]. Translated by Paloma Fresno-Calleja. Zaragoza: Prensas de la Universidad de Zaragoza.
Freud, Sigmund.1924. *Freud: Collected Papers* Vol. 1. New York-London-Vienna: The International Psycho-Analytical Press.
—. 1985. *The Complete Letters of Sigmund Freud to Wilhelm Fleiss*. Translated and edited by Jeffrey Moussiaff Mason. Cambridge, MA: Harvard University Press.
Gabrielle, Cindy. 2015. *The Unharnessed World: Janet Frame and Buddhist Thought*. Newcastle upon Tyne: Cambridge Scholars Publishing.
Gardner, Helen, ed. 1966. *The Metaphysical Poets*. London: Penguin Books.

Gifford, Henry. 1962. "On the New English Bible." *Essays in Criticism* 11: 466–70.

Gordon, R.K. 1967. *Anglo-Saxon Poetry*. London: J.M. Dent & Sons.

Grace, Patricia. 1975. *Waiariki and Other Stories*. Auckland: Penguin Books NZ.

—. 2001. *Dogside Story*. London: The Women's Press.

Guerber, Helene Adeline. 1912. *Contes et Légendes*. London: George Harrap & Co.

Hayward, John, ed. 1958. *The Faber Book of English Verse*. London: Faber & Faber.

Holloway, Judith. 2001. "Unfortunate Folk: A Study of the Social Context of Committal to Seacliff, 1928–1937." In *"Unfortunate Folk": Essays on Mental Health Treatment 1863–1992*, edited by Barbara Brookes and Jane Thomson, 153–67. Dunedin: University of Otago Press.

Hopkins, Gerard Manley. 1967. *Poems and Prose*. Edited by W.H. Gardner. London: Penguin Books.

Houlahan, Mark. 2002a. "'Think about Shakespeare': *King Lear* on Pacific Cliffs." In *Shakespeare Survey 5: King Lear and its Aftermath*, edited by Peter Holland, 170–80. Cambridge: Cambridge University Press.

—. 2002b. "Shakespeare in the Settlers' House." *Journal of New Zealand Literature* 20: 112–24.

Hughes, Ted. 1995. "The Art of Poetry 71 [Interview]." *The Paris Review* 134: 55–94.

Ireland, Kevin. 2005. *Mr. Sargeson at Home: Frank Sargeson Memorial Lecture*. Hamilton: University of Waikato.

Ihimaera, Witi. 1991. "A Maori Perspective." *Journal of New Zealand Literature* 9: 53–54.

—. 1992. "Listening to One's Ancestors. An Interview with Paul Sharrad." In *Australian and New Zealand Studies in Canada* 8. Calgary: University of Toronto Press.

James, Clive. 2013. *Dante: The Divine Comedy*. London: Pan Macmillan.

Jones, Lawrence. 1987. *Barbed Wire and Mirrors: Essays on New Zealand Prose*. Dunedin: Otago University Press.

—. 1989. "Continuing Accomplishment: Novels in 1988." *Journal of New Zealand Literature* 7: 106–30.

—. 2003. *Picking up the Traces: The Making of a New Zealand Literary Culture 1932–1944*. Wellington: Victoria University Press.

—. 2008. *Nurse to the Imagination: 50 Years of the Burns Fellowship*. Dunedin: Otago University Press.

Kafka, Franz. 1986. *Die Verwandlung* [The Metamorphosis]. London: Routledge.

King, Michael. 1995. *Frank Sargeson: A Life*. Auckland: Penguin Books NZ

—. 2000. *Wrestling with the Angel: A Life of Janet Frame*. Auckland: Penguin Books NZ.

Kristeva, Julia. 1986. "Word, Dialogue and Novel." In *The Kristeva Reader*, edited by Tori Moi, 34–61. New York: Columbia University Press.

Kundera, Milan. 2017. *"Die Weltliteratur."* In D'haen et al, *World Literature*, 289–300.

Lawn, Jennifer. 1990. "The Many Voices of *Owls Do Cry*: A Bakhtinian Approach." *Journal of New Zealand Literature* 8: 87–105.

Leeming, Owen. 1963. "Review of *Scented Gardens for the Blind*." *Landfall* 68: 386–89.

—. 1964. "Review of *The New Poetic* by C.K. Stead." *Landfall* 71: 287–88.

Lewis, C.S. 2013. "The Literary Impact of the Authorised Version: The Ethel M. Wood Lecture", delivered before the University of London, 20 March 1950, in *Selected Literary Essays*, edited by Walter Hooper, 126–145. Cambridge: Cambridge University Press.

McIntosh, Tracey. 2005. "Māori Identities: Fixed, Fluid and Forced." In *New Zealand Identities: Departures and Destinations*, edited by James Lui, 38–51. Wellington: Victoria University Press.

McLeod, Marion. 1992. "Shafts of Parody and Sly Wit." *New Zealand Listener*, September 5: 52–53.

MacNeice, Louis. 2011. *Varieties of Parable*. London: Faber & Faber.

Manhire, Bill. 2008. "Introduction." In Janet Frame, *Storms Will Tell*. Tarset: Bloodaxe Books.

Mercer, Gina. 1994. *Janet Frame: Subversive Fictions*. St. Lucia: University of Queensland Press.

Millar, Paul. 2010. "Introduction." *James K. Baxter: Selected Poems*. Manchester: Carcanet Press.

Miller, Alice. 1985. *Thou Shalt Not Be Aware: Society's Betrayal of the Child*. Translated by Hildegarde & Hunter Hannum. London & Sydney: Pluto Press.

—. 1997. *Breaking Down the Wall of Silence: To Join the Waiting Child*. London: Virago Press.

Mills, Tom L., ed. 1943. *Verse by New Zealand Children*. Wellington: Progressive Publishing Society.

Morrell, W.P. 1969. *The University of Otago: A Centennial History*. Dunedin: University of Otago Press.

Mount Helicon: A School Anthology of Verse. 1933. London: Edward Arnold.

Natusch, Sheila. 2004. *Letters from Jean*. Wellington: Nestegg.

Padel, Ruth. 2004. *52 Ways of Looking at a Poem*. London: Random House.

Palgrave, Francis Turner, ed. 1940. *The Golden Treasury of the Best Songs and Lyrical Poems in the English Language*. London: Oxford University Press.

Panny, Judith Dell. 1993. *I Have What I Gave: The Fiction of Janet Frame*. New York: George Braziller.

Paterson, Don. 2006. *Orpheus: A Version of Rilke's Die Sonette an Orpheus*. London: Faber & Faber.

Plath, Sylvia. 1989. *Collected Poems*. Edited by Ted Hughes. London Faber & Faber.

Propp, V., 2013. *Morphology of the Folktale*. Austin, TX: University of Texas.

Rilke, Rainer Maria. 1946. *Sonnets to Orpheus*. Translated and edited by J.B. Leishman. London: The Hogarth Press

—. 1947. *Rainer Maria Rilke: Fifty Selected Poems with English Translations*. Translated and edited by C.F. MacIntyre. Berkeley, CA: University of California Press.

—. 1986. *The Complete French Poems*, translated and edited by A. Poulin Jr. St. Paul, MN: Greywolf Press.

—. 1992. *The Notebooks of Malte Laurids Brigge*, translated by M.D. Herter Norton. New York: W.W. Norton & Co Inc.

Rhodes, H. Winston. 1957. "Review of *Owls Do Cry*." *Landfall* 43: 327–31.

—. 1972. "Preludes and Parables." *Landfall* 102: 135–46.

Roberts, Priscilla, ed. 2012. *Cuban Missile Crisis: The Essential Guide*. Santa Barbara, CA: CLIO.

Sage, Lorna. 2001. "Angela Carter: The Fairy Tale." In Lorna Sage, *Moments of Truth: Twelve Twentieth-Century Woman Writers*, 221–48. London: Harper Collins.

Sargeson, Frank. 1964. "Shakespeare and the Kiwi." *Landfall* 69: 49–54.

—. 2012. *The Letters of Frank Sargeson*. Edited by Sarah Shieff. Auckland: Random House.

Sarraute, Nathalie. 1959. *Le Planétarium*. Paris: Gallimard

—. 1990. "The Art of Fiction 115 [Interview]." *The Paris Review* 114, 152–84.

Sarti, Antonella. 1998. *Spiritcarvers: Interviews with Eighteen Writers from New Zealand*. Amsterdam-Atlanta, GA: Rodopi.

Scott, Keith. 2011. *Dear Dot I Must Tell You: A Personal History of Young New Zealanders*. Auckland: Activity Press.

Shelley, P.B. 1994. *Selected Prose and Poetry of Shelley*. Edited by Bruce Woodcock. Ware: Wordsworth Editions.

—. 1904. *The Complete Poetical Works of Shelley*. Edited by Thomas Hutchinson. Oxford: Clarendon Press.

Smith, Stevie. 1987. *Stevie Smith: Collected Poems*. Edited by James MacGibbon. London: Penguin Books.

Spivak, Gayatri Chakrovorty. 2005. *Death of a Discipline*. New York: Columbia University Press.

Steiner, George. 2017. "A Footnote to *Weltliteratur*." In D'haen et al, *World Literature*, 114–21.

Sturm, J.C. 1996. *Dedications*. Wellington: Steele Roberts.

Thomas, Dylan. 1988. *Collected Poems, 1934–53*. Edited by Walford Davies and Ralph Maud. London: J.M. Dent & Sons.

Thurber, James. 1983. "The Little Girl and the Wolf." In *Fables for Our Times: And Famous Poems Illustrated*, 3. New York: Harper & Row Inc.

Warner, Marina. 2014. *Once Upon a Time: A Short History of Fairy Tale*. Oxford: Oxford University Press.

Warwick Research Collective, The. 2015. *Combined and Uneven Development: Towards a New Theory of World Literature.* Liverpool: Liverpool University Press.

Whitman, Walt. 2009. *Leaves of Grass*. Edited by Jerome Loving. Oxford: Oxford University Press.

Whitmarsh, W.F.H., ed. 1937. *Ils Ont Chanté : An Anthology of French Verse for Schools.* London: Longmans, Green & Co.

Williams, Mark. 1990. *Leaving the Highway: Six New Zealand Novelists*. Auckland: Auckland University Press.

Wilson, Janet. 1993. "Post-modernism or post Colonialism? Fictive Strategies in *Living in the Maniototo* and *The Carpathians*." *Journal of Postcolonial Writing* 11: 114–31.

—. 1998. "The Inner World: Living in Janet Frame's Maniototo." In Zoppi *Routes of the Roots*, 631–49.

Woolf, Virginia. 2002. *Moments of Being*. London: Random House Pimlico.

Wratislaw, A.H., trans. and ed. 1977. *Sixty Folk-Tales from Exclusively Slavonic Sources*. London: Elliot Stock.

Yeats, W.B. 1998. *Selected Poems*. London: Folio Society.

—. 2000. *Collected Poems of W.B. Yeats*. Ware: Wordsworth Editions.

Zipes, Jack. 1988. *The Brothers Grimm: From Enchanted Forests to the Modern World*. New York-London: Routledge.

Zoppi, Isabella Maria, ed. 1998. *Roots of the Routes: Geography and Literature in the English-speaking Countries.* Rome: Bulzoni Editore.

ibidem.eu

Zeitfracht Medien GmbH
Ferdinand-Jühlke-Straße 7,
99095 - DE, Erfurt
produktsicherheit@zeitfracht.de